SAILING AROUND THE WORLD:

Volume 2,
Finding our way home

Howard & Judy Wang

Howard & Judy Wang

Copyright © 2017 Howard & Judy Wang
Wang Publishing Services, Santa Barbara, CA
All rights reserved.

Library of Congress Control Number: 2017916134
ISBN-10: 1977782817
ISBN-13: 978-1977782816

DEDICATION

We dedicate our story to pioneers, inventors, and explorers who took risks so that we may all journey. We are forever grateful to our parents and mentors for instilling in us an internal compass to navigate in sunshine and in storm.

Howard & Judy Wang

Contents

ACKNOWLEDGMENTS 3

A Note to Readers 5

1. Passage to Darwin 7

2. Exotic Indonesia 44

3. Navigating the Straits 65

4. Plying the Indian Ocean 76

5. Sailing the Pirate Alley 89

6. The Red Sea Escapade 95

7. The Nile Flows North 130

8. It's All Greek to Me 152

9. Knights of Malta 174

10. The Mediterranean Sea 182

11. The Rock and the Canary 196

12. An Impromptu Port of Call 209

13. Dashing Across the Atlantic 224

14. The Caribbean Sea 238

15. Guna Yala 249

16. The Panama Canal 262

17. North to Costa Rica 278

18. The Precarious Bash North 291

19. Completing the Circumnavigation 297

Epilogue 302

About the Authors 303

Howard & Judy Wang

ACKNOWLEDGMENTS

We thank you, our friends and family, who encouraged and cheered us on during our journey. We are grateful for the complete file of our email preserved by Maureen Stonehouse, our daughter, and Susan Hill. Gratitude is due to Mark Wang for the homecoming photo taken in San Diego and to Filip Lembregts for the screenshot of Laelia in the Miraflores Locks. We are indebted to Bruce Thompson, *The Forecaster*, our weather guru, for his weather advice during Laelia's Atlantic crossing. Bruce also edited the early chapters of the manuscript and set the book on a favorable tack. We thank the late Don Anderson, *Summer Passage*, for his weather forecasts during our passages in Mexico and the Pacific Islands. If you enjoy this book, thank Alice Chaffee, our editor, who improved the flow and made the book readable. The authors are fully responsible for any deficiencies in these pages. We also thank Maureen, our daughter, for building the website to show the color photographs.

Howard & Judy Wang

A Note to Readers

Our sailing adventure around the world took us to forty-two countries in eight years. This book, in two volumes, is about a different way of life, discovering faraway lands, and meeting uncommon people. One day at a time, we learned as we went and did the seemingly impossible. Volume 1 begins with an account of how we almost met our doom, and tells how two novices managed to sail from California to Sydney, Australia. Volume 2 describes our arduous journey home by way of the pirate alley, the Suez and Panama Canals, and bashing upwind along the Pacific Coast.

There is a website, <SailBoatLaelia.com>, to show photos we took along the way, a glossary, and a page on Frequently Asked Questions. All maps are north up. The book is in American English, but local spellings are used, when appropriate, for place names.

We wish you an adventurous journey, with fascinating discoveries, in the comfort of your armchair. Sit back, relax, and join us on this journey.

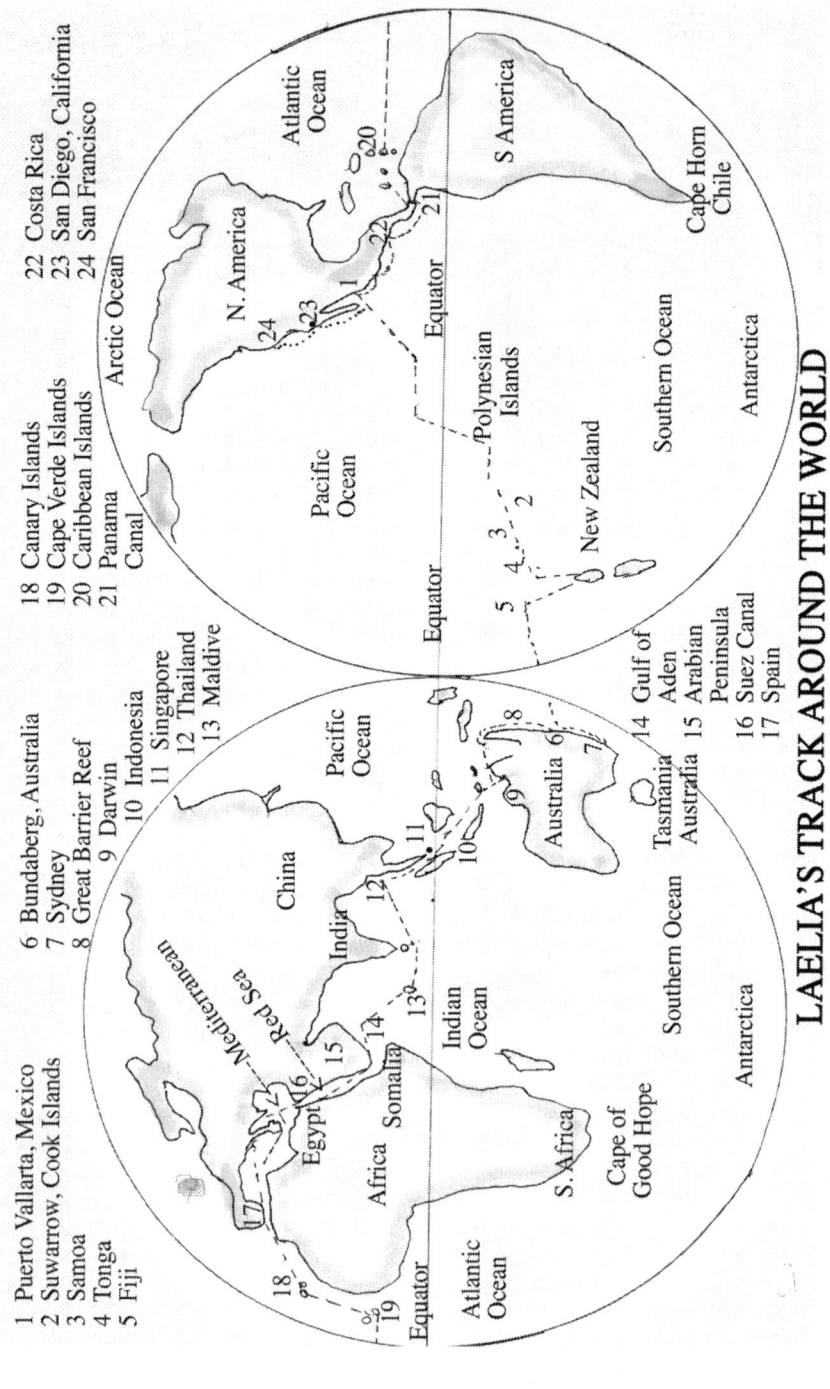

LAELIA'S TRACK AROUND THE WORLD

1. Passage to Darwin

Departing Oyster Cove Boatyard (32 44.071 S, 151 57.104 E), 12 February 2008. Departing Lemon Tree Passage Marina, Port Stephens (32 43.844 S, 152 2.463 E), 21 March 2008. Rounding Cape York (10 29.655 S, 142 17.914 E), 28 June 2008. Arriving Fannie Bay, Darwin, Northern Territory, Australia (12 25.692 S, 130 49.323 E), 03 July 2008.

Our Australian Home

"Aaaahhh..." I screamed, rushed back in, and slammed the sliding glass door shut.

"It...it's furry and warm," I said, still shaken as I turned on the porch light. There they were...a couple of furry beasts hanging on the bird feeder. They were Australian bushtail possums (*Trichosurus vulpecula*). Unlike the California opossum I knew with sparse hair, these Australian marsupials had luxuriant fur. They stared at me unafraid with big dark eyes. I had just discovered why the birdseed in the feeder was disappearing so quickly.

While Laelia was "on the hard" in the boatyard, we toured every State and the Northern Territory in Australia by car. We rode the Ghan (the Australian Railroad in the outback), toured a billabong (a seasonal lake), flew over the diamond mine, took photos of Quokkas (a small marsupial on Rottnest Island off of Perth), and slept underground in an opal mine. Along our trip there were koalas, wombats, wallabies, kangaroos, platypus, and Tassie Devils. We saw for the first time the indigenous black kangaroo paw (*Macropidia fulginosa*), a flower that grows only in a few square-miles north of Perth and the giant lily, *Victoria amazonica*, at the Adelaide Botanical Garden.

As our 18-month visa was coming to an end, we worked furiously to get Laelia ready for launch at the Oyster Cove Boatyard. We re-stitched the sail and patched the canvas. The diesel engines were serviced and the rudderstocks dropped and inspected for corrosion. We gave Laelia five coats of bottom paint to keep the barnacles away.

While Laelia was being worked on, we lived in a small rented home where a flock of lorikeets visited the feeder everyday. I was inspecting the feeder, in the dark, when I chanced upon our furry marauders.

Heading north
After launching from the boatyard in February, Laelia stayed at the Lemon Tree Passage Marina in Port Stephens for several weeks until we sold the car. By then it was high time for cruising boats to migrate north along the East Australian Coast. It would be an arduous passage to the far north of the continent where the cyclone season does not end until mid-May. Our destination was Darwin, the jumping-off point for Indonesia.

The passage to Darwin was expected to be difficult because of the strong current and extreme tides in the Cape York region and the Gulf of Carpentaria. The land had a sparse population with few facilities. The remoteness of the region and the lack of a good guidebook in our possession made the passage daunting. Furthermore, the weather in the Gulf of Carpentaria is notoriously unreliable with sudden tempests and huge seas.

Sailing north along the East Coast of Australia was vastly different than our sail south a year and a half earlier. The East Australian Current, at as much as two to three knots or more, was now against us as we headed north. Sudden storms were also a constant risk. The strategy was to sail by short hops from port to port with an eye on the weather. We kept track of safe havens along the way in case conditions turned ugly.

It can be demoralizing to be crashing mightily ahead through the waves with the engine working at its maximum, but making minimal progress against the fierce headwind and contrary current.

The forecast at the time was for a five-day stretch of thirty-knot winds and three-meter seas. This would be our first time at sea in more than a year. I thought that it would be wise to err on the side of caution.

I wanted to wait a few days for the wind and swells to ease a bit before we actually ventured out to the open ocean. We did untie the dock lines at the marina so we could ease into being at sea. We went across the bay to hook onto a mooring ball at Fame Cove, about five miles from the dock, inside Port Stephens. Now we were on our own.

It was a serene little cove, well sheltered from the storm and with its shores dotted with low trees. There was plenty of bird life squawking and a herd of five or six wild goats feeding on a point of land not far from us. We could see the resident bottlenose dolphins chasing fish. Occasionally a fish would jump out of the water in a desperate attempt to get away.

At the time, there was not enough sun shining on Laelia's solar panels to supply the electricity we needed. The wind turbine had been tied up while Laelia was stored in the boatyard. Now it was time for it to produce some electricity. I cut the rope that secured the blades of the turbine and it started spinning.

Judy said, "I smell smoke. Do you smell it?"

"Mmm, I'm not sure. I don't see any fire or smoke on land near us," I said as I sniffed. "I'll check the engine room." One thing I knew for certain was that it's never a good sign to smell smoke on a boat. I didn't think there could be a fire in the engine room. We were anchored and the engines were turned off, but there were fuel hoses in there. It couldn't hurt to check every possibility.

Just as I opened the engine compartment hatch, I got hit in the face with a big puff of black smoke.

Yikes! Troubles.

Smoke or fire is easily the most frightening occurrence on a boat. There is no place to run for safety. Fiberglass burns well and flames could reduce Laelia to the waterline in a matter of minutes.

In the engine room, the fuel line looked intact and there was no diesel leakage, but the voltage regulator for the wind turbine looked crumpled. It had melted and was still hot to the touch. I quickly turned the battery switch to off and the smoke soon dissipated.

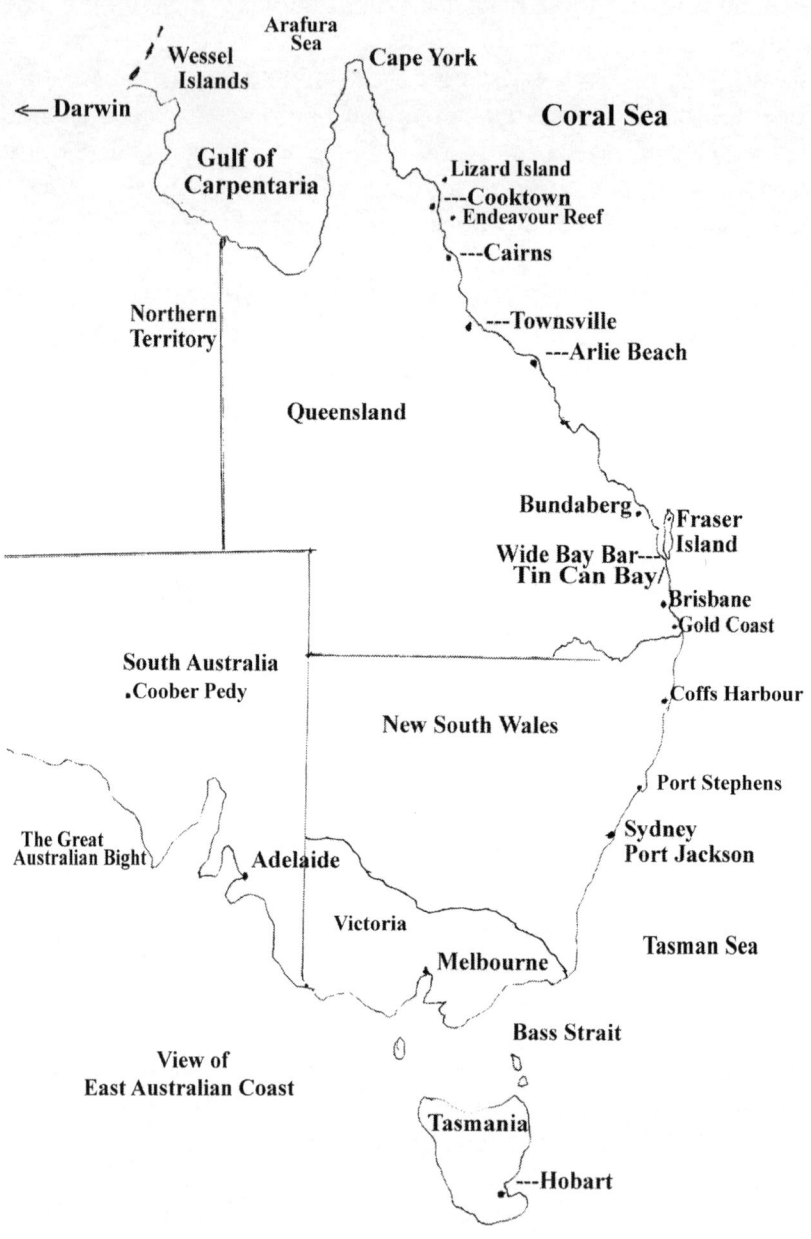

It seemed that the wind turbine, instead of charging the battery, had drained the battery bank and burned up the regulator. There must have been a short circuit in the wind turbine.

Well, that is certainly not an auspicious beginning for our journey.

A little later in the afternoon, Judy baked poppy seed muffins to warm the salon. It also helped to chase away the odor of burnt electrical insulation. I was preparing dinner, frying some onions over the propane stove in the galley. The counter was still full of provisions that had not yet been stowed so there wasn't much space for cooking. There were cooking utensils crowded together and some fried onions were on a paper plate next to the stove.

"I smell a wood fire," Judy said.

"Not again? There's no wood fire around here."

"Maybe there is a bush fire on shore," Judy said.

"With this wind blowing outside, it's hard to smell anything from on shore." I was being my skeptical self.

As I sniffed, it really smelled like there was a wood-burning stove near by. Then in one instant we both saw the paper plate near the stove bursting into flames. It burned with some intensity because the oil from the fried onions had made the paper plate very flammable.

"Here's the fire extinguisher," Judy said as she handed the red cylinder to me.

"That would ruin the onions," I protested as I shut the stove off.

It crossed my mind that the fire extinguisher cost about $100 and would cost that much to recharge it again. Luckily, the paper plate was not enough fuel for the fire to continue and was quickly beaten into submission and smothered under a kitchen towel.

"The onions still taste pretty good," I said as I sampled the food.

That was how we started our first day at sea for this leg of the journey…well, not exactly at sea, but it was at least afloat and it wasn't dull. We had had two crises already and we had not even set sail yet; it did not bode well. Perhaps we needed more practice at this boating thing.

We managed to sleep through the night at Fame Cove without any further adventures. The next morning was bright and sunny, though blustery. Waves and white caps were visible in the well-protected water. We were tied to a 24-hour-only public mooring ball, it would be courteous for us to move on. We decided to move across to Salamander Bay, a few miles away, but still inside Port Stephens. It was a little closer to the open ocean...the Tasman Sea.

Salamander Bay was well protected from wind and we felt comfortable. Our plan was to ease Laelia into the tail end of the blow as the wind and the sea calmed down a little. At sunset, we checked the weather forecast again.

Oh-oh. It seemed the forecast had an update: If we left the next morning according to plan, we would have missed a favorable weather window although a narrow one.

We could depart immediately to salvage much of the remaining southerly wind. It was approaching low tide. It would be slack water if we left right away. If we waited much longer, we would have to fight the incoming tide on our way out to the open ocean.

Just as I was getting myself to the bow to release the mooring lines, we heard a voice at the stern of the boat. A couple in a "tinny" (aluminum dinghy) had come over from their boat. We could tell they were locals. We never miss a chance to meet the locals wherever we go. The timing was not quite right, but we wanted to meet them. We told them we were leaving right away, but come aboard for a quick chat anyway.

They even brought over a bottle of Champagne for us. They told us that they usually lived in Sydney, but came to their boat frequently. They saw us tying up at the mooring ball and the US flag we were flying, but waited for us to settle down before coming over for a visit. This lovely couple was being so very thoughtful. We enjoyed talking to them as if we had known them for years. Time was short, but it was congenial and a lot of fun. They presented us with a Sydney flag: a bright green field with a boxing kangaroo...a yellow kangaroo wearing bright red boxing gloves. It was a very special Sydney Olympic Flag. What a send-off! We all promised to stay in touch. They returned to their boat and we departed Salamander Bay. The tide was beginning to come in, but the current was not yet too strong. We went through the passage into the Tasman Sea with no difficulties as the night descended.

The problem with leaving port 15 hours earlier than planned was that we were not able to go through the proper departure preparations. Judy took her seasick pills as soon as we decided to leave, but she would normally have taken them the night before and would have taken a second dose before departure.

As soon as the boat entered the open ocean, it was like being thrown into a different world. The proverbial washing machine would have been a joy ride by comparison. By this time, Judy was feeling the motion and needed to go to sleep. Fortunately for her, she could sleep just by putting her head on the pillow. By now she had confirmed many times over the neurological fact that a sleeping brain does not suffer from seasickness.

For the first hour or so, we had to head east against an ESE wind and SE swells in order to clear the large boulders at the headland, an obstacle we didn't anticipate. With the wind on the nose, it felt much stronger than twenty-five knots and we could hear it whistling through the rigging. Swells were about six feet, but at close intervals and came relentlessly one after the other. The wind loosened the white foam at the top of the waves sending a spray lashing at the boat. It looked as if the waves would bury Laelia under, but each time the boat leapt up against the wave then crashed down on the other side.

Occasionally, Laelia would smash into a big wave with a loud thud and come to a dead stop. As the seawater washed over the deck, ever so slowly, Laelia would start moving forward again. We went up and down on those swells like riding a rollercoaster.

After we cleared the nearby islands, we were able to turn north and put the wind and swells on our starboard quarter. That made the motion better, but not by much. Now the waves were looming from behind Laelia and lifting the boat up. Then, from time to time, the boat would surf down a steep wave at high speed. As the boat accelerated, the water roared under the bridge deck making sounds like horse hoofs in a stampede.

In strong wind, Laelia sailed nicely at seven plus knots according to the paddlewheel transducer that reported water speed passing at the bottom of the boat. Unfortunately, the GPS reported that we were only going around 5 knots SOG (speed over ground). It meant that we had a 2-knot current against us. This was not unexpected. With the earth's rotation, the ocean current travels from east to west; all that water has to go somewhere as it collides with the Australian Continent.

By the middle of the passage, after about 15 hours, the wind calmed down. This was both good and bad. With lighter wind and the persisting current, we could no longer maintain a 5-knot progress SOG. On the other hand, the swells also calmed considerably, making life worth living again. Judy was able to stay up and stand watch while I slept. We turned on at least one engine to keep the boat speed respectable. At just over the equivalent of US $6 per gallon for diesel, it was quite a luxury.

During the second night, with calmer seas, we were in a much better frame of mind to appreciate the night sky. Orion was visible and Crux (the Southern Cross) followed it across the sky. It was satisfying as each lighthouse was identified during the night, knowing that we were able to navigate through the night without modern electronics. To see a light across miles of dark churning ocean and to make a positive identification was reassuring. It provided a connection with something needful and vital inside us. Despite the aloneness in the ocean, the light provided that link to the rest of humanity. It was in that frame of mind we came across the Smoky Cape Light. It gave a sequence of three flashes repeated every twenty seconds, and its height allowed the beam to be seen at 26 miles away. It was a very bright light telling us we were getting close to our destination at Coffs Harbour. It was comforting and calming.

The land mass was called Smoky Cape because Captain Cook observed smoke coming from the point of land when he sailed past this patch of water 238 years ago. It was smoke from bush fires set by the Dunghutti Aboriginal people in their traditional way of managing the land. We continued as the sun came up. Before long we arrived at Coffs Harbour in bright daylight and blue skies.

Mutton Birds
On our way north we made a point of stopping at Coffs Harbour Marina where we had been forced to sail into a storm previously. The marina was very accessible from the open ocean. Breakwaters bridged the mainland to a near-shore island, creating a marina in between the two. There were no sandbars to cross or rivers to navigate. It offered good protection for small craft and fishing boats.

We liked the marina, but regretted one unfortunate result of the development. The breakwater produced a land bridge to the little island. Feral animals could now invade what once was a safe haven for the mutton-bird nesting ground.

These birds are also called shearwaters because of their habit of gliding very close to the water surface. It is common to see them flying low over the water in large colonies. They were so numerous at one time providing meat and oil that it was like "sheep on wings," hence the name mutton bird.

In earlier days, Charles Darwin wrote, "...there were birds in the hundreds of thousands in a flock making the sky black as they flew overhead."

These shearwaters are true pelagic birds migrating across thousands of ocean miles around the world every year. They migrate annually from California and Cape Horn to breed in Mexico on the offshore islands. The Manx shearwaters (*Puffinus puffinus*) migrate between UK and Brazil. The short-tailed shearwaters (*Ardenna tenuirostris*) in Tasmania migrate all the way to the Aleutian Islands and the Artic then return by way of the Pacific Islands and Japan. At Coffs Harbour the wedge-tailed shearwaters (*A. pacificus*) migrate to the Philippines.

The local Aboriginal dreamtime stories tell that the moon, the guardian of this sacred island, keeps mutton birds available for the Gumbaynggirr people who live in this region. "Tides, rip tides, and floods" would punish those who abused their privileges.

There was a nice walking track (trail) on the island. We were able to see ground burrows where the mutton birds kept their young. Both parents hunt during the day and return after dark to feed their chicks. The parents wait until their chicks are full of fat before flying off heeding their inborn migratory urge. The young chicks, abandoned and barely able to fly, manage to flock together and eventually make their own migration from instinctive knowledge.

The little island is a part of the National Park System where mutton birds were protected. There were park signs that warn visitors to stay on the track (trail) and not to disturb the burrows.

It was a wind-swept little island with no trees, but lots of low shrubs to provide some shelter for the burrow entrance against predators. We also observed many traps set by the National Park Service to remove rodents. The Park Service was also making an effort to control non-native weeds that were less favorable to the mutton birds.

It seemed strange that Australia still allowed commercial harvesting in Tasmania of mutton bird chicks (babies) for their flesh, feathers, and oil although with only a short 30-day season. The harvest was justified based on traditional cultural practice of the Aborigines. Although Aborigines did harvest mutton birds for sustenance, commercial harvesting was only introduced in more recent times by the sealers and their Aboriginal families.

While we were waiting for favorable weather, we took in some of the sights. There was a World-Heritage temperate rain forest near enough for a day trip. Dorrigo National Park was high up in the mountains inland from Coffs. We rented a car and went exploring. The drive up reminded us of the drive to Yosemite with long sweeping roads along the precipice and twisty hairpin switchbacks on the steep slopes of the mountain.

The park had miles of boardwalk with some sections suspended among the large gum trees. The most spectacular was the Skywalk where we shuffled out onto this cantilevered structure jutting into the thin air over the valley. While peeking down at the void, I got that twinge of fear. We could see miles of the valley and felt the wind as if we were floating on air.

Back along the forested track, we saw a moderately sized bird walking among the grass. It had black feathers and a red wattle. We later identified it as a bush turkey that many people here considered a pest. Apparently these birds would use their claws to dig up an entire patch of lawn to find tasty grubs in the soil underneath.

We also came across half a dozen monitor lizards about one meter in length sunning themselves at the edge of a grove of trees. All of them seemed to be molting with patches of rather tattered looking skin. Many bird species could be found here, including some rare species, but we were neither there at the right time nor sat still long enough to be proper bird watchers.

On our drive back, we stopped at the Smoky Cape Lighthouse. The fairly extensive keeper's house and facilities had turned into a B&B. It was such an alluring location with a commanding view high over the Tasman Sea and white beach dunes on either side along the coast. We would have stayed the night there, but there was no room at the inn, a wedding party was in full swing when we arrived. As we walked around the small park near the lighthouse, we spied a joey. I stalked by stealth to get a photo while the mother roo watched us suspiciously, but not alarmed.

All of a sudden, as if the joey decided to put on a show, it ran...well, no it hopped, in circles around us at first. Then it reversed course and continued to circle. Then it went the other way. For a finale it went into figure eights. It moved fast, allowing me time to snap mostly blurred photos. I had considered climbing on the picnic table to avoid getting trampled, but Judy thought that would have been undignified.

We read the plaques at the park. "The Smoky Cape Lighthouse was the most elevated lighthouse on the New South Wales Coast." First lit on 15 April 1891 and was the last lighthouse where architectural excellence was still an important consideration. It was included "on the Commonwealth Heritage list for its: historic connection with James Cook's voyage, dramatic coast terrain, accessibility to visitors, and high quality architectural skill and innovation..."

Of course Captain Cook never had the benefit of this lighthouse. He only observed smoke from bush fires set by the Aboriginals to hunt and to keep the grasses low for traveling on foot. Over the many thousands of years, the ecology of Australia had adapted to include fire as an integral aspect of its life cycle. The burnt gum trees may look forlorn and dead, but would put out green shoots after the first rain in the season. Many trees required fire to initiate seed germination. Even today, the Aboriginals still carry out regular burns over many parts of Australia.

We drove through smoke as well as fires along the highway, especially in the Northern Territory. At places where we stayed long enough, we watched greenery sprouting along the trunks of apparently "dead" trees only days after a heavy rain. This is a form of land management that prevents heavy build up of fuel on the forest floor. Fires set off in the wet season every three to four years are never so intense as to cause serious harm.

In the more populated parts of modern Australia, where burns were not practical or not carried out regularly, devastating and tragic bush fires had killed people and destroyed homes. It is probably in the psyche of every Australian to respect the ferocity of the bush fire. In every town large and small, there are Volunteer Fire Brigades that respond to local fires.

Passage to Brisbane

We waited in vain for two weeks at Coffs Harbour for favorable winds to visit Lord Howe Island. Instead we were getting great ESE winds for sailing north. Finally we could resist no longer and gave in to heading north instead. The first leg of the trip was fast, Laelia zipped along at 9 or 10 knots with just the jib. Not wanting to put too much strain on the rigging, we put two reefs on the jib to slow the boat down to 7.5 knots.

We had a fast passage to the Gold Coast Seaway in Queensland. The Seaway is the main navigable entrance to Broadwater and Southern Moreton Bay. As we made our way through the channel, we saw surfers taking advantage of the occasional breaking swells. It was disconcerting as it would have been most inauspicious to run over a surfer fresh upon arrival.

We ended up at the Southport Yacht Club, one of those marinas where motor yachts were like warships towering above the docks. Some locals told us that the Gold Coast is the equivalent of Miami and Fort Lauderdale rolled into one.

We checked out the local scenes, the giant malls. Malls big and small are about the same the world over, but these malls have great food courts. The Gold Coast was most famous for its dance clubs (some call them drinking clubs). The young adults and some not so young ones would drink and dance, then stagger back to their hobbit holes after the bewitching hour. The music was loud and the behavior worse as the night progressed. We were advised by a number of people not to go on weekends.

One taxi driver said that he avoided that scene after dark. "If someone wants to be dropped off there, I would drop him off, but I leave the area as soon as possible."

I thought we should check out the place as an interesting anthropological curiosity. After dinner each night, as the sun went down, Judy and I would look at each other and say, "Let's go some other night."

We met a couple, Jan and Eddie, who stopped by our boat when they saw the American flag on Laelia's stern. They invited us to join them at dinner at a Surf Lifesaving Club. Eddie took time to tell us about the local waterways and how to navigate in a number of tricky areas. It was most helpful to know specific sandbars where boats often ran aground. Local knowledge is golden.

We left Southport on a windy Tuesday morning. The VMR (Volunteer Marine Rescue) at the Seaway Tower was broadcasting a strong wind warning for our area...Hervey Bay and Moreton Bay. Yes, the wind was blowing hard, but the water was not rough. Laelia was sailing in water sheltered by a couple of large sand islands, so the sea state was fairly comfortable despite the strong wind. Southport was at the southern end of the Broadwater that included a network of shallow sandy estuaries at the delta of three converging rivers. The keyword here was "shallow." Laelia twisted and turned through these shallow passages. At one point, the navigable channel was only a few feet deep.

We followed Eddie's advice carefully, allowing us to make good time through the maze of sandy estuaries without running aground. It was a windy, overcast day with lead-gray clouds overhead, but armed with local knowledge, we avoided major mistakes. It took much of the anxiety out of our passage.

The only excitement was when we got caught between two fast ferries in a narrow channel. We were on what appeared to be a large expanse of water very much like a lake, but there was only a very narrow channel deep enough to accommodate boats other than runabouts. We got in the narrow, twisty channel in an especially shallow area.

We saw the first ferry at a distance going towards a different direction. Even supposing that the ferry was coming our way, we thought we could get through the narrow channel long before it arrived. We were wrong. The ferry was almost upon us as we were still carefully winding our way through the maze of a channel. There was no escape. A lot of water was all around the channel, but the chart indicated one meter or half a meter of water outside the channel and we could see little patches of sand exposed here and there. In one area we could see birds walking around on water, but we knew they were actually walking on sand in only inches of water. The ferry couldn't pass us...the channel was too narrow. It was speeding towards us.

Oh no! We are going to get mowed down and crushed into a thousand pieces to become fish food.

I abandoned all caution, pushed up the throttle, and raced ahead, hoping not to run aground as we rounded the tight curves. With hearts pounding and mouths feeling dry, we finally could see the end of the channel with one more marker about 100 yards away.

What is that up ahead of us? Yikes! Crikey! Another ferry dead ahead coming at us.

It looked exactly like the one that had been chasing us. Both were identical blue and white ferries, each sporting a big vehicle ramp jutting high up on the bow and loaded with trucks and cars.

Ay-yah, this has to be a plot to catch us in a vise of two ferries. Oh my! What can we do? Help!

Wait...the on-coming ferry was not quite in the channel...it was moving fast, but just outside of the channel marker. *Hah! It can't enter the channel.*

Of course! They are not going to collide head-on...obviously.

The approaching ferry had to stay out of the channel until the ferry behind us, the chasing ferry, was out of the way. They had done this before and knew where there was deep water.

It dawned on me that, if the ferry had enough water under it, Laelia would probably be fine too. We waited until Laelia, going in the opposite direction, passed the oncoming ferry port to port. We made a very sharp U-turn to port and dropped immediately behind the ferry we had just passed. As we completed the U-turn, the chasing ferry went whooshing by us, still hissing with frustration for letting us escape.

We completed our escape with another U-turn to follow behind our original pursuer. Of course we were not trying to run it down or even catch up. We could only follow in its propeller wash for a few minutes before it was out of sight. At least we got to live another day.

It was already dark when we arrived at a quiet anchorage in the lee of St. Helena Island National Park, a little island in Southern Moreton Bay not far from the mouth of the Brisbane River. We dropped anchor between two green flashing navigation markers and turned on the anchor light. With Laelia the only boat anchored there, we put on a second light in the cockpit to make sure we were visible to passing boat traffic. The island provided shelter from the strong SE wind. Had it not been for the wind, the chop, and the darkness we could have made it over to the park by dinghy for a stroll and to check out some of the old buildings. Instead, we cooked a pork roast with star anise, honey, and light amounts of soy sauce...yum!

We got up early the next morning to catch the slack water for going up the Brisbane River. Sunrise was at 0605, high water at 0645. It would take more than an hour to get in the river channel, so there was no chance of riding the flood tide up the river in daylight. We were satisfied with a few hours of slack water to arrive at a designated anchorage near the Botanical Garden. We had little boating experienced on rivers so this was something new and a fun experience. As we went under the Gateway Bridge, despite the 70-meter high bridge clearance, it looked as if our mast (only 20 meters) was going to hit the span. Of course it didn't. Still, we held our breath as Laelia went under the bridge.

It was uneventful going up the river. We had an opportunity to place ourselves right smack in front of the cruise ship, Sun Princess, for more exciting boating adventures. We resisted that urge and, instead, stayed out of the way to one side on the Brisbane River until the stately Princess went towering past us.

The one unsettling event was that, as the Princess passed by us, we could see both the radar image on the screen and the ship directly. Judy was in the salon looking at the radar screen with a quizzical expression.

"How come the Princess is on our port side?" Judy asked.

"No, it is on our starboard side," I replied, thinking she was having trouble with her left and right or port and starboard.

"I know the ship is on the right, but it is on the left side of us according to our radar," Judy protested.

I went and looked at the screen.

"Hmm…something is seriously wrong with our radar," I admitted.

Our radar had never worked very well. We would have been in bad trouble had it been foggy or at night. Perhaps it was time to get serious about this radar business. At night or in poor visibility, having a reliable radar could ward off such disaster as getting run down by a ship.

We dropped anchor at the Port Brisbane anchorage under the shadow of the Brisbane Botanical Garden. We couldn't stay ashore too long because of the unsettled weather condition and the constant swinging of Laelia on her anchor with the tidal cycle. We did, however, walk the Garden and enjoy the Teahouse where "brekkie" (breakfast) was served all day.

Running the Wide Bay Bar

We learned from Eddie and Jan at the Southport Marina about "the most dangerous sandbar in Australia." That was the reputation of the Wide Bay Bar located near the southern end of Fraser Island. Boats had been rolled in the surf and lives lost attempting to cross this treacherous sandbar. It was just as well we didn't know anything about those awful stories when we exited there fifteen months earlier. At the time, we just blindly followed a fishing boat across the bar.

Much later we read in a newspaper article, entitled "Patrolling the Toughest Bar in Queensland" by Ross Kay: "It is described by some as the most dangerous bar on the Eastern Coast of Australia, and it has never even served a drink."

We had absolutely no experience in dealing with big, turbulent sandbars like that. Years ago, while standing on *terra firma* in Astoria, Oregon, we observed the sandbar at the mouth of the Columbia River. It made an impression and instilled in us a healthy respect for the power and deadly danger of the turbulent water at these bars.

The Wide Bay Bar is not a single sandbar, but a series of them. As ocean swells and wind-blown current hit the shallow sand, breaking surf threatens to roll and swallow even large vessels. The sand shifts frequently. There is no permanent channel and there is always a chance for vessels to run aground. Boats spun parallel to the swells are ripe for rolling over.

This time around heading north, we could no longer plead ignorance. To enter the Great Sandy Strait at the Wide Bay Bar, we needed to have high water at slack or flood tide. The prevailing SE wind at this time of the year (May) would have been helpful too.

Unfortunately, when we arrived at the Wide Bay Bar early in the morning, there was an unusual west wind. We could see lots of breaking surf all across the entry area. We cruised up and down waiting for slack water. More importantly, we were trying to find the leading light that marked the channel.

"I can't see the leading lights on the beach," I said. "Maybe we should check with the VMR."

"VMR Tin Can Bay, VMR, VMR, this is sailing catamaran Laelia," Judy hailed on the VHF radio. By this time, we were not shy about talking to the VMR.

"Laelia, this is VMR Tin Can Bay, go ahead." The radio was very clear.

"We are having a problem locating the leading light at the entrance to Wide Bay Bar. Can you help?"

"The beacons have been discontinued, but I can give you the updated GPS coordinates."

"Ok, I'm ready," Judy replied.

The voice on the radio proceeded to give the three sets of numbers. The GPS coordinates gave us the starting point and the mid-point where we were to turn and adjust course to aim for the final set of coordinates.

"Let me know when you completed the turn and heading for the washing machine. By the way, a fishing boat had gone out about half hour ago. But, it is not yet high tide right now. If you are uncertain, you can wait another half hour for possibly better conditions. VMR Tin Can Bay on standby."

We had been waiting for some time already and felt the strain of getting pushed around by the waves. We wanted to go before we got seasick. A few other sailboats had arrived. No doubt they were listening in on the conversation and were probably waiting to see how we fared.

There were breakers everywhere, but we thought we could see a path clear of the largest ones. We decided to make a run for it. First, we punched in the GPS coordinates in the chart screen and got the boat pointed in the proper direction before speeding up. We pushed the throttle all the way to the maximum RPM allowed for the engines. With both engines at full blast, Laelia leapt at waves and crashed ahead. The roar of the engines was drowned out by the noise of the wind and the breaking waves. Indeed, there were breakers on all sides, but we had a clear course.

About one third of the way in, I saw a large breaker rolling towards Laelia from the direction of the stern. Laelia was moving swiftly, but the breaker was faster. The breaking surf came within ten feet of the stern where I was standing. As the breaker peaked, the undertow was sucking water away from in front of the wave creating a shallow area just before the breaking surf. I could see that shallow spot of water. For a moment, all I could see was sand with very little water over it.

Wow, Laelia almost hit bottom...that would have been a

disaster.

All this happened faster than the time it took to talk about it. Soon, we were at the waypoint to make a course adjustment into the "washing machine." There was white water everywhere with confused waves. Swells were breaking in every direction. Spumes of white foam flew from the tops of waves.

"VMR, VMR, Thanks for the advice. We are in. I can see why you call this the washing machine," Judy reported.

Crossing sandbars will always be high risk, but, this time, we felt some sense of control. Being in communication with VMR was a big help. Our previous experience gave us some idea of what to expect. Still, it was a tense experience.

We took Laelia to an anchorage not far from Tin Can Bay for the night. The next morning we drove the dinghy to the Tin Can Bay Harbour to see the feeding of wild dolphins. On the way, I managed to run the outboard into a shallow spot.

"Good grief, we are aground," I said.

"How did you manage to run a dinghy aground? It must really be shallow here."

"Well, it takes talent," I replied.

I tipped the outboard to get the propeller out of the mud, then used the oar to pole ourselves to deeper water.

At the Tin Can Bay Jetty (a jetty is a wharf in Australia) children and adults were standing knee deep at the water's edge waiting for the dolphins. Right on time, several dolphins came and accepted the offering of small fish from the children. These were the rare Australian humpback dolphins, *Sousa sahulersis.* (The classification was revised in 2014.) They could catch fresh fish anywhere; it was not clear to me why they would accept stale, dead fish for breakfast. Perhaps it was a social occasion. The children certainly were excited to meet and feed the dolphins. The tradition started when an injured dolphin was nursed back to health in 1950. Now, several generations later, individual names were given to the nine dolphins in the pod. The tourists came a long way to be close to the "wild" dolphins. The policy was that male and young dolphins received no food. The males weren't fed because of their tendency to fight. No food for the young because of the risk of encouraging dependence. At the time it was a low-keyed, small-town affair with friendly supervision by volunteers.

We went over to the neighboring VMR building where they had a rotating schedule of volunteers working on the radio. They also had boats for going on rescue missions in bad weather or in the dark of night to help fellow boaters. We brought with us a six-pack of "stubbies" to say thanks for the help. (Stubbies are beer in short-neck bottles.) It was a different watch officer on duty at the time and not the one Judy talked with on the radio. He was very surprised by the visit and the stubbies.

"No one has ever done that before," he said.

"We appreciate the help we received from the VMR," I said. "And if it is alright with you, could we have a photo of you?"

He was quite pleased to pose for us. We felt good about the visit; we always like to leave a good wake as we pass through on a boat or in life.

This time around, the passage through Great Sandy Strait was relatively easy, having been through the area once before going the other direction. By this time, we were also very good at navigating shallow sandy channels. We saw turtles and a few dolphins along the way.

We calculated the tides right this time and arrived at the shallows before high water. We only had to wait a short time for high tide before transiting the shallow bottleneck at the Great Sandy Strait. While waiting, we dropped anchor a little aside from the main channel and ate lunch. Just as we were about to pick up anchor to continue, we spied a fleet of motor cruisers parading towards us from the horizon. They were large motorboats of thirty-five to fifty feet in length, all white and in formation...one after the other with not much more than two or three boat-lengths in between. They were much faster than Laelia so we waited for them to pass. They went by us within thirty feet. We had to wave at all twenty-two of them.

We found out later that they belonged to the Riviera Cruising Club on their annual cruise. We saw them all anchored in a neat row later just before we departed the Strait into Hervey Bay. They anchored every night so it was easy for us to get ahead of them despite their speed. Getting ahead of them was important because that many boats could use up a lot of dock space at a marina or moorings at a small anchorage.

We continued our journey to Port Bundaberg. It was a night

passage up the Burnett River. We arrived at 0200 hours in the morning, too early to get in the marina, so we anchored in the river and waited. We had an appointment to replace the errant radar and install the AIS (automatic identification system) to Laelia's navigation display. The AIS is required for every ship over 60 feet to report, over the VHF radio, its name, course, speed, and GPS coordinates. The AIS boosted safety at sea by avoiding collisions. Laelia, at forty-two feet, was not required to install the AIS, but it was in our interest to inform ships of our location.

Port Bundaberg to Island Head Creek

We were anxious to find a good technician to install the new radar. While we were still at sea, we contacted a number of marine electronic shops by email about our radar problem. We got not only a prompt reply from Rampant Marine Electronics in Bundaberg, but also a knowledgeable diagnosis. To expedite, parts were ordered before Laelia's arrival. We were even offered the use of their family car. For boaties with no automobile, the offer of wheels to haul provisions is the ultimate kindness. Bundaberg, based on our experience, was the friendliest marina facility we encountered.

At the diesel mechanic's shop, I ordered a couple of alternator belts, but when they arrived, the belts showed a different part number than what I had been using.

"Are you sure these are the right sized belts?" I asked.

"The only way to find out for sure is to put one on," said the mechanic as he grabbed his tools and went to the dock with me and changed the belt on Laelia's starboard engine.

While he was at it, the mechanic inspected the engine for possible problems. He also taught me how to use a 19-mm box wrench to turn the crankshaft on my engine to make it much easier to spin the new belt onto the pulley. Considering how I struggled, swore, and sweated profusely every time I changed one of those belts, the lesson of a shortcut was like revelation from heaven.

He did all that for free. He wouldn't accept any payment. All I could do was to bring him a bottle of red wine before we left Bundaberg.

On our last night in Bundaberg, we were invited to see the tropical garden at the radar technician's home. It was a garden of cycads, triangle palms, Pandanus, timber bamboo, and elkhorn ferns. There was much more, but I was overwhelmed by the sunset from Dave's house overlooking the Burnett River. He pointed out the different birds that inhabited the trees in the vicinity of his home from the big balcony as we watched the red glow of the sunset. The pizza that came out of the kitchen was also terrific. *Maybe that is why the people in Bundaberg are so friendly... life is good in this town.*

It was time to move on north along the Queensland Coast. The weather forecast was for three days of favorable SE wind before a trough was to pass through with a NE/NW gale. We decided to head for Great Keppel Island on an overnight passage.

The Island was named by Captain Cook and is now part of the Great Barrier Reef Marine Park. It has crystal clear, productive water. The beach stretched for miles right in front of the anchorage. The navigation was easy without fringe reefs, but the anchorage was exposed to a NE blow. We upped anchor the next day at the first light of dawn and sailed for a more protected anchorage at Island Head Creek, part of a military training area.

Much of the nautical chart for this area was blank, un-surveyed. So we used a hand-drawn map in the guidebook. The Creek looked like a large lake at high tide, but we could detect sand banks lurking just inches below the water surface in many areas. At low tide, large sandbars showed. The navigable channel varied from 85 feet deep to where we eventually anchored in 11 feet of water. The next day we watched the depth meter as the tide went out. It showed at first 12.9 feet, then dropping to 8 feet, before going down to 6 feet. Judy was joking that I could walk around the boat and scrub the hull. Large swatches of sandy beaches showed up near the boat. Then the depth meter showed 5.3, 4.7....

It was too late to escape. If I turned on the engine now, it would probably suck in a lot of sand with the cooling water. The depth meter went to 3.7 feet. We kept telling ourselves that Laelia is a catamaran and even if grounded it would still stay upright. That was certainly true, but I would just as soon not be grounded. As time went on, Laelia started to swing around ever so gently to face the exit as the tide started to come up. That was reassuring.

We spent much of the day doing chores. Judy made new mosquito screens to put over hatches...nets sewed on to tubes filled with pebbles. I was threading an electric cable through the engine room to the lazarette. It sounded simple, but it was a dirty and sweaty job.

I went in the water under the boat to check the zinc, but I didn't stay long. No one had said anything about crocodiles in this creek, but we hadn't talked to anyone in many days. The guidebook warned that creeks within twenty miles from here were infested with crocodiles...big salties. Some boats carry firearms to shoot crocodiles when they become aggressive or try to come aboard although crocodiles are protected in Australia. We didn't carry any firearms and would just as soon not meet up with a hungry old croc.

Just as a good sunset was developing, we saw a sleek Hallberg Rassy (Hallberg Rassys are primo bluewater yachts) wandering into the harbor entrance. I could tell, even at that distance, that it was too far outside of the deep-water channel. That boat no doubt had a seven-foot keel. Laelia, with much shallower draft, had gingerly hugged the rocky cliff to stay in the deepwater channel when we came in. The skipper of the Hallberg Rassy was about twenty yards too far from the rocks and very near the sandbar that was exposed earlier in the day at low tide.

"What is that Hallberg Rassy doing? He's heading straight for the sandbar," I exclaimed.

"I think he's already aground," Judy said.

"Mmm, you're right, I can hear him grinding his bow thruster trying to turn the boat around."

It was pretty much obligatory for us to help under the circumstances although I would have preferred some rest after all the chores. Judy and I lowered our dinghy in the water and clamped on the larger 15-horse outboard in case I needed to push the distressed boat.

As it turned out, we didn't have to do anything heroic. All he wanted was for his wife to use my handheld depth sounder to check out the water around and in front of his boat. So I ran the dinghy around his boat for his wife to check the depth and guide him back to deeper water. He was running his engine churning up the sand and yelling gruffly at us to go this way and that way. He was rude. His wife in the dinghy kept apologizing to me for her skipper's poor manners. Eventually his boat was afloat again. He left without a word.

I suppose he was lucky. He got stuck just about an hour before maximal high tide for the day. Had he not gotten free when he did, the ebb tide would have laid his boat on its side. Anyway, the day ended peacefully with Laelia the only boat in the huge harbor.

An Event at the Endeavour Reef
Early in the morning, we departed from the Marlin Marina in Cairns. The forecast was for fifteen to twenty-five knots of wind and much stronger gusts to the north of us. We started sailing with one reef on the main expecting sudden gusts. After a while, I became impatient with the persistent light wind. It was relaxing, but sailing at less than four knots was not very inspiring. So we shook out the reef and raised the main all the way. Laelia was able to move ahead faster. Before long the wind began to strengthen and Laelia pushed ahead at 8 to 9 knots. As it got dark, the usual lull in the wind didn't happen. In fact we hit a couple of evening squalls when the wind picked up strength and shifted in direction. It was never fun reefing the mainsail in the rain or in the dark.

We were already in the Great Barrier Reef. The reef system had three general zones, the outer, the middle, and the inner reef waters. We stayed in the inner waters so the swells were much less than in the open water...the Coral Sea. The downside of staying within the barrier reef was that we had to stay within the shipping channel to avoid running aground on the reef in the night.

The shipping channel stayed straight as long as the reef terrain allowed, but the channel made sharp turns to avoid reefs and coral islands. There were small islands and occasional isolated rocks in the middle of the channel, but they were clearly marked by beacons.

As we turned with the contour of the channel, we had to jibe the main in the mostly SE or ESE winds. Jibing a large mainsail in strong wind could be risky and hazardous. As we were sailing down wind, the main was let out a lot to catch the wind coming from astern Laelia. When we jibed the main, we would turn the boat and move the boom from one side of the boat to the opposite side. If that was allowed to happen spontaneously and uncontrolled, the sudden whipping motion of the main sail across the stern of the boat could be very powerful and break any number of parts in the boom and mast assemblage. In an uncontrolled jibe, anyone whose head got whacked by the boom probably wouldn't live to tell about it. So it was always important to keep the sail under control during a jibe.

During one of these maneuvers, I erred in letting the jib (the foresail) get away with too much slack. The jib protested the neglect by wrapping itself around the wire forestay in a tangle and proceeded to whip itself to pieces in the wind. I cringed each time the sail slapped and crackled. I went up to the bow wearing my tether to see what could be done. It was dark and raining. The raindrops felt like sharp needles as they hit me in the face while cold water flowed down my back. Any attempt to unwrap the jib from the forestay against strong wind was clearly impossible. I couldn't even hold on to the jib sheet as it tried to rip my arm out of its socket. Eventually, we managed to furl the jib part way. The hope was that we could fix the problem in daylight before the jib demolished itself completely.

By now, we were sailing with only the big mainsail about twenty nautical miles south of Cooktown. On our east side was a large coral reef. Judy was on watch. She noticed on our new radar screen the presence of a large ship heading our way. We could identify the ship by name listed on the AIS screen.

Judy called the ship on the VHF radio. "Sea Witch, Sea Witch, this is sailing vessel Laelia, Laelia."

"Laelia, this is Sea Witch. You're on my radar loud and clear. Over."

"Sea Witch, is passing port to port acceptable? Over." Judy made the suggestion.

"Port to port is good. Sea Witch out," replied the watch officer.

"Laelia out."

It was important that the ship's watch officer saw Laelia on the radar and knew where we were and that we intended to stay on the right side of the shipping channel.

While in Bundaberg I had installed an "active radar reflector" on Laelia's mast. The device receives the radar signal from a ship and re-transmits an amplified radar echo in all directions. It was like making a little "pussycat" (Laelia) look like a big "tiger", at least on the radar screen. Anyway, we call our active radar reflector "Tiger." We were pleased that all our expensive new gadgets were working.

After Judy established contact with the cargo ship, it was my watch as Judy went to sleep. The 200-meter ship was just passing our port beam as agreed. The chart-screen showed that Laelia at the edge of the channel had a good separation from the passing ship. All of a sudden, the image on the chart-plotter showed Laelia heading straight for the reef.

What's going on?

It seemed that the autopilot had stopped working and Laelia had turned and headed into the wind. I tried to hand steer, but by then the boat had lost too much speed and the rudder was no longer effective.

I could see black clouds overhead in the night sky obscuring a bright three-quarter moon. From the increased wind strength and its altered direction, I realized that we were in the middle of another squall. The rain was pelting down.

I started both engines to get enough boat speed to allow the rudders to do their job. Even as we were gaining some speed, we still could not hold our course going down wind with following swells. With the slightest over-steering, the boat would head into the wind again towards the big reef. We did this a number of times with Laelia spinning around in circles away from the channel.

"What's going on?" Judy became alarmed.

"Good, you're awake," I said, "I can use some help. Keep an eye on the chart screen so we won't get too close to that reef."

"That reef over there? It's a big reef. It's labeled Endeavour Reef on the chart," Judy said.

Endeavour Reef ...that sounded familiar.

Each time Laelia spun around, the mainsail made terrible whipping sounds as the sail protested the punishment. Luckily, we always kept a "preventer" on the mainsail to avoid accidental jibes. Laelia was out of control and kept spinning around any number of times before I realized that the big mainsail was still all the way up, but with the jib more or less furled, the sail plan on the boat was terribly unbalanced. So on the next spin around, as Laelia was heading into the wind, we lowered the mainsail.

After that the autopilot together with the two engines was able to hold a course. By then I was wet, cold, and felt thoroughly miserable. Even in the dark of night, with no one watching, what happened was not pretty. It was certainly not a proud sailing moment. The only good thing was that we were able to unwrap the jib and furled it properly.

"Hey, Endeavour Reef...wasn't that where Captain Cook ship wrecked?" I asked.

"Right, that's why they named the reef for his ship, the Endeavour," said Judy.

"Is that why Laelia was hell bent on crashing into it?" I said, "Or was it Captain Cook's ghost trying to snatch Laelia?"

"It can't be. Beside, Captain Cook didn't die there," said Judy. "He managed to bring the Endeavour limping across the water to Cooktown for repairs."

"You are right. Had Captain Cook not survived at the reef, Australians would most likely be speaking French or Dutch today."

As it was, Captain Cook and his crew spent forty-eight days repairing his ship on the shores of the Endeavour River in what is now called Cooktown. During that period, contact was first established with the Indigenous People. Joseph Banks probably had a great time exploring the area. Of interest to zoologists was that the ship's crew encountered the kangaroo for the first time.

Even as we continued with the passage, I had questions about our catamaran's performance. I had sailed Laelia with only the main before without problem, but not now. Something was not right with the steering. I left notes in the log: the autopilot is not the same and the steering seems to wander with a greater excursion. I thought perhaps the rudder sensor was worn. It remained an unsolved mystery for many hundreds of miles.

Lizard Island
After Port Douglas and Cooktown, there would be few opportunities to re-provision until well after Cape York. There are Aboriginal settlements at Cape Bedford and at Lockhart River. In an emergency, we could probably find a phone at the settlements.

The skipper on another boat smashed his hand in the spinning blades of his wind generator. A number of cruising boats escorted him and his boat to Lockhart River. At the Aboriginal clinic, there was only a nurse on duty at the time; they waited 72 hours before a doctor finally showed up. By then it was too late to stitch his open wounds. I only saw his heavily bandaged hand when he arrived in

Darwin. It was somewhat of a miracle that he recovered from the broken bones and deep lacerations.

Within the Great Barrier Reef there are anchorages on the mainland and those nestled around islands, where cruisers can get a good night's sleep. It was possible to sail only during daylight hours by anchoring every night along the way.

We decided not to stop so often because it would take extra time to detour to an anchorage and to secure the boat for the night. We could cover more distance each day by sailing around the clock. We did stop at a few of the extra special places that were not just anchorages, but "destinations." Lizard Island was such a place.

While we waited for a weather window, I had time to write.

This is Tuesday, 17 June 2008. We are anchored at Lizard Island about 400 nautical miles south of Cape York. We are about 150 feet from the beach at Mrs. Watson's Bay with the anchor rode taut as a violin string. It has been and still is windy. The wind is 20 knots even in this protected anchorage. We hear the wind shrieking in the rigging and see white caps all around.

It is quite comfortable here. We will wait out the strong wind over this weekend before heading out to Escape River. That will be our last anchorage before rounding the notorious Cape York. In the meantime, if the wind generator keeps spinning and the sun shines on the solar panels, I may have enough electricity to keep the laptop working and write more about what happened to Mrs. Watson, for whom this bay was named.
Howard and Judy
Laelia, anchored at Lizard Island, 14 39 S, 145 27E

Five days later I wrote:
This is Sunday, 22 June 2008. We are still anchored at Lizard Island. All night long the wind blew at 20 to 30 knots. With sunrise, the wind has not shown any sign of moderating. It looks like we will still be pinned down here for the next 2 or 3 days. The anchor is holding, the anchorage is sheltered from swells, and we still have some fresh vegetables. The wind generator is working hard and we have plenty of electricity. So we really can't complain too much.

A Canadian couple and I walked up to Cook's Lookout about 320 meters above the anchorage. The National Park Service provided excellent markers and interpretive signs. It was a steep rock scramble for the first half followed by a more gradual walk along the ridge.

At the top of the mountain, there was a panoramic view. A few nearby reefs were clearly visible, but we could not see the outer barrier due to the haze.

We saw lizards. Captain Cook wrote in his log in 1770: the only land animals we saw here were lizards which occasioned my naming the island Lizard Island.

The ones we saw were about one meter in length from head to the tip of its tail. They seemed well fed and alert.
Howard and Judy
Laelia, anchored at Lizard Island

There were quite a number of boats seeking shelter at the anchorage. At one time there were twenty plus boats. It was a very social time. We had at least one potluck dinner and any number of happy hours on the beach when the swells were not prohibitive to make a beach landing by dinghy.

One boat had been there for almost a month. It was a family of four with two young children. They were looking for a break in the SE winds to head back to Cairns to repair a broken chain-plate that held the mast upright.

We were pinned down for nine days at Lizard Island. In that amount of time we were able to explore the area. There was a Research Station operated by the Australian Museum. Judging from the display of doctoral theses in the library, a fair number of graduate students from different universities had completed their dissertation projects at the station. The primary emphasis at the station was on the larval development of fish in the reef, but the station would accommodate any qualified researcher who had the funds.

I was surprised that very little was studied about their namesake, the monitor lizard on the island. The caretaker who led the tour at the station thought that monitor lizards at the Island were probably no different from those on the mainland since

Lizard Island had not been isolated from the mainland for all that long (about 6 to 10 thousand years). Lizard Island was connected to the mainland during the last mini ice age when the sea level was lower.

The station was mainly busy in the southern summer with a full house of researchers and students. In late June and July during the Southern Winter, the SE trade wind was dominant and it was quite dry and comfortably cool. Many Australian cruisers consider Lizard Island their northern terminus. They would arrive here in September and return south with the NE winds in October well before the start of the cyclone season.

We went to see what could have been Mrs. Watson's home. Back in 1880 her husband was away fishing for trepang or beche-de-mer. I knew these creatures as sea cucumbers, an *echinoderm* related to the sea urchins and sea stars, but very slimy and shaped like a cucumber.

The Watsons used Lizard Island as a home base and processed their catch there. Mrs. Watson, formerly Mary Phillips, discovered that one of her two Chinese servants, Ah Sam, was missing when he was tending the vegetable garden. Ah Sam's body was never found, but his pigtail was discovered on the mainland some months later.

About a month after Ah Sam's disappearance, the Aboriginals attacked Mrs. Watson and Ah Leung who was seriously injured by a spear during the initial ambush. Although Mrs. Watson repelled the attackers with her gun, she decided that their situation was hopeless. During a lull in the fracas the two of them, carrying Mrs. Watson's newborn infant, escaped by sea.

The details of the story were only discovered in a diary kept by Mrs. Watson, where she described in excruciating detail their ordeal and impending death from thirst on the small, parched island now named Watson's Island. We saw the island on the chart as we sailed through that region of the Great Barrier Reef.

Lizard Island only had water because rainwater was trapped in a large rocky basin where *Pandanus* palms thrived. The excess water flowed along a small seasonal creek draining into a tidal mangrove swamp before entering the sea at Mrs. Watson's Bay.

As we looked at the ruin of the house in bright sunlight and felt the cooling wind, it was hard to imagine the tragedy unfolding in so peaceful a place. I grieved for Mrs. Watson. She was a courageous woman who faced death unyielding and wrote her diary to the gut-wrenching end.

What a pioneer like Mrs. Watson never dreamed of was that her little family had stumbled onto an Aboriginal sacred site where they came by dugout canoes at regular intervals for special ceremonies and to feast on dugongs, turtles, and shell fish. It was likely that this was a ceremonial site for initiation of boys into adulthood. Although unintended, Mrs. Watson committed a serious transgression. Lizard Island was not the uninhabited paradise that Mrs. Watson had thought it to be.

At present the Lizard Island National Park is on Aboriginal land being leased back permanently to the government. The Park is co-managed with Aboriginals living traditionally in that region. The Dingaal people, who consider themselves custodians of Lizard Island, ask visitors "to respect the land and all that it provides."

Rounding Cape York
To sail from the East Coast of Australia to Darwin, we must round the notorious Cape York. It is a remote and desolate land with little service. We were on our own. We approached the long passage with a strange mixture of foreboding and excitement. Perhaps that was fear…I was not sure.

The eponymous peninsula was described as "one of the last remaining wilderness areas on Earth." The map showed isolated Aboriginal settlements, National Parks, and conservation reserves dotting the pristine landscape. Special permits and local knowledge were required for non-Aboriginals. I tried unsuccessfully to obtain a permit from the Aboriginal Council to visit the settlements.

Cape York is where the Coral Sea meets the Arafura Sea. From there, Papua New Guinea is only 70 miles across the Torres Strait to the north. The strait is shallow, scattered with islands and bars. There is a strong current in the Torres Strait due to a difference in sea levels between the Coral and the Arafura Seas. Together with extreme tidal movements in this part of the world, the current could be as much as seven knots or more. The treacherous condition was a serious challenge to navigation.

When we finally left Lizard Island, it was windy and gray. We continued to sail in the inner Great Barrier Reef heading north.

Although Laelia was in the shipping channel, it was not entirely risk free. We had received reports from other cruisers of seeing sailboats abandoned on the reef.

Cape York Peninsula and a part of the Northern Territory

The overwhelming advantage of sailing the inner reef was the calmer water. Even Captain Cook and his hardened crew on the Endeavour, after their desperate escape, went back in the barrier reef to avoid the rough water in the Coral Sea. Thanks to calm seas in the Inner Barrier Reef, Judy and I could both eat normally and were comfortable.

As we sailed north, we frequently encountered patrol boats and low-flying airplanes.

"Catamaran, catamaran Laelia. This is the Australian Border Protection…how many persons on board?" The VHF radio came alive and we could hear the roar as an airplane made a low pass over us.

"This is catamaran Laelia. Two POB. Over." Judy answered.

"What is your call sign?" The voice continued, but the plane was no longer visible.

"The call sign is Whiskey, Charlie, November, 4632. Over." Judy gave our FCC-assigned radio call sign.

"Your destination?"

"Destination is Darwin."

The encounter was straightforward. We had filed a notification with Immigration and Port Authority before departure. I was certain that Laelia was on a list with all the particulars. The name "Laelia" was in large letters on the bow. The plane no doubt also had an infrared detector that counted the number of warm bodies on board Laelia even as he was asking the question. The questions were to confirm our truthfulness. The radio call sign was another way to identify our authenticity.

The waterway in the north of Australia was infested with smugglers, asylum seekers, and drug traffickers. We never anticipated the number of times we were overflown and the number of patrol vessels in these waterways.

One dark night, we heard over VHF channel 16, "Vessel in the shipping channel heading south. Identify yourself." We recognized the voice of our friend Janet. There was no answer. We also detected the mysterious vessel clearly on our radar, a large target on the screen. It was only a few miles ahead of us, but the vessel was not broadcasting an AIS signal. That was odd. It could be an armed smuggler. We were getting worried for our friend. These illegal vessels were armed and didn't care to be noticed. I had no doubt that they had little regard for innocent lives.

"We are a sailboat heading north on your opposite course. You are less than a mile from us. Identify yourself." Janet was not letting up.

The mysterious vessel was not moving at a high rate of speed. That was odd too. Illegal vessels don't tarry... they have a drug or human cargo to deliver…quick in and quick out.

"This is the Australian Defense Force Patrol. What is your boat name? And Home Port?"

"Uh oh...big surprise." Both Judy and I had the same response.

"This is…uh…Rebirth II. Home Port…" Janet didn't realize she was challenging a navy ship. The inquiry went on in considerable detail. I gathered that it was a patrol vessel from the Royal Australian Navy sharing duty with the Australian Customs.

Now that I knew the location of the Navy Patrol, I took an alternate channel to avoid any possibility of an encounter. Our friend Janet might have blown the stealth patrol's cover if there were any illegal vessels within the 12- or 15-mile range of the VHF radio.

The twists and turns in the marked channel kept us busy and the radio kept us entertained. Night watch was not so boring, but it was not the best way to get a good night's sleep.

In order to tackle the Cape in our tip-top faculties, we decided to get some rest at an anchorage. It was also important to time our navigation according to the changing currents at the Cape. Our plan was to anchor at a safe haven nearby and to time our arrival at the Cape for optimal streaming conditions.

We arrived at the Escape River, a decent anchorage close to the fearsome Cape York. There were two problems with this anchorage…we only knew about one of them. We were warned that there was a shallow rock in the channel on the approach to Escape River. Unfortunately, we didn't have an accurate location for the rock because the radio transmission was a bit garbled. We discovered the other problem as we were sailing up stream in the wide expanse of the river.

"What the hell is all that fuzzy stuff ahead of us?" I asked. "It looks like a large patch of weeds."

"No…don't run into it. It's an oyster raft," said Judy, still looking through the binoculars.

"Damn…the chart shows some kind of commercial operation only on the south side of the river."

"Well, they must have expanded since the chart was made. The place is full of oyster rafts now," Judy said.

"It's a pain in the neck with all these obstacles…What a hassle," I grumbled to no one in particular.

Judy used binoculars to scan for a clear path in between the rafts. We ended up weaving up stream to drop anchor in a small bay with no oyster nets.

It was a quiet anchorage with no other boats around, very peaceful, not a sound, and not a soul. I was surprised that there were no guards. The oyster rafts probably were worth many millions of dollars in investment.

There was no Internet, no phone signal, and the SSB radio was heavy with static. We might as well be on the moon. I worked a long time to coax a weather report out of the radio.

We did chores on the boat to get ready for the next day. I checked the engine oil, all the filters, and made sure the alternator belts were in good condition. I studied the charts. We had learned previously from an Australian catamaran named This Way Up to check the time of maximum stream at Hammond's Rock. That was most helpful as none of our information mentioned the practical tricks of timing the strong currents.

All this area was crocodile country...not just crocodile, but man-eating salties. So far we hadn't seen any. The way to find them was to go on deck after dark and shine a flashlight (or a torch as the Aussies would call it) at the mangrove by the water's edge. All those bright red dots would be reflections from the crocs' eyes.

The next morning, we headed out the Escape River in late morning. We took a shortcut by way of a narrow strip of water about ten miles north of the river between Albany Island and the mainland. By taking the shortcut, Laelia avoided the heavy traffic in the Adolphus channel. Soon after we passed Alpha Rock, a prominent landmark in the channel, I spied a ship in the distance in front of Laelia heading our way in the Torres Strait.

"I'm turning on both engines just in case," I said. "There is a ship that could come pretty close to us."

"The ship is already on the AIS screen and it's on a collision course with us...it's a cargo ship called Star Bird," Judy said.

"I'm changing course ten degrees to starboard...you call him on the radio. I think port to port will work for us."

"Star Bird, Star Bird, this is sailing vessel Laelia, Laelia." Judy hailed the ship on the VHF radio.

"Star Bird here. You a sailboat? I see a large target on my radar," The ship's officer replied.

"Yes, this is the sailing vessel Laelia. What's your intention? I suggest we pass port to port. Is that ok with you? Over."

"Yeah, port to port's good. Star Bird out."

"Laelia out."

After dark, we passed the Booby Island Lighthouse that was on the Australian Heritage list. More importantly, the white flash at

7.5-second intervals told me that we had just exited from the Torres Strait shipping channel. We were now in the Arafura Sea. From here, there were two ways to reach Darwin. We could hug the Coast of the Gulf of Carpentaria. Or, we could sail directly across the Gulf in open water. The first option would allow us to anchor each night and not have to stand night watch, but it would take many days. The latter option would be faster, but we could encounter bad weather at sea. The Gulf is notorious for its erratic and unexpected storms.

After consultation with Judy, the decision was to take our chances and sail directly across the Arafura Sea heading for the northern most point of the Wessel Islands. The Wessels are a string of islands at the top of the Arnhem Land Region in the Northern Territory of Australia.

While crossing the Gulf in the Arafura Sea, we could hear the radio transmissions from other sailboats reporting their many adventures as they hugged the shore of the Gulf. We were taking a shorter route, but had our fingers crossed for decent weather.

Our original plan was to stop and rest at one of the Wessel Islands. The wind was good and Laelia sailed too fast and, as a result, our timing was off. We arrived in the vicinity at about four in the morning. It was still pitch dark. It is never a good idea to anchor in unfamiliar water at night. On top of that, although it was legal for us to anchor, we had no permit to land on any of these islands to stretch our sea legs. A favorable wind was blowing. I waved at the Wessels as Laelia shot past.

Laelia was now sailing at the top of Australia, heading west...destination Darwin. Shipping traffic was still our main hazard. Our radar signal detector kept flashing red, indicating ships nearby. We came close to a tanker, Pacific Leo, east of Croker Island, but passed without incident. More ships were around, but posed no immediate danger.

Later, as we passed the Croker Point Lighthouse, it flashed at 5-second intervals through a heavy mist. We were not lost, but the light was enormously comforting...it made me feel... connected.

Soon after passing the Lighthouse, we were overflown by another plane identifying itself as Australian Coastwatch. The queries were becoming more detailed and lasting a long time.

As Laelia approached the western-most point of the Peninsula,

Cape Don, we had to stop. There were only about a hundred miles between Cape Don and Darwin, but in this region, there are additional considerations to navigation. The daily tidal range is around 30 feet or more, creating a peak current of as much as five to seven knots. Laelia's boat speed could be significantly affected. It was worth a short wait to avoid fighting a contrary current. So we stopped and had lunch in a little bay before rounding the Cape into the Van Diemen Gulf.

We did a good job of catching the favorable current, but ended up going too fast. Laelia arrived at Darwin just before dawn. We anchored a few hours outside of Darwin to wait for daylight.

The huge tidal range made it necessary for marinas in Darwin to have locks. I had seen locks in rivers and in canals, but this was the first time I had seen locks at a seaside marina. Without locks, the marina would drain empty at low tide, pouring boats and docks out with the sea. It seemed to us like way too much bother to go in and out of locks. We decided to anchor in Fannie Bay. A large number of boats were already anchored, getting ready for the passage to Indonesia.

We learned quickly the art of securing the dinghy after making a beach landing. With 30-foot tides, the water level moved a long distance up and down the beach. When we rode the dinghy to shore in the morning at low tide, I would drag the dinghy a long way to the top of the beach and set the anchor in dry sand. By that evening, the water level would be high up the beach, but with the dinghy accessible at the water's edge.

One evening, we had two embarrassed novices asking us for a lift to their boats that were anchored almost a hundred meters out in the water. It was low tide when they anchored their boats at the water's edge. Now, at high tide, we could barely see their boats out there bobbing in the dark. They didn't want to swim to retrieve their dinghy. Of course we did the only decent thing to help a couple of fellow mariners in distress.

It was a time of preparation for the long passage to Southeast Asia. Days were occupied by boat repair and provisioning. Our big to-do was replacing a worn cone-drive in the transmission.

Late at night, wafting from the shore, the bass didgeridoo wailing in the dark was like the spirit of ancient magic. The melody grabbed at the soul and haunted the mind. The seductive drumbeats...stirred up irrepressible yearnings of the wild. The enchantment permeated the anchorage as I drifted into my dreams.

2. Exotic Indonesia

Departing Fannie Bay, Darwin (12 25.692 S, 130 49.323 E), 26 July 2008. Arriving Nongsa Point Marina, Batam Island, Indonesia (01 11.803 N, 104 05.817E), 24 September 2008.

Crossing the Timor Sea
Judy and I decided, after the Baja-Haha Rally to Mexico, that rallies are inherently unsafe because the high concentration of boats increases the chance of a collision at sea. On the plus side, rallies are a good way to meet like-minded people. Judy has always been more social and enjoys gatherings of people. There is definitely the camaraderie among cruisers who are willing to help each other. We enjoy the company of others who share our interest.

There was also a practical incentive. Sail-Indonesia Rally billed itself as a way to streamline the official check-in process at Indonesian ports. We had been to Indonesia before and were aware that the Indonesian bureaucracy can be cumbersome. So we signed up online for the Rally.

There were 117 boats in the Rally. On the first leg, we were all supposed to depart from Darwin, Australia for Kupang in West Timor, Indonesia, on 26 July 2008 at 1100 hours. Many people took the start time seriously and went up to the starting line for the signal. *Ha, we know better...we'll wait.*

The idea was that by waiting, we wouldn't have to tangle with more than a hundred other boats all scurrying to depart or to risk getting run over by some eager-beaver hotshot. But, waiting was difficult as others left in a big hoopla. We only managed to wait until noon before pulling anchor and departing Fannie Bay.

As it turned out, leaving an hour later didn't make much of a difference. It was a strange psychology. As soon as the other boats sailed away, I was anxious to get going. Then, as soon as I saw another boat sailing in our vicinity, I started to trim sails for maximum efficiency. Before long, by nightfall, we were in the middle of the pack. All night long we could see navigation lights all around us. We had to be extra vigilant to avoid a collision. Night watch was more stressful in a rally.

Our new radar was proving its worth. I set the screen at a scale to keep track of boats near us. We were usually able to correlate the radar targets on the screen with navigation lights visible on the water. Unfortunately, not all sailboats were detectable on the radar screen. It depended on how well the vessels reflected the radar signal. During night watch, it was crucial to scan for navigation light by eye. When in doubt, the binoculars were helpful for seeing faint lights on the horizon. The radar and AIS (automatic identification system) were both valuable, but they were better at tracking ships than at spotting fiberglass or wooden sailboats. Despite the heavy traffic, we managed the first night, then a second night with no incident.

There were oil-drilling platforms that were not marked on the chart, but they were well lit and showed brilliantly on radar as well. Similarly, the cargo ship was a piece of cake with our new radar. Cargo ships and tankers follow international protocols regarding navigation lights and all of them broadcast an AIS signal. Local fishing boats with no lights were a serious problem.

In the Timor Sea there were fishing platforms and fish attractors made of bamboo poles. These bamboo structures were completely invisible to the radar. In addition, there were also logs floating in the sea like crocodiles waiting to take a bite out of Laelia. Tugboats usually displayed distinctive navigation lights, but they often towed barges with no lights. The steel towline was invisible in the dark and could change its length to suit the prevailing towing condition. Running into a towline would probably be fatal. As a result, night watch was exhausting in these waters.

"The rewards of cruising in these waters outweigh whatever difficulties one may have to face," declared the author of the guidebook. Admittedly, the islands are exotic, but the many hazards required serious and intense vigilance.

Eventually, we arrived! It was in the dark of night. Heavy clouds obscured the crescent moon. We couldn't see the anchorage, but we were approaching the GPS coordinates provided by the organizers of the rally.

Had we been sailing alone, we would never have sailed into an unknown anchorage in the dark without reliable information. By this time, we knew better. It seemed being in a rally had led to dependence. It was an uncomfortable realization. We were told, "It's a big anchorage with plenty of room." That was not sufficient information for entering the harbor at night. I should have been better prepared.

It was difficult to see the other boats already anchored in the harbor. The shore lights of Kupang blended in with the anchor lights and were indistinguishable.

"Stop..stop...I think there is a boat in front of us," I said. "I can't see anything, it just feels like there is something in front of us."

"Why don't we just drop anchor here and worry about it in the morning?" Judy suggested.

"Yeah, let's quit before we bump into someone. It's already two o'clock. It'll be daylight soon."

Perhaps it was the lack of sleep. Our night vision was completely shot. Our minds weren't at their tip-top best. I still can't explain why we didn't get a searchlight to check things out. After we anchored, we were dead to the world for a few hours.

First thing the next morning, Judy looked out the salon window. "Oh! Look where we anchored...we are on top of another boat!"

"Wow, what a boat. It ain't just any boat...it's a Deerfoot 70," I said.

We had no idea that we almost crashed into a million-dollar yacht during the night.

We scanned the anchorage for another spot to move to, but came up with nothing. The anchorage was completely full. Boats had been arriving throughout the night.

"Well, I guess we'll just have to stay put. If the wind doesn't shift, we'll be OK," I said.

Laelia Is Impounded

"Permission to come aboard," cried Paul from his dinghy. He had arrived a day before us and anchored not far from Laelia.

"Permission granted," I said. It was a customary exchange of formalities.

"Have you heard? The entire fleet has been impounded by the Indonesian Customs." Paul was shouting before he even got on board.

"Impounded? What for? I don't understand," I said.

"Impounded! That means none of the boats are allowed to leave this anchorage. They will be pasting an official legal notice on every boat in the fleet. It's like being arrested and locked up," Paul explained loudly.

"They can't be serious," I said.

"Yes, they are! It's a serious matter. The impoundment will be on official records worldwide...like a criminal record." Paul was red in the face and gesticulating. He continued, "It's outrageous. I'm not going to put up with this."

"What's the problem that needs to be resolved?" Judy asked.

"I was told that it's about the Temporary Import Tax. Private yachts are exempt, but the rally is considered a commercial operation...so every boat in the fleet has to pay a bond and the tax." Paul seemed to calm down a little.

"That's silly. The only reason we paid to join the rally is to have that sort of bureaucratic stuff taken care of by the organizers," I said.

"Well, apparently the Indonesian organizer didn't do some paperwork to extend the exemption to the rally boats." Paul said.

"I'm sure things will settle out somehow. Let's go ashore and look around," I said.

There were two ways to go ashore. We could dock at the floating platform and get to the beach by a narrow ramp or we could do a beach landing in our dinghy. There was a fair amount of surf activity making the beach landing a challenge, although a group of boat-boys were available to help. Still, given the choice, the platform was much preferable to a wet landing in the surf.

I dropped Judy off at the floating platform. I had barely left to tie up the dinghy before I heard my name being shouted over the roar of the outboard.

"Howard! Come back..." Judy was shouting.

"What's the problem now?" I muttered.

"I can't get to the beach...the ramp is gone." Judy was still standing on the platform.

I could guess who had moved the ramp. The boat-boys were getting good tips by helping with the beach landing. With boats tying up at the platform, the ramp was a threat to their rice bowl.

With the ramp gone, we had to do a beach landing. Judy detested having to jump out of the dink quickly and getting her shoes all wet and full of sand.

Kupang and the Customs

We were ashore to explore the local scene. The Kupang town center was just a short walk away.

"Salamat pagi." I greeted the vendor good morning.

"Salamat pagi." The vendor, sitting cross-legged by the doorway of a building, returned the morning greeting and gave me a big smile. I could see that she was missing at least three front teeth. She was probably no more than 40 or 50, but weather beaten and wiry. She was very thin. She pointed to the items she was selling...not much, just some bananas and a few squash.

"Berapa?" I asked.

She waved the sign with the price. It was in the thousands of Indonesian Rupiah, but only the equivalent of twenty to thirty cents. I paid her in Rupiah and she gave me all her bananas. By this time, a younger woman who was asleep a few feet away woke up. She hollered loudly at me, wanting me to buy from her as well. So I bought a few items from her. Both vendors thought it was great fun and were laughing aloud. No doubt, I had overpaid them. I was laughing too, feeling pretty good that my Bahasa Indonesia was still operational.

"Terima kasih." I thanked them for the purchase and they responded with the same courtesy.

"Salamat jalan." They wished me goodbye (literally good walk).

"Salamat tinggal." I wished them a good stay.

Indonesian culture is very gracious with a long history, despite the obvious poverty at the time, especially in Timor. Bahasa Indonesia is a Malay trade language that helped unite the thousands of islands that each had its own distinct language. It is a user-friendly language... easy to learn with an intuitive grammar.

When we returned a few hours later, I surmised that there had been plenty of complaints about the missing ramp.

"Look, the ramp is back," Judy said happily.

"Hurray! No more beach landings." We both cheered, but were premature.

We ate lunch at the beach restaurant under the shade of a big tree where many cruisers hung out and traded stories over a beer. We befriended a young woman who could speak good English and was willing to help me with my Bahasa Indonesia. She was studying to be a journalist. We later met her father, a dignified gentleman. I think he wanted to see what kind of people would travel across the ocean in little boats. We kept in touch with her by email for several years.

Overnight, the entire platform at the beach lost its anchor and drifted away. I had my suspicions that there was foul play and had no doubt about the culprit, but nobody claimed responsibility.

There were probably serious behind-the-scene negotiations this time. By afternoon, the platform was reattached, but only for unloading passengers; no dinghy was permitted to tie up at the platform. In addition, there was a set-fee payable to the boat boys for landing and for looking after the dinghy. The "rice-bowl tempest" was settled. Everyone was relieved, except for one or two of the boat owners.

"It's extortion! They don't own the beach," declared one cruiser.

"The fee isn't much...the boat boys do provide a useful service," said another.

"That's not the point. It's the principle of the thing," the first cruiser retorted.

I didn't want to rile him up any further by joining the discussion. There wasn't much we could do as short-term visitors. All we could do was to fit in for a few days until we sailed away. I could live with the negotiated settlement: Judy got a dry landing at the dock, I paid a little money, and the boat boys earned some cash. I was certain that bringing in the authorities would end up costing even more money.

There were more than a hundred boats anchored in the harbor. Quarantine, Customs, and Immigration Officers were very busy checking-in all the boats. It was two days later before they came to

Laelia...we were among the last dozen boats to get checked in.

As soon as the officers arrived on board, they wanted to glue the impound declaration on the hull over the gelcoat. By that time I had heard the tale of woe about how difficult it was to remove the glue from the painted surface.

"It will probably be more visible if it is glued on the window," I said.

"Ok, that's good," the officer agreed.

They were very polite and pleasant, but did have to follow a strict bureaucratic procedure. Every document had to have at least two copies for each of several departments. Our printer-copier on board had a very busy exercise. They wanted us to formalize our crew list with the boat stamp that we had never used before. There was no ink on Laelia for the rubber stamp. I ended using some printer ink to stamp some smudges on our Crew List and Alcohol Declaration. I kept a straight face, trying hard not to laugh at such anachronism. Had I even smirked, it would have been a serious faux pas.

As soon as they were out of sight, I removed the sticker from the window before the sun baked it on permanently. I then discovered on the sticker some fine print about serious penalties for removing it without official authorization, but it was too late.

The afternoon wind picked up with considerable vigor. At least a dozen boats dragged anchor, stirring up plenty of excitement. One boat was anchored too close to our stern. We had hoped it would move somewhere else, but didn't say anything. After all, Laelia was anchored pretty close to the Deerfoot. All of a sudden, the boat disappeared from behind Laelia.

"Oops... what happened to the boat behind us?" Judy asked.

"Uh...it was there just moments ago," I replied. "There it is...about 100 yards down wind... still moving...it's dragging anchor."

"Pan-pan...pan-pan...pan-pan...two boats are dragging anchor in the anchorage." The VHF radio came alive with the alert. Someone had the presence of mind to send the alarm.

"You better go help them." Judy said.

As I jumped in the dinghy, there were already three dinghies speeding ahead of me toward the two sailboats. I stayed close in case they needed more hands. One of the boats adrift had no one on board. The rescuer had to climb aboard the moving vessel and figure out how to start the engine. Our neighbor was actually on his boat and could rescue himself and help to untangle the anchor chain. He came back to where he had anchored before, but a few yards farther back.

By this time, the bureaucratic nightmare was only part way through. Several tents were pitched on the beach, this time for checking out of Kupang. It was more paperwork, but in reverse. We had to come ashore and queue up to fill out forms and have documents stamped for permission to depart...contingent on a settlement of the dispute. We didn't know it at the time, but the dispute was in the national news in Jakarta and in Australia.

I was never certain whether the dispute was ever resolved, but we were told that all boats were free to depart Kupang.

Before we left Kupang, the provincial government provided a feast for the fleet. It was a buffet with many local dishes. There were speeches, dancing, and singing, followed by a choral performance by school children.

"Hey, it's a great feast and it's all free," one of the cruisers next to me said happily.

"Yeah, it's a feast alright, but why are they feeding several hundred people for free?" I asked. I was thinking of the abject poverty of the people I saw in town. There was clearly inadequate dental care and the lack of clean water. Yet they were spending money on cruisers who could well pay for the feast.

I sampled a little of everything in the buffet. Judy was more circumspect, taking only food she could recognize and liked. Some of the other cruisers were shoveling heaping amounts of food onto their plates. They acted as if they had not eaten for days. Obviously, they had no consideration for people behind them in the food line. I was disgusted and felt ashamed for their bad manners.

The children in the chorus sang as we ate. We applauded when they finished. Then the children went to the buffet line for their dinner. If I had been ashamed earlier, I was mortified now. I could see that there was nothing left except rice. I was embarrassed.

What kind of people are these cruisers?

"What do the local people think of us?" I asked Judy.

"They probably think we are all pigs." Judy didn't mince words.

We were also treated to a tour of a unique village that was the pride of the island. It was a very special village. We were told that this village had long ago refused any assistance from the government, even turning down the offer of having electricity brought in. The villagers grew their own food and raised sheep for wool, and used the wool to weave attractive fabrics. Everyone in the village worked, man, woman, and child.

They sang to welcome us and again when we left. The boys performed a re-enactment of a legend to entertain us. Not surprisingly they made sure we all visited their fabric shop, where many of us bought colorful hand-woven fabric. The income reportedly would be used for items they couldn't make on their own. It was quite a showcase of a little utopia. Too bad the village boundary didn't include the rest of the island.

Anchored Next to a Smoking Volcano

We had an overnight passage from Kupang and were now anchored quietly behind a reef under a smoking volcano. There were many volcanic peaks all around, evidence of a cataclysmic past. The little bay was in front of the small town of Lewoleba on Pulau (Island) Lembata in Indonesia.

During the passage, we discovered that the Savu Sea between Timor and Lembata Islands was a busy shipping channel. Ships plied between Western Australia and the Pacific through this corridor. As we were heading north, we first noted, on our AIS, a ship destined for Dampier, Western Australia, coming from the NE. We had our "Tiger," our active radar reflector, turned on to make sure the ship saw us on its radar screen. It was still 12 miles away steaming at 14 knots. Our closest point of approach (CPA) was 2.5 nautical miles. That was a comfortable distance.

Then we saw another ship heading our way from the SW going to Japan at 18 knots. It was most likely a giant ore ship. Right behind it was a third ship on a parallel course, but a few miles to the north. I felted trapped as these big fast ships were converging on poor little Laelia...all within the hour.

We were motor sailing at 5 knots with just the jib. The wind was abating causing the jib sheets to flap and make crackling sounds. The noise was annoying so I furled the jib. That was fortunate because little did I know that we would soon need to do some fast maneuvering without being encumbered by any sail. Just then yet another ship was noted on the AIS, coming from the north on its way to Kupang. It appeared to be on our track steaming straight at us. We were boxed in.

The ship from the north was truly the danger. I wasn't absolutely sure that there would be a collision, but I wanted to get out of the way. I steered Laelia to port at full throttle. It took half an hour of running like a scared rabbit before I saw with binoculars a convincing green navigation light on the approaching ship assuring me that we were on the ship's starboard side. We passed starboard to starboard (right side to right side). Navigation lights are red on the port (left) side of the vessel and green on the starboard (right) side.

We were pleasantly surprised when we arrived at the empty anchorage in bright sunshine. It was delightful to be the only boat there. We arrived early because Laelia had skipped one of the ports on the rally itinerary.

While on shore on Lembata Island, a young man approached us and introduced himself as a journalist. Apparently, our friend in Kupang had alerted him of our arrival, not knowing that I had a serious aversion to reporters. I hated being quoted out of context to make a story more interesting.

This young journalist was very personable and seemed sincere. He was curious how people could sail across oceans. We invited him on board. He asked many questions about our preparations, of storms we encountered, and he wanted to know how we navigated through strange places.

"It seems very daunting. Not just about all the preparation, but with all the troubles you have already encountered," he said.

"Well, it may seem that way, but it's really not that difficult," I replied. "It is daunting when the events are all mentioned together, but take it one day at a time and it just happens. We dealt with each incident the best we could as it occurred."

"I don't know...I don't think many people can do that." He frowned and looked at me earnestly.

"Look at it this way," I said, "you tell a ten-year old boy that he has to go to school for so many more years. After that, if he is lucky, he will find a job and work for 30 years. He will need to get up every morning and deal with all the problems like bullies, the police, tax collectors, cyclones, epidemics; the boy probably would refuse to get out of bed that day."

"I wouldn't blame him," agreed the journalist.

"Yet, most of us do exactly that...one day at a time. We try to do the best we know how every day. Before we know it, we're there," I said.

He was quiet. I continued, "Life is lived one day at a time and, with some effort, it can add up to be something wonderful. The sailing life is no different."

He brightened up and said, "Sedikit sedikit, lama lama, menjadi bukit." (Indonesian proverb: bit by bit, after a long time, it builds a mountain.)

Anchorage at Lewoleba, Pulau Lembata, Indonesia

I showed him a photo that I had taken from the boat early that morning, showing several sailboats in the quiet anchorage with morning fog drifting over the palms and homes ashore.

"That's Lembata? I never knew it's so beautiful," he exclaimed. He had never seen the island from the sea.

"It's the same place you see every day," I said. "Just from a different perspective."

Within a few days, the rest of the fleet caught up with Laelia.

Again, the rally fleet was treated to a display of the local culture, followed by a parade through town and the surrounding area.

We had the choice of riding tandem on the back of motorbikes or on an open truck. We ended up in a truck with a crowd. The truck's springs were not designed to carry the weight of so many bodies. Out of town, the roads were either full of potholes or were simply unpaved dirt roads. We waved as we went through residential areas and farms with rice fields. At times we stopped to take photos of children and the farms. Then back in the truck rumbling through hills and dales. My body was never so thankful when the parade was finally finished.

The Island of the Komodos

Laelia was heading for Rincah, one of the smaller islands in the Komodo National Park. We wanted to see a Komodo dragon. Of course they are not really dragons; they are a species of large monitor lizards (*Varanus komodoensis*).

Laelia was anchored in a very narrow, finger-like inlet with shallow mud banks on the sides. Water was very deep in the center of the channel. We had to pay out all 200 feet of our anchor chain in the water.

It was our 45th wedding anniversary and there was a windstorm at sea. The water in this protected anchorage was relatively peaceful compared to the boiling cauldron just outside the inlet. From the boat, we saw monkeys on the beach at low tide and a lone sea eagle soaring above diving for fish.

The reason we were delaying setting foot on land was because there was a large Komodo sunbathing on the small dinghy dock. To get ashore, we would have to leap over the lazy lizard. Judy and I thought that it would be rude to disturb its mid-morning nap.

The Komodo appeared sluggish, but we knew it could move lightning fast to snatch a bite of a leg or to whack someone with its tail. A woman told us that she had seen a dragon snatching a monkey in the flick of an eye and tearing it apart.

Eventually we went ashore when the big Komodo vacated the dinghy dock. We were walking towards the Ranger Station a few hundred yards away along a walking trail. It was a pleasant walk after having been cooped up on the boat for days.

"Look...over there." Judy suddenly stopped on the trail. A large dragon was heading in our direction, walking quickly on all four legs extended like a cat.

I hope he's not terribly hungry.

"Maybe we should go back to the boat," Judy said.

Before I could decide whether we should start running, the Komodo veered ahead of us and crossed the trail, still running on all fours. It was not a galloping motion, but kind of a quick cat-like trot or canter. I managed to snap my first Komodo photo.

We looked around the Ranger Station and at the shacks that backpackers could stay in overnight. It was not exactly the average B&B in Carmel by the Sea, but it was definitely safer than sleeping outdoors. The shacks were under trees that provided shade from the harsh midday sun.

"Watch out, Judy...you're about to step on a dragon," I said.

"Oh...I thought it was a tree root." Judy backed off.

All the English-speaking guides were already on tours. We got Yusuf, the Ranger, to be our guide. For our protection, he carried a stick. It looked like a two-pronged trident, but it was just a flimsy tree-branch.

"Are you sure that stick is enough to keep us from getting eaten by the Komodos?" I asked without much conviction.

These lizards can be ten feet long for a big male with a powerful tail that constitutes half the total length of the animal. It can whack the prey with its tail then sink its razor-sharp teeth into the stunned prey. If necessary, its head would swivel, using its teeth like a can-opener on the prey. Even a small bite could be fatal because of the rich mix of deadly bacterial culture in its mouth. The Komodo had been known to stalk an injured prey for days until the deer or buffalo collapsed from the infection resulting from the bite.

"Don't worry, I point the stick, and it backs off." Yusuf seemed very assured that his magical tree branch would keep us safe.

"I show you," he said, and demonstrated the technique on a nearby dragon. He pointed the stick with the fork close to the Komodo's mouth. The big lizard flicked its yellowish forked tongue like a flame at the branch a few times. It opened its mouth to show its teeth...and moved back a few steps. It probably wasn't hungry enough to bother with the stick.

We visited a mound of dirt...a Komodo nest, which was guarded by the female to keep other Komodos and predators away. The eggs were five or six feet deep in one of the several holes. The extra holes served as decoys. The female usually laid the eggs in September and would guard them for about four months before going away. The young would hatch around April and survive by hiding in trees and eating insects that were plentiful at that time of year.

While on the tour, we saw sea eagles, several falcons, a pair of megapodes, a water buffalo, and Macaque monkeys, but we found only droppings from the Timorese deer.

We invited Yusuf and another guide to Laelia for tea after they were off duty. They had many questions about our journey and about places we had visited. They had never been invited on board any of the thousands of yachts that had anchored at the island.

We gave them each a pair of sunglasses. They were pleased, but they wanted to give us something in return. I suggested that they could sing a song. They thought that was a good idea. We enjoyed their song although we didn't understand the lyrics. We were still in touch with them years later by email.

Several years after we departed from Rincah, we received a message from Yusuf: *"One of our friends was attacked by a 4-year-old dragon. It came in our front office and bit his leg and his hand... he recovered after five months and is working again."*

Before we departed Rincah Island, I dove in the crystal clear water to inspect the zinc on the propeller hub. That was when I discovered that we were missing the port rudder. It had snapped off at the hull. With only one rudder on the starboard hull, there was much less steering power...a nagging problem that had plagued us for some time. Laelia most likely had lost its port rudder at the Endeavour Reef in Australia when it was spinning out of control. For most of the last two months, Laelia had apparently been sailing with only one rudder instead of two.

"We need a new rudder," I said to Judy. "Bali is probably our best bet." We needed a heavy gauged stainless steel bar for the rudderstock and supplies for molding a fiberglass rudder. Replacing Laelia's rudder was now our most urgent goal. We wouldn't be able to stay in the rally anymore.

We had already missed several ports on the rally list. We didn't like the over-crowded anchorages and the way the islanders were being taken advantage of by the organizers. Anyway, the rally was becoming a hindrance to our freedom of movement. Most of all, I didn't need the rally to expedite the paperwork. Indonesian bureaucracy was actually easier to negotiate on my own.

The Best Cup of Coffee in the World
Indonesia is a nation of thousands of islands. Strong tidal currents can be swift in the straits between islands. The proper method was to use transits of the moon to predict the tidal stream. But mostly I did it by trial and error...we waited if the current was too strong. The worst we experienced was three knots, although the current could be as much as five knots or more at other times.

Eventually, we left the dry barren islands behind in the east. We were crossing the Wallace Line that ran through the Lombok Strait between Lombok and Bali. Alfred Wallace described the ecological divide in 1859 as an abrupt change in abundance and diversity on these islands. From this point on westward, the islands are lush with greater diversity of life.

We had to navigate through the outer reefs to get to the Serangan Harbor. The current was fierce and we could see breaking surf on either side of Laelia. Both engines were laboring and Laelia was crabbing along fighting a cross current. As we passed the barrier reef, there were anchor lines from a variety of ships and fish traps. Both Judy and I were on high alert to anticipate obstacles. We managed, one hazard at a time.

The anchorage was formed between Serangan Island and the southern shore of Denpasar City in Bali. The island is connected to Denpasar by a bridge and a lot of shoal water that provides for a protected harbor.

Through the marina, we got in touch with an Englishman, Robert, who said that he could fashion a new rudder for Laelia. He was building a catamaran for himself in a small boatyard. We brought drawings and provided dimensions for the rudder.

Robert invited us to see his almost completed catamaran.

"Wow, this is a huge catamaran," we exclaimed as we climbed aboard the vessel.

"It has nine staterooms," Robert said proudly. "It is seventy feet by fifty feet wide."

"It's wider than Laelia is long!" Judy said.

"That's incredible...it's big enough to fit three boats like mine on this," I said. "When will you be launching your boat?" I asked thinking maybe there would be a nice party soon.

"We'll launch on Wednesday..." He said with an impish grin.

He probably had been saying that for years. The boat was practically finished with the shining gelcoat already painted...a bright pink. It would be an amazing boat if he would ever launch it. *Perhaps he is afraid of something.*

Almost as if she had heard what I was thinking, Julia, his wife said, "Robert worries about his heart slowing down on him. He thinks one of these days, it will stop completely."

"Well, he probably can use a pacemaker," I said.

"That's it...that's what the doc thinks I need," Robert said. "But I don't want them to cut me open."

"It's not an open-chest procedure," Judy chimed in. "Howard will show you his pacemaker."

I unbuttoned my shirt at the top. "Here...it's just under the skin. The pacemaker is no bigger than a cigarette lighter," I said.

"Maybe it's not such a big surgery," Julia piped up, hopefully.

"Oh...in that case, I'll have to fly back to engage the National Health Service," said Robert.

While our new rudder was being built, Judy and I went traveling. Semarang on the North Coast of Java was one of the ports visited by the Chinese Admiral Zheng Ho, a Chinese Muslim, in the fifteenth century. (His nicknames were Sinbad, San Bao, or Sam Poo, meaning three treasures in Chinese.) The city still celebrates the event in July and August and has a parade each year. We were not there at the right time for the parade, but visited the Chinese temple depicting the courageous deeds of his fleet. There were carvings on the wall portraying how the admiral rescued a princess from the pirates and delivered her to her wedding by naval escort. It was a lot of rich and colorful history going back six hundred years.

On a different outing, we were touring an Orchid Garden with a couple from another boat. We came to a billboard in big letters: "Kopi Luwak." It was the sign for a coffee shop.

"Hey, look they have the best coffee in the world here," I said.

I had learned about Kopi Luwak from the movie, *The Bucket List*. In that movie, Morgan Freeman was telling Jack Nicholson about the civets eating whole coffee berries and leaving behind droppings of naturally fermented coffee beans. As a result the beans gave extraordinary flavor to the coffee.

Surprised, Jack Nicholson exclaimed, "You are shitting me!"

Morgan Freeman, who could hardly contain his glee, said, "No, the cats beat me to it."

Of course civets (*Paradoxurus hermaphroditus*) are not cats although they are sometimes referred to as civet cats or Palm Civets.

"I'm going to get a cup of Kopi Luwak. Anyone else?" I asked.

Judy and the other two appeared dubious. I figured that we were not likely to revisit the place again and one of us had to give it a try...no risk, no gain. I am not addicted to coffee, but this was a once-in-a-lifetime opportunity.

After I had taken the first sip and didn't roll on the ground clutching my throat, all three of them decided they would have a sip from my cup. The coffee was strong and smooth, but not so good as to deserve to be on anyone's bucket list.

We visited the World-Heritage Buddhist monument, Borobudur, not far from the region of Yogyakarta. It was built during the 9th Century when Java was still a Hindu kingdom. It was a massive structure, mountainous in proportions. It was abandoned because of a decline in interest, as the population converted to Islam, and the falling volcanic ash. Eventually, the tropical jungle secluded the mountainous monument for 500 years.

The compound surrounding the monument was open only from sunrise to sunset. In order to watch the sunrise from the top of the monument, I made a reservation at the only hotel within the compound. The hotel provided devotees with flashlights to make the pilgrimage trek up the monument, starting at around four in the morning. Judy slept as I shut the door behind me. It took most of the hour for the climb. The steps were not exactly easy-risers or built according to any ergonomic building code. I settled myself in a vantage spot facing east for a good photo. The sky became lighter as the appointed hours came and went.

Where is the sunrise?

It was a cloudy morning...no glorious sunrise over the stupa. Life is not always fair. I have learned to accept disappointment as well as the joy of success. It was a peaceful time at the top of an ancient Buddhist/Hindu shrine. I can treasure that. Happiness is to

SAILING AROUND THE WORLD

be content with what we have. I reached through the stone lattice and touched the Buddha statue in the stupa for "good luck."

When we returned to Serangan Harbor, the rudder had already been delivered to the marina. With the help of the marina staff, we installed the rudder on Laelia.

Judy became ill from something she ate. She vomited, had diarrhea, and couldn't hold down any liquid. She became weak and stayed in the bunk on Laelia. This went on for several days.

"I think you better go to the clinic to find out what is the problem," I said.

"I'm too tired to get out of bed," Judy replied weakly. "There is no way for me to climb in and out of the dinghy."

She was right in that it was a long process not just to get out of bed, get dressed, get in the dinghy, and to climb on the dock. That was what we did every day, but she was so very weak at that point. Even if we had gotten to shore, there was still an hour's taxi ride to the clinic in Denpasar.

By the next day, she was visibly worse. It was beginning to look serious. It would be very difficult for me to carry her in and out of the dinghy. If by chance she should fall in the water, it would be the end for her.

"Judy, it's serious. You're going to die if you don't get help," I said.

She seemed to understand. Slowly, excruciatingly so, she managed to put on some clothes. I helped her stagger to the stern of Laelia and put on an inflatable life vest. She got in the dinghy for the short trip over water then literally crawled onto the dinghy dock. We waited for the taxi. We had never been to a clinic before in Indonesia and had no idea what it would be like.

I gave the taxi driver the address.

"I know..." He gestured at his head to assure me that he knew the place. The taxi ride seemed to take forever, but the driver knew exactly our intended destination.

The clinic was a breath of fresh air. It was immaculate and modern. Judy was put on a gurney and her vital signs were taken. An IV bag was set up. By the time Judy received her second bag of saline solution she was already feeling better.

"She is very dehydrated," the doctor said.

I could see that Judy was out of danger. I didn't know it at the time, but the clinic had been at the center of the emergency medical actions after the 2002 Bali bombing. That little clinic could do a lot more than treat a severe case of dehydration. The staff at the facility saved many lives.

"It's been a few hours, she is still weak. She needs to drink the soup and keep it down before she can leave," the doctor said.

It was a lesson we both could understand. The internal environment of the body is normally well regulated, but a simple condition such as dehydration can be fatal.

A Little Storm in the Channel

It was time to depart Indonesia because our visa was about to expire. Our final port in Indonesia would be Pulau Batam, about 15 miles south of Singapore. From Bali, it would be a passage of around one thousand miles in the Java Sea to get to Pulau Batam.

We soon discovered that the Java Sea was busy with shipping traffic. The log showed that we made radio contact with Hereford Express to pass port to port and, an hour later, with English Bay, again to pass port to port. The cruise ship Sun Princess was heading for Darwin, passing Laelia three miles away. Around sunset, there were numerous fishing vessels heading back to shore. After dark there were at least three ships passing within a few miles. Night watch was not dull. It required constant vigilance.

On the second night, the traffic became much lighter. There was no wind, and consequently we were motoring at low speed. I finished a visual sweep of the horizon and found no sign of vessels.

Bang! Crash...followed by sound of things scratching on the starboard hull. I looked up and saw a bamboo structure scraping its way aft. Laelia's deck was about six feet above the water line. The bamboo structure was around eight or nine feet above the water. It had no lights and no sail and it was caught on the stanchion on the stern deck. I went to inspect it. The structure was made from a lot of 3-inch diameter bamboo poles lashed together. It was too heavy to haul on deck.

I stopped Laelia to release the structure from the stanchion. It soon started to drift away. Within a few minute it was no longer visible. It was probably a portion of a fishing platform blown away by a storm.

I checked for damages; no water was gushing into the hull. However, the bow stanchion on the starboard side was torn clean away. Laelia was still seaworthy, but repairs would be needed later. I switched on the engines again to continue our passage.

On the approach to Batam, Laelia was motoring north in the channel between a row of several small islands and the island of Bintan. There was a contrary current in the channel pushing Laelia back. All night long, we had been dodging fishing vessels and tugs towing large barges full of gravel. By daylight, the traffic was still heavy, but the weather was changing. A storm was brewing.

The wind started to howl and the waves, driven by the wind, began to build. The current also increased as the wind mounted. I increased the throttle to maintain boat speed. The rudder is most efficient when the boat speed is high. In this sudden change in the sea state, the worst thing that could happen was for Laelia to take the waves on the beam. The catamaran was most prone to capsizing when the waves were coming from the side. These waves were building into enormous sizes of fifteen feet and more, greater than half the width of Laelia. It was important to keep control of the rudder to avoid turning sideways and rolling over.

The lightning was followed quickly by rolling thunder, and the rain started to pelt down. It was a heavy tropical downpour.

The throttle was at maximum, but we were making little progress against the combination of 25-knot head wind, three knots of contrary current, and tall oncoming waves. Laelia's speed over ground was not much more than one knot despite both engines churning mightily.

"I don't know how long the engines can keep up at this pace," I said.

"Both engines are at 3600 RPM, but we seem to be standing still in the channel," Judy noted.

"I know. If there is a lull in the storm, I would turn the boat around and go to the little anchorage we passed earlier."

At that moment, a tug came close to Laelia on our starboard side, followed by the long steel cable and the barge. It was a colossal barrier. On Laelia's port side was an island. We were trapped. Had I deviated from our course at that moment, Laelia would either run aground or be mowed down by the barge.

Just then, I noticed a line caught on Laelia's bow cleat dragging in the water. If the line should catch on the propeller, the engine would grind to a halt with dire consequences. I quickly attached my tether to the jack-line (a safety line) and headed forward to retrieve the stray line.

As I was teetering on the bow to disentangle the line, I saw a mountainous wave coming at me. All I could do was to hold on to the cleat, the only handhold available...the stanchion had been torn away days ago.

The wave was rising higher and coming faster. It buried me under. It felt warm.

I seemed to be under water for a long time. Then I heard a popping sound. My auto-inflatable life-vest, activated by seawater, had inflated. As the bow came out of the wave, I was wrapped in a bright yellow, doughboy-like vest.

Later, Judy said, "I saw the whole thing. I yelled at you to hold on when I saw the giant wave. Then you disappeared completely under the water."

It was a frightening situation. I could have gotten washed off the boat. Even with the tether on, it would have taken quick action and a struggle to drag me back on board...assuming no serious injuries.

Judy continued, "Next thing I saw was the yellow vest popping up on the bow."

Still dripping wet, I waited for a lull in the wave action to turn Laelia around. As soon as we anchored in a little bay out of direct force of the wind, the whole world seemed to calm down. It was as if the storm had finished. We ate lunch and waited. We were able to proceed an hour later and arrived at the Nongsa Point Marina on Batam Island in late afternoon.

3. Navigating the Straits

Arriving Keppel Bay Marina, Singapore (01 15.906 N, 103 48.783 E), 28 September 2008. Arriving Ao Po Grand Marina, Phuket, Thailand (08 04.154 N, 098 26.668 E), 21 December 2008.

The Strait of Singapore
"How can we get across without getting crushed?" Judy lamented.

"Well, it's like crossing a busy highway. You study the traffic and dash across when there is an opening," I said.

"Yeah, but when there is a break in traffic in one direction, there are ships coming the other way. There is never a quiet time with no traffic," Judy said.

The shipping traffic is separated just like vehicles on a super highway. We were heading north. So we needed to cross the eastbound lane first, then the westbound lane.

We heard from boaters that the best place to cross the Strait of Singapore was to follow the ferry-crossing lane. We followed a ferry for a short few minutes, but the ferry was a lot faster than Laelia and soon was out of sight. We were left to cross the busy Strait all by ourselves.

At the time, there was a break in the eastbound traffic and Laelia was already in the lane. We could see at least three westbound ships, one after the other, coming from our right. We were committed, with Laelia in the midst of crossing the eastbound lane and the engines at maximum RPM. It was clear that the first ship to our right would cross Laelia's bow at a short distance in front of us. What we needed to do was to maintain Laelia's momentum and sprint across the westbound lane without getting smashed by the next two speeding ships, a container ship followed by a tanker. It's a game of "chicken" with only one possible loser.

It was too risky to try beating the container ship across its bow and a much safer bet to cross the ship's path at its stern. That would give Laelia the most time to sprint across the channel before getting hit and demolished by the tanker. Our lives depended on timing. These ships would neither be able to change course nor slow appreciably to avoid smashing Laelia into little bits. Our fate was in our own hands.

"Aim for the stern of that container ship," I told Judy who was at the helm. It put Laelia on a diagonal course in the shipping lane. With the container ship steaming along, Judy continued to adjust course to aim at its stern. The idea was for us to cross close behind the container ship to give Laelia more time to cut across the shipping lane ahead of the next ship, the tanker.

It was also important not to get too close to these ships, because these big monsters put out a huge wake as they steamed along. In the worst-case scenario, the wake with a height measured in meters could knock a sailboat down on its side. Being afraid was not an option. It was crucial to have a plan and stick to the plan to the best of our ability. Knowing that both engines were well maintained was an important boost of confidence.

It was a morning with plenty of adrenaline rushes, but we made it across the Strait of Singapore. We then motored along the shore looking for the designated anchorage to meet with the Singapore Customs vessel.

"Where is the customs anchorage? Let's take a look at the chart screen," I said as I adjusted the GPS chart screen.

Suddenly, the chart screen went completely dark. I poked at the buttons and turned the dials frantically to no avail.

"What do you know...we are navigating the world's busiest patch of water completely blind," I exclaimed.

We had paper charts, but with no identifiable landmarks to fix Laelia's position accurately. Much later, we discovered that our chart screen quit because there were too many ships in the vicinity. The AIS software saturated the memory buffer with information from hundreds of ships and crashed the computer. The chart screen was trying to reboot with no success. Had the system been able to talk, it would have said, "Help, it's too much. I give up!"

Finally, by sheer guesswork, we found and checked in with the Customs. On our way to our marina, Laelia entered Cruise Bay...the last bit of water before the Keppel Bay Marina. As we entered the little bay, we saw a towering cruise ship, at about one hundred meters away, moving slowly towards us. Apparently it had just left the dock. It gave five loud blasts, "Baaa, baaa, baaa, baaa, baaa." That was a nautical alarm warning us that we were in imminent danger.

The alarm was deafening and intimidating, but I didn't think Laelia was in any real danger, even if the ship deliberately tried to run us down. With the ship operating at slow speed, it simply couldn't accelerate that fast. We quickly turned away into the marina entrance and got out of harm's way.

About half an hour later, at the dock in the marina, we received a personal visit from the Cruise Bay Harbour Master. Apparently, we were supposed to receive permission from him on channel 18 over the VHF radio before entering the Bay.

Well, no one had given us that information.

Of course, ignorance was a poor defense. All we could do was humbly apologize and promise never to get in the way of their cruise ships again. It was important that we show respect and beg for mercy...the Harbour Master had all the power to crucify us at that moment.

All of that was more excitement than we could tolerate in one day. So we hoofed over to the Harbour-Front Mall...Singapore malls are the size of small cities, all air-conditioned. We found a map of the mall to navigate our way around. Believe it or not, there were three ice cream shops along the food section on the map.

Swenson's, Ben & Jerry's, and Haagen Dazs were the choices. Judy walked towards the shops very bravely with much resolve. The sprucely attired Indian man at Haagen Dazs invited her to sample their ice cream. She politely thanked him and moved on. All was well until three shops down when we spotted a Ben & Jerry.

She said, "Wow, we can have Cherry Garcia!"

"Hmmm...." I said. "It's already five o'clock. If we eat ice cream now, how are we going to have room for dinner?"

Well, there was no answer to that question. Five more shops down the way there was Swenson's with their funky Tiffany stained-glass lampshades and all the other trappings. Not a word was said as we walked past. The silence was deafening. I thought perhaps I was in some kind of doghouse.

Please understand that this was our first day in Singapore after two months in Indonesia. Indonesia has all these things in big cities, but we didn't visit many big cities. Indonesia also has very beautiful five-star resorts with magnificent and exotic shops, but never three ice cream shops right in a row. While in Indonesia, we mostly got our feet wet making beach landings and getting "Mee Goreng" (fried noodles) from street vendors. Much of Indonesia was still a developing country at that time. Most of the local people we met, in small towns, had a lower standard of living.

After much negotiation, we decided to give up going to Billy Bomber's hamburger place in Holland's Village and settled for a Carl Jr. hamburger instead. After that we returned to Haagen Dazs and the day ended peacefully.

The next night, we went to Holland's Village. It was a lot more upscale than it had been ten years earlier when we lived there. Now there was an entire street blocked off to accommodate outdoor seating. Billy Bomber's was no more; instead there was now a Hog's Breath Cafe at the same location. We found a Shanghai restaurant nearby that served steamed dumplings in little bamboo steamers and hand-pulled noodles.

While in Singapore, we had the chance to visit with Singaporean friends. We invited them to come to our boat for breakfast. We knew that by noon it would be too hot on board Laelia. (It was not uncommon for Judy and I to eat lunch at the mall and watch a movie...any bad movie. The malls are always well air-conditioned.)

With prospective guests in a few days, I felt that we needed to fix the air-conditioner on Laelia. While the contractor was directing the workmen to repair the broken stanchion on the bow, I crawled in the hull working on the air-con. It was mostly to repair the plumbing for the cooling water and to prime the saltwater pump.

Even with the air-conditioner working, I could feel the ambient temperature rising in Laelia's salon as the morning wore on. Fortunately, the breakfast went well and we had a good visit. We released our captive guests before beads of perspiration appeared on their brows.

While Laelia was docked in a secure marina in Singapore, we went back to California for a quick visit in the fall of 2008. Our return flight to Singapore in November tested our patience and good humor. The second leg of our flight, from Japan's Narita International to Singapore, was held up by mechanical problems and as a result we were bused to a hotel overnight in Tokyo. There we encountered a modern Japanese toilet, or rather a toilet-bidet combination, involving many unfamiliar buttons and levers. I described this in a letter to our friends, adding the following admonition: "Whatever you do, do not lean on the toilet seat to inspect the plumbing. The unit is really not designed as an eyewash..."

When we finally got back to Singapore we were in trouble, this time with Singapore Immigration. Arriving at the airport we unwittingly checked into the country as American tourists instead of "merchant seamen." The penalty could have been as much as two thousand dollars each. As I wrote our friends: "It was a long story, but to make things legal, we had to ride the ferry to Batam, Indonesia and check back into Singapore properly as a couple of sailors. Anyway, we avoided paying a fine by taking a round-trip ferry ride. Talk about inflexible bureaucracy."

The Malacca Strait
It was a 30-hour overnight passage from Singapore to the Admiral Marina at Port Dickson, Malaysia. We went by way of the Malacca Strait, a body of water situated between the Island of Sumatra and the West Coast of Malay Peninsula.

Laelia was in historic waters as we headed north on the west coast of Malaysia. Long ago, nine-masted treasure ships, some as much as 400 feet in length, dominated the Malacca Strait. Between 1405 and 1433 AD, during the Chinese Ming Dynasty, Admiral Cheng Ho commanded six expeditions to promote trade with Southeast Asia, India, East Africa, and possibly also Australia according to Aboriginal accounts. With each expedition there were anywhere from 25 to 30 thousand persons on board 50 to 100 ships of varying sizes.

After his daring exploits in what is now Indonesia, the admiral's fleet continued on past present-day Singapore to the Malacca Strait. Fast forward to 2008; after departing Singapore, Laelia sailed the same territorial waters, retracing the path of Cheng Ho's armada.

The admiral had befriended the Sultan of Malacca and made Malacca River the base for his fleet. In the ensuing centuries, Malacca declined and the river became silted. The nearest marina was at Port Dixon where we berthed Laelia. From there, we made a pilgrimage by land to the historic town of Malacca to visit the Cheng Ho Museum, where many of the fleet's artifacts were on display. It was a captivating chapter in nautical history, but little noticed by historians.

Our journey in the Malacca Strait was among heavy traffic of fishing boats, tankers, cargo containers, and tugs towing barges. I kept Laelia on the outer edge of the shipping lane, running the engine almost the entire distance. It was simply too risky to tack across the fast moving shipping traffic by sail. Among our greatest concerns were barges with long towlines not visible in the gloom of night.

Historically these waters were infested with pirates. As recently as a few decades ago ships went "missing" en route and were never seen again. Presently, the combined navies of Singapore, Thailand, and Malaysia have made the waterways here safe.

Although pirates were the least of our risks in the Strait, by the time we reached northern Malaysia there were plenty of discussions among cruisers about the prospect of encountering pirates at the Horn of Africa. For most skippers and their crews, a decision would have to be made soon. The choices were to head north by way of the Red Sea and the Suez Canal or to sail south to round the Cape of Good Hope in South Africa. Fear and doubt, mixed with bravado, were expressed at various happy hours.

"Which way do you plan to go? Suez Canal or South Africa?" asked a young man named Jake.

"Well, I don't know yet. I was thinking of sailing up the Red Sea and transiting the Suez Canal. It would shorten the trip by about 5000 nautical miles," an Aussie answered and continued, "That's why the Suez Canal is such a big deal to the world economy."

An old single-handing sailor from Ireland chimed in: "You know that the Somali pirates have been acting up in the Gulf of Aden recently. They are taking a ship almost every week."

"Sure, but they haven't been messing with sailboats…at least not yet," said the Aussie. "There just isn't enough money in these sailboats to be worth the trouble. Everybody knows that cargo ships and tankers are worth hundreds of millions and paying a million or two in ransom is nothing to these companies. In comparison, the pirates wouldn't get more than a few hundred dollars out of my boat."

"It'll be me luck for the pirates to attack me boat just to get their jollies," said the old Irishman. "I rather favor a passage rounding South Africa myself. Sure, it would add thirty or forty days to the trip, but what's the hurry? There's a strong south-setting current on the East Coast of Africa that should save a few days."

"I know about the Agulhas Current," the Aussie replied. "If the wind is north or northeast, it is terrific, but if the wind shifts to southwest against the current, it is big trouble. What happened to the luck of the Irish?"

"Yeah, that's right. That's also why they have some of the best weather routers in South Africa. Those chaps are known to forecast the time of the wind shift to within half an hour. When they say go, you sail like a bat out of hell and, when they say stop, you duck into a harbor." The Irishman continued, "I'm saving me luck for good weather rounding the Cape."

After a few more beers, the topic turned to weapons.

"I'm heading north. The word is that it's legal in Oman to buy weapons. I plan to pick up a semi-automatic rifle there for my boat," said Jake.

"I heard that too. Suppose I have a gun and know how to use it, how do I know whom to shoot and when to open fire?" asked the Aussie.

"I don't have that kind of problem. I'll fire first and ask questions later," declared Jake.

Everyone was silently sipping more beer. Apparently, the thought of actually encountering pirates and opening fire on them called for some reflection.

Having weapons on board was a topic Judy and I had already discussed. We reckoned having firearms on Laelia would be more of a liability and would probably add little to our safety. We would need to declare them at every port, adding to the paperwork and delay. In most countries, if we got caught with an undeclared firearm, we could face long jail times.

In any event, I knew that I would never be able to shoot people without unequivocal knowledge of their malevolent intent. I had thought through the possible scenarios. For certain, I would have lost the element of surprise by the time I could identify a pirate. "Shooting first and ask questions later" is easier said than done. If I mistakenly killed an innocent person, how would I answer to local authorities or my own conscience? I could end up rotting in a foreign prison for murder.

On Laelia our only weapons were two machetes: a long one I

kept in the salon and a short one next to my pillow. I imagined they might be useful in a last-ditch, hand-to-hand combat if it came to that, although I had no experience in such things except what I had seen in movies.

I had bought the two machetes in a local "Ferreteria" in Mazatlan, Mexico long ago. The long one was the kind used for whacking shrubs in the jungle and the short one was called a coconut knife about half a meter long. They were too big to put in a shopping bag. I carried one in each hand as we walked back to the marina from town. I noticed that even in broad daylight, people approaching me from the opposite direction would cross the street to avoid me.

An Interlude in Thailand

We were aware of the violent attacks of militant Muslims against Thai Buddhists in an ethnic separatist insurgency by Pattani Malays near the Thai-Malaysia border on the mainland. Our destination was Langkawi Island, a tax-free zone, although near the border, there had been no bloody attacks.

We berthed Laelia at the Yacht Club Marina at the tax-free Langkawi Island, where we provisioned for the Indian Ocean passage and beyond. Cruisers stocked up especially on wine and beer. Even non-smokers like us bought cigarettes. We were advised that cigarettes were needed as gifts through the Red Sea and the Suez Canal. I didn't particularly like the idea of encouraging smoking, but neither was I eager to reform the world. Cigarettes were safer than wads of money to carry on the boat.

Just north of us, one of the cruisers was knifed to death on his sailboat while his wife was tied up. The story we heard was that two Burmese boat slaves swam to the victim's sailboat trying to steal a credit card or some cash. They were desperate escapees from a cargo ship where they had been held as captive crew for more than a year. They had no intention of killing anyone, but when the cruiser fought back, he was killed in the fight.

Apparently, it was not uncommon for certain cargo ships to impress helpless locals to work on ships by force. The unwilling crew was unpaid with no passport and no means of survival in a foreign country. It was slavery on the high seas.

From Langkawi, it was a short hop to Phuket Island in

Thailand, a tourist Mecca that was especially hard hit by the Boxing Day tsunami in 2004. In Phuket, about 4000 people had died, half of them international tourists. All told the toll was close to a quarter million involving eleven countries surrounding the Andaman Sea. We arrived just before Christmas four years after the natural disaster. From what we could see, much of the obvious damage in Phuket had been restored, but some remnants of the tragedy were still conspicuous.

Phuket is a sailor's dream...good food, skilled boat works, gentle breeze, friendly people, and breath-taking surroundings. The distinctive limestone karsts thrusting straight out of the shallow sea reminded us of giant haystacks. There are only a few places in the world that have such unusual geological formations. The unique scenery was in a Bond movie, The *Man with the Golden Gun*, where our hero maneuvered a low-flying seaplane between these rocky pinnacles. Instead of a plane, we explored the sea caves at the base of the karsts by kayak.

There is a unique village, Koh Panyee, built completely on stilts over water. It started with only two Muslim Malay families of nomadic fishermen more than two hundred years ago. At the time, Thai law didn't allow foreign nationals to own land, so they built their dwelling on stilts adjacent to a large limestone outcrop. Now the village consists of 360 families and more than 1,500 persons. In addition to fishing they also have a thriving tourist business and a legendary football (soccer) team.

We are celebrities! Our Thai friends came to visit us at the marina, but we didn't expect them to bring a camera crew from a TV station to interview the intrepid seafarers. There was nothing we could do but to play along and answer questions.

Before we left Thailand, we went to see the Simon Cabaret, a fun and talented song and dance extravaganza with an international reputation. It was a long-running show in Phuket where all the beautiful showgirls and gorgeous dancers were what the Thais referred to as "katoey or lady boys." They are transvestites, but we thought they were more than just female impersonators. We speculated on how "lady boys" could have such curvaceous anatomy. My guess was that it involved more than just cross-dressing, because most of the costumes were revealing. I speculated that estrogen creams or perhaps implants were involved. Perhaps even more was done to alter their bodies with hormonal treatment. There is a lot we don't know.

If that was true, I wondered about the harmful effects to their physiology. It seemed excessive to push the artistic boundary to such an extreme. Were the performers compelled by artistic motives or by economic necessity? We had no information.

We would have liked to stay in Thailand much longer, but the journey beckoned. The annual cycle of wind and waves yonder waits for no one. Tardiness brings misery and danger. It was time for us to say "Sawadee krup and Sawadee kah" (goodbye, in male and female voices respectively, in Thai).

4. Plying the Indian Ocean

Departing Ao Po Grand Marina, Phuket, Thailand (08 04.154 N, 098 26.668 E), 22 January 2009. Arriving Hulhumale Anchorage, Maldive (04 13.051 N, 073 32.123 E), 03 February 2009.

A Rough Neighborhood
After considerable pondering on the tradeoffs between the risks of piracy versus the thousands of extra miles by sailing around South Africa, we decided to take a chance and head for the Mediterranean by way of the Red Sea and Suez Canal. The best wind for sailing northbound in the Red Sea is in the early part of the year. For that reason, we needed to depart Thailand in January to arrive in time for the Red Sea passage in the spring of 2009.

The first leg, according to our plan, was from Thailand to the Maldives, about 1,500 nautical miles (NM) across the Indian Ocean. Then, from the Maldives it was another 1,400-NM north to the Arabian Sea to Salalah, Oman. The third leg was a short hop of 600 NM along the southern coast of the Arabian Peninsula, from Salalah to the Port of Aden in Yemen.

For planning purposes, I usually assumed an average speed of five knots or 120 NM a day. In between passages, I allowed a week for catching up on sleep, provisioning, refueling, and perhaps a bit of sightseeing. So overall the trip from Thailand to Aden could take six to eight weeks.

The Port of Aden, at the strategic southern entrance to the Red

Sea, is only a few miles across the Gulf from Somalia. We knew this segment of the passage would be dangerous, but at the time pirates were attacking only the rich shipping traffic and had not attacked sailboats.

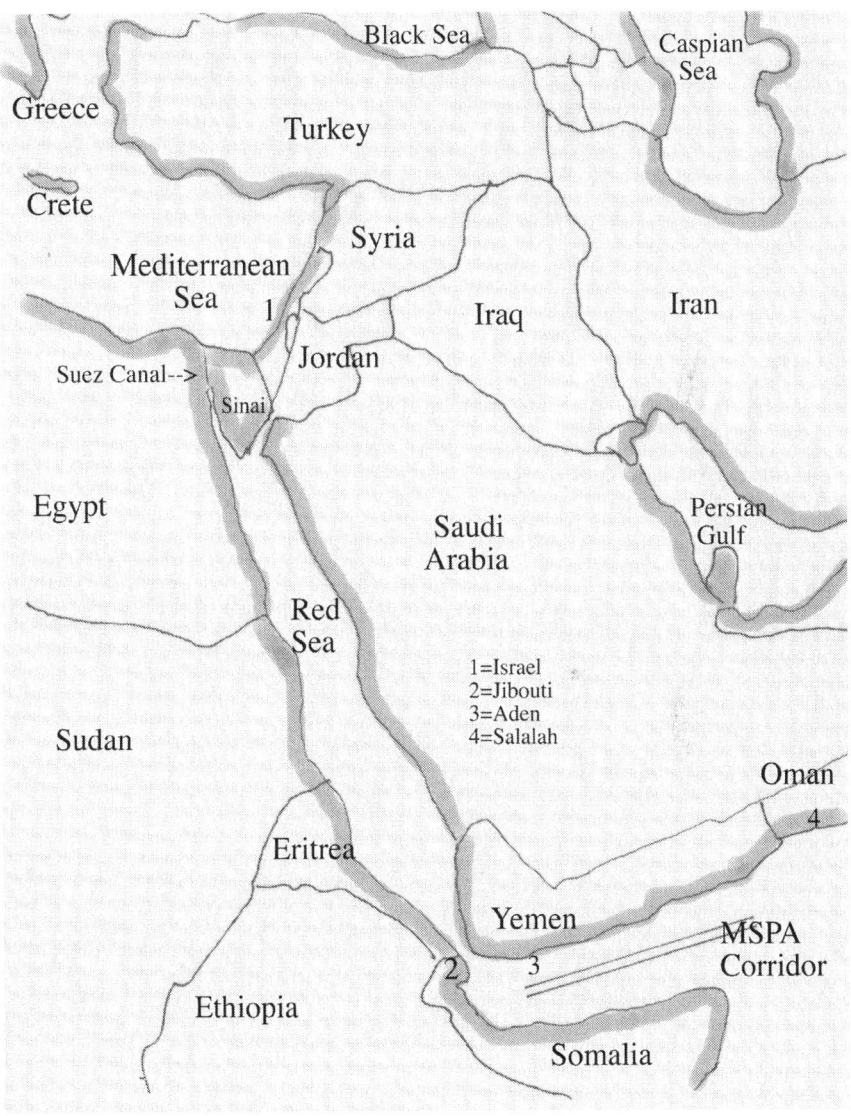

Countries in the Vicinity of the Red Sea

We departed Thailand on a sunny January day heading towards the southernmost point of Sri Lanka and India. The Northeast Monsoon usually dominates at that time of the year. We had wind that fluctuated about ENE while we were heading WSW. The saying "may the wind be always at your back" is actually not as good as it sounds. I had greeted people with that saying myself, but sailboats don't perform well with wind directly at their backs. The best point of sail for Laelia is on a beam reach with wind coming from the side. Of course, regardless of the condition it is normal for sailors to whine about the wind.

The wind was too light and the waves rolled Laelia side to side, so the sail didn't set right. Every now and then, the slack sail would catch the wind and fill suddenly with a loud snap. Crack! Each time I heard it, I could almost feel the stitches bursting along the seams of the sailcloth. With the boat moving at two knots, we rejoiced when the GPS showed Laelia moving at three knots.

Wow, we are gaining! Then, I became impatient.

Hmmm, I can run faster than that. How are we going to sail 1500 miles at this pace?

Subsequent days went by better. The wind improved so we now aimed for five knots instead of three. We saw flying fish. They were amazing to watch as they broke suddenly out of the water and stayed in the air for four or five seconds...sometimes longer. I even saw them changing course more than once in mid-flight. It was always a little sad to pick them up each morning off the deck, stiff and dried with their greatly enlarged pectoral fins neatly folded on their sides. I took some pictures of a few of them before tossing them overboard. One night, a flying fish came through the stern rail and hit me in the leg; I was able to quickly toss it back in the water. Perhaps it lived.

I only had one squid land on the deck this passage. That was good, because they tend to stain the deck purple for a long time. Only one pod of dolphins was sighted early in the passage in the Bay of Bengal. It was a pod of six or seven individuals about seven feet in length and fairly light colored. Again, by contrast, we frequently saw dolphins and pilot whales in the Pacific and often in groups of several hundreds or thousands.

We saw no sea birds after we departed Thailand. It was not until 180 NM from the Maldives that we saw the first bird life again...a frigate bird. It was circling Laelia, but later went diving for a small patch of flying fish. Frigate birds raise their young on deserted atolls where there are few predators. There are plenty of atolls in the Maldives not suitable for human habitation, but good enough as rookeries for birds.

We speculated on the reason for the lack of seabirds on this passage. At places where monkeys are plentiful, birds are under heavy pressure. Monkeys are able to reach bird nests for the eggs when other food sources become scarce.

On the second day out of Thailand, a breezy sunny day, Laelia was moving along at a pleasant seven-knot pace. It was my birthday. I went below to the stateroom to sleep while Judy was on watch. Awakened from a sound sleep, I thought I heard a loud crash followed by a sort of whistling sound.

Then I heard Judy yelling, "Come quickly, we have a problem."

I jumped out of the bunk and rushed up to the cockpit to see lines dangling everywhere and sails billowing in the cockpit.

Sails billowing in the cockpit?

Sails are supposed to be high up on the mast. The boom had also crashed down on top of the dodger roof and was resting on one of the solar panels. It didn't take us long to figure out that the halyard holding the mainsail aloft had parted. Without the halyard, the boom had crashed down, followed by the mainsail sliding down on the sail track making that whistling sound. The reefing lines were dangling in the cockpit, but most of the mainsail had actually ended up in the sail-bag. Only a small part of the sail was fluttering in the cockpit, but it was a shocking sight just the same.

In the scheme of things, this was only a minor disaster compared to being de-masted or having the boat flipped upside down, but it was not exactly a happy occurrence.

We had to switch to Plan B. We had installed a block (nautical jargon for a pulley) on the masthead several years earlier when we had a chafing problem with Laelia's halyard. We thought we had solved the chafing problem, but perhaps we were premature in that assessment.

The spare block had only a leader line through it. I sewed a spare 14-mm halyard end to end to the leader and wrapped the splice with tape, then threaded it through the block by pulling on the leader. That was how a backup halyard was installed on Laelia. All this took about two hours as Laelia sailed along at a stately pace with just a jib. With the mainsail hauled all the way up on the backup halyard, Laelia again moved smartly forward at a respectable speed. Life was good again.

As we approached the coast of Sri Lanka to round the southern point of the Indian subcontinent, the shipping traffic began to increase. In these ocean passages, ships posed the greatest hazard. The sailboats that disappeared "without a trace" probably were sunk as they got run over by a ship. There had been at least one photo on the Internet where a ship arrived in port with a sailboat still snared on the ship's bow bulb.

Fiberglass boats do not reflect radar signals well. Most sailboats carry a radar reflector on the mast, but the reflected signal was often too weak and not reflecting in every direction. We installed an active radar reflector (Tiger) that amplifies and rebroadcasts the signal in all directions, to make sure ships could see Laelia on their radar screens.

Laelia also had an AIS (Automatic Identification System) transceiver that ploted the ships' positions on our chart-plotter screen. The same unit also sent out a signal that put Laelia on nearby ships' navigation screens. It was one of the best inventions to avoid collisions at sea. We made use of every piece of technology available.

Within two hundred miles east of Sri Lanka we started seeing a large number of ships. By the time we were within a hundred miles, we never saw less than a dozen ships in a 25-mile radius. There were designated shipping lanes with a traffic separation scheme south of Sri Lanka, but no one seemed to pay attention to the lanes. Some ships appeared to be pretty aggressive in how they encroached on other ships' safe zones.

These ships were monstrous, anywhere from 360 to more than 1,000 feet in length, cruising at twenty to twenty-five plus knots. A few ships reported their length in nautical miles instead of meters. None of these vessels could stop quickly or change course without miles of clearance. One time we met four ships coming at Laelia head-on and I had to quickly decide what course Laelia should take in order to securely squeak by between those behemoths.

On another late night, I judged from the GPS position and

course of the ship heading approaching from the west, that we could pass port to port, with Laelia about one mile to the north. I thought it would be a routine passage of vessels. To my surprise, the other ship changed course to port and brought us on a clear collision course. I checked the positions and courses again to make sure of the situation before I got on the VHF radio to call the ship by name. His intention was to continue on his new course, although he could see on his radar and AIS that we were on a collision course. He didn't care.

I had no choice but to take evasive action. With my heart pounding, I could see the ship passing by less than a hundred yards from Laelia. It was too close for comfort, but we avoided disaster. It was a good incentive to continue to stand watch day and night.

That same night we had another encounter with a clearly malicious ship. Each time I changed course to avoid a collision, the ship, following not far behind Laelia, would also change course exactly to defeat my goal. It didn't just happen once or twice, but five times. It wasn't my imagination, because the course changes were clearly displayed on the AIS screen each time. Finally, I steered in a completely different direction so that the other ship would have to make a drastic course change to continue stalking Laelia. That ended the dangerous antics and the ship disappeared into the gloom of night.

The crew in the Indian Ocean represented a pretty mixed bunch, with many different accents on the radio. Some were possibly intoxicated. One or two were singing over the VHF radio, and others made obscene remarks. We heard them cursing at each other. I had to shut down our radio for some respite.

We were relieved as we finally got away from the heavily traveled area and sailed on by ourselves. It was a long night, but we survived to see the sunrise again.

Looking for the Eclipse

On the 26th of January 2009 there was to be a sun eclipse. It was not just any old eclipse, but an annular eclipse. The moon was expected to block out the center portion of the sun, leaving a bright ring of light. The rarity of the event made it worthwhile to put in a little extra effort.

We built a pinhole camera out of a carton with a piece of

notebook paper for a viewing screen. As the appointed time approached, we pointed the box with the pinhole at the sun. Lo and behold, there was a bright spot on the screen looking like the sun...well, it was bright and round. We took photos using the macro setting on the digital camera.

While we waited for the eclipse, we took a few more pictures each looking just like the one before. Clouds came by. We yelled at the clouds to move on. I have a personal history with sun eclipses; almost every time that I have tried to view one, there was sure to be a brief rain shower. But, this was the Indian Ocean during the NE Monsoon; good dry weather is the norm. It didn't look like there would be any rain.

By now we had taken a dozen photos. We waited patiently, but it was already five minutes past the time of the eclipse.

That was strange. Unlike human events, these astronomical events are very punctual.

We had no less than eight or nine timepieces on board Laelia, so we had the exact time. Perhaps we got the local time mixed up with the UTC time. (Universal Time Coordinated is the same as Greenwich Mean Time or Zulu time.) Actually, there is only a single UTC time anywhere in the world. Some of our clocks were on UTC time for getting on scheduled radio nets. For daily living on board, we generally kept the time of the departure-port until near arrival at a port in a new time zone.

I had hoped that we could report to our friends at home an observation from the Indian Ocean of the Annular Sun Eclipse of 2009, but it was not to be. Much later we discovered that Laelia was too far north to see even 10% of the full eclipse. To see the full eclipse at our longitude, we would have had to be in the Southern Hemisphere.

No sun eclipse, but we did get the Big Dipper (Ursa Major) back. Actually we had the Dipper back for certain as early as Magnetic Island and at Cairns when we were still in Australia. Our first sighting was only the handle of the Big Dipper in Bundaberg, Queensland, Australia. It was a feeling akin to discovering a long-lost friend when we first realized that it was our most familiar constellation.

We are on our way home!

Orion was upside down when we were in Australia, but now the constellation was on its side. In the early morning hours, we had the Dipper on our right and the Southern Cross (Crux), now low in the southern sky, on our left. I wasn't sure how soon we would be saying goodbye to Crux, which had been our constant companion on night watches for the last few years.

I reached for the binoculars to take a close look at Crux. The fifth star in the Crux as shown in the Australian flag was not as easily visible except for those with good eyesight. Even with my eyeglasses on, my cataracts still attenuated my vision, but it was quite bright as seen through the binoculars. We would miss seeing our friend at some point as we headed north from the Maldives.

After a few days, activities took on somewhat of a routine. We ate, slept, stood watch, and did the necessary boat chores. With just the two of us, we didn't keep a strict watch schedule, but we slept alternately whenever the chance presented itself. At any one stretch of time, one of us was always asleep.

As we rounded Sri Lanka and started heading WNW and NW, I expected the strong NE trades to become blocked by the island of Sri Lanka. I resisted the urge to reef the big mainsail. I thought the wind would subside, but it kept up a blustery blow and increased in strength to gusts of 25 knots. It was a little worrisome because the wind was from the NE and now that we had turned, the swells from the NE and the wind were both on the beam (on the side of the boat). Laelia, a catamaran, didn't heel like monohull boats, but it did roll side to side with these swells.

Experts had told me that cruising catamarans do not flip over. Well, no doubt experts were correct, but I didn't want to be the first to find out that there are a few special conditions when bad things could happen. Anyway, I went and put a reef on the big mainsail and furled the jib.

We had lunch and I went to sleep. Less than an hour later, I woke to see Judy unfurling the jib. The wind was dying...we were now in the island's wind shadow. We put all the sails back up and wallowed around in a light breeze before turning on the engine. After a few hours, the breeze picked up strength and soon Laelia was pushing ahead at eight plus knots. It felt good to have Laelia moving with such power and grace.

That went on for some hours before we suddenly heard a crash. Without even going out to the cockpit to inspect, we knew the halyard had failed yet again, and it's the backup that failed this time. It was getting to be a bad habit.

There was the jumbled mess, reefing lines dangling in the cockpit and the boom once again resting on the same sad solar panel. It turned out that the block holding up the halyard at the masthead had a broken stem...the metal pin that connected the block to the shackle snapped.

Now what do we do? Hey, this time it is a serious problem. We have no more backups.

Continuing to our planned destination was in doubt. Uligamu (an atoll in the northern Maldives) was up wind and would require the mainsail, which we could no longer hoist without the halyard. We could motor all the way there; it was only 250 NM away. On the other hand, we knew from radio chatter that Uligamu was quite remote, with an unreliable fuel supply and only a mini-mart type of grocery store. What was the chance of finding a rigger there to fix Laelia's halyard problem?

Male (mah'-lay), 200 NM south of Uligamu, was the Capital and the biggest city in the Maldives. We could sail there with just the jib. The chance of finding a rigger and buying more rope in Male was better. That turned out to be the winning argument.

Male and the Maldives

Our first sighting of Male from the sea was a little shocking. After twelve days of not seeing any land, we were suddenly confronted with a skyline of high-rise buildings, eight to ten stories tall, shooting up from the horizon. Male is on a small island on the southern rim of Ari atoll. The island is no more than one nautical mile long by half a nautical mile wide. The entire country is made up of atolls and small islands all of them at sea level. The recent tsunami had caused some devastation according to reports although we saw no obvious signs of damage.

The president of the Maldives was on the news not too long ago looking to purchase some other place to relocate the entire quarter million of the country's inhabitants. Apparently, if global climate change comes to pass as predicted, the Maldives will be no more in thirty years...except for ripples. The pristine water will remain and the reefs, if they survive, will continue to be excellent dive sites.

As we headed to Male, a port we had not planned to visit, we realized we had no information about the place. We had charts and such, but no information on clearance procedures at the port. Fortunately, there was an Australian boat, s/v Sunburnt, a few hours ahead of us going in that direction. They gave us, over the radio, the GPS waypoints where we could anchor and wait for the CIQ (Customs, Immigration, and Quarantine) clearance.

Six officers arrived on Laelia to complete the check-in procedure. The state of our health and the sanitation of Laelia's galley were all part of the clearance. No live pigs or dogs were allowed. It is a hundred-percent Sunni Muslim country and no pork was allowed on shore.

The officers were very professional, polite, and friendly. Check-in was no problem except for filling out all the forms, signing, and officiating the signature with Laelia's boat stamp. Luckily we had made boat stamps in Fiji and also in Indonesia when we discovered that these items were important for bureaucratic occasions. After the check-in, we were permitted to proceed to the Hulhumale Lagoon, where we dropped anchor in 45 feet of water.

So far that was the good news. The bad news was that beginning that year, 2009, all foreign boats had to be represented by an agent. The fee was substantial and it was quoted in Euros. It was an unexpected expense, but we had no choice.

As long as we had an agent, we decided to put him to good use. With his help we located a rigger, an electrician, the fuel tender, and received all manner of information within minutes. Our agent was a stocky middle-aged gentleman prematurely bald. He was well traveled and knowledgeable about world affairs and carried himself with dignity. He lived alone. His family was in Singapore so his children could attend better schools. He believed that education was the only way to get ahead in the world. This man certainly spared no effort for the sake of educating his offspring.

The only rigger on the island turned out not to be a professional rigger, but a skipper on a charter catamaran. He had gained experience with rigging work from repairing the catamaran under his care. He went up on Laelia's mast top for three hours until after dark. Each time when a ferry went by, Laelia rolled and the mast swung, but our guy held on and got a new halyard threaded through the mast. While we had his services, we had another backup halyard installed with an even bigger block at the top of the mast. That was just part of thinking ahead of the next disaster.

Judy and I were invited to tea on the skipper's catamaran the next afternoon. It was a new boat built in South Africa and was very well designed, with three double en suite guestrooms. We suffered a bit of boat envy. I offered to trade boats with him, but he thought I was joking.

The skipper and his two-person crew did all the sailing as well as meal preparation. They knew the best dive and snorkeling sites as well as secret underwater caves. Most of the waters in the Maldives have not been surveyed since the 1880s. Local skippers familiar with the area have a distinct advantage. Guests who went to some of the out-of-the-way atolls raved about the marine life such as turtles, dolphins, and an occasional manta ray or two. As far as I could tell, the tourist trade was the country's primary source of income. There were literally hundreds of resorts, most of them 5-star, scattered across the archipelago on secluded tiny little islands with pristine water. The coral reefs and the rich marine life made these locations some of the world's premier dive and snorkeling sites.

I was waiting ashore near the dinghy dock. A boy about six showed up admiring our dinghy which was sporting a new red cover made in Thailand. I asked him what he thought of our little boat. He was not terribly articulate so I went back to my bench. Just then his mother, in her long robe and headscarf, rushed over, looking relieved that her boy was still safely on the dock. I told her that the boy was admiring my boat.

She said, "Yes, he is very adventuresome. He will talk to strangers." *Mmm, I must be the stranger. I suppose I do stick out a bit around here.* She told me that it was Friday... no school. They were waiting for the boat to an island picnic.

Most people I met had a difficult time figuring out my nationality. It was hard for them to accept when I told them that I am an American. In their minds Americans look like Europeans. I had to explain many times (in Indonesia, Malaysia, and Thailand as well) that I was born in China, but that my parents had immigrated to America when I was young. As they were still puzzling over that, I would mention that America has people from many different places. If that didn't bring out any sign of comprehension, I would mention Tiger Woods or Martin Luther

King. Then they would break out in a big smile, "And Obama!"

It was hard to estimate how much the election of Obama changed America's image in the world. Many of the people we met in the street knew little about America. However, they did have TV images etched in their minds of the Rodney King beatings. Some of the older people remember images of police dogs used against civil rights marchers years ago. Somehow, a country with those negative images turned around and elected a black man as president forced people to re-evaluate their notions of our country. It reflected well on America as a people and a nation.

Our SE Asian friends pointed out that the great quality of the American political system is that despite the rancorous election campaign, the parties are able to work together after the election is over. The selection of Hillary Clinton as head of "Foreign Ministry" impressed those who were more knowledgeable about America. The Clintons commanded tremendous respect among Austral Asians. Most everyone with whom we had a chance to talk politics acknowledged that what happened in America definitely had a big effect on them as well. They felt the election of Obama was very positive for the world.

One young man put it very simply and rather emotionally. "He has to be better, he is more like me," he said as he pointed to the skin on his chocolate brown arm.

Our attempt at provisioning, in Male, was a little disappointing. Most of the local produce was limited to coconuts, bananas, potatoes, squashes, and cucumbers. Even the tomatoes were apparently shipped from China. There were also bananas from India, but very limited amount of leafy vegetables.

I was happy that the halyard problem was solved. The backup halyard now had a super, humungous Garhauer block at the top of the mast. The weather forecast was for light wind, but we didn't care. We were ready to depart and motored out of the atoll.

On the Way to Salalah

It would have been nice to visit Uligamu, others have raved about the snorkeling. To go to Uligamu would be a bit of a bash north against a NNE or NE wind. It would also involve more navigating through the many other atolls and some un-surveyed areas. On the other hand going directly to Salalah, Oman, would be a nice NW passage with a more or less beam reach all the way there.

We passed one lone turtle as we departed and saw a few dolphins and one lonesome sea snake. It was a very calm day. There was no wind, consequently no ripple on the water. With such a smooth water surface, even a lone ripple was very noticeable. There it was, a wedge of ripple cutting through the surface about ten feet from the boat. It looked more like a blade of grass floating vertically in the water with one end at the surface. Unlike a blade of grass, it kept moving along and the lower portion wiggled from side to side. It was no longer than 10 inches, yellowish with darker markings on the back. It was not fast, but persistent. It was too far away for a picture by the time the camera was at hand.

Laelia was heading north for the Arabian Sea not far from the pirate-infested Gulf of Aden. We were still in the Indian Ocean and had the choice of stopping over in Port Salalah, Oman, or making a left turn into the Gulf of Aden. Judy and I listened to the radio chatter reporting that the anchorage in Salalah was overly crowded and that the holding was poor with vessels dragging anchor.

"Tell me again why we are going to Salalah?" I asked Judy.

"Well, some boats are planning to buy weapons in Oman to protect themselves against pirates. Also, it's a good place to top up our fuel tank in case we need to dodge pirates," she replied.

"We already decided not to buy weapons," I said. "You are right that it would be very bad to run out of fuel in the pirate alley, but we have enough...I checked. Do you want to stop at Salalah?"

"Not really," Judy answered. "The harbor sounds crowded and the holding is poor. I don't need to go to another country just to check it off the list."

"Besides, Salalah is out of our way. It would delay our entry into the Red Sea by almost a week. We are already late in the season for the Red Sea passage. Maybe we should skip Salalah,"

"That's fine with me. I don't mind at all," Judy agreed.

So the decision was made to change course for the Port of Aden. I adjusted the autopilot to veer west to bring Laelia parallel to the Yemeni Coast on our starboard, with Somalia south of us on our port side.

5. Sailing the Pirate Alley

Departing Hulhumale Anchorage, Maldive (04 13.051 N, 073 32.123 E), 09 February 2009. Running the MSPA corridor (14 29.500 N, 53 E), in the Gulf of Aden, between 20 to 24 February 2009.

Gulf of Aden
The Gulf of Aden, a strip of water about 120 NM wide, funnels the shipping traffic between the Indian Ocean and the Red Sea which leads to the Suez Canal. The Gulf had for years been riddled with miscellaneous small-time piracy. When necessary, the cargo ships and tankers paid ransoms quietly. Only in recent years were some of the more brazen attacks on shipping traffic publicized in the media. The publicity, the increased cost of insurance, and the real possibility of a catastrophic oil spill prompted naval patrols in the Gulf since 2008.

I had downloaded the latest GPS coordinates for the Maritime Security Patrol Area (MSPA). It was a corridor to accommodate two-way shipping traffic in the Gulf of Aden situated between Yemen to the north and Somalia to the south. A multinational naval task force under US command had been patrolling the corridor providing some safety, although there were still successful armed attacks by Somali pirates from time to time.

The approximately 450-NM long corridor had two 5-NM wide channels with a 2-NM traffic separation zone in between. The westbound traffic was to stay in the more northerly channel.

We heard on the radio net that a group of sailboats sponsored by the Blue-Water Round-the-World Rally were staying in the traffic separation zone. I wasn't sure that was such a safe strategy. Considering the number of ships in the area powering at twenty to thirty knots and pirates moving even faster, the corridor was like a racetrack. Only there were no checkered flags, no beacons, and no dotted line on the water to physically separate the traffic. There was no legal requirement for ships to stay in the lanes.

Any vessel in the separation zone would need to watch for shipping traffic going in both directions. If Laelia, heading west, stayed on the northern border (right side) of the westbound channel, I would only have to worry about fast ships from astern. And, if the traffic got too nasty, I could escape out of the corridor.

```
    12 00 N, 45 E         MSPA Corridor            14 30 N, 53 E
    ─ ─ ─ ─ ─ ─ ─ ─ ─ ─ ─ ─ ─ ─ ─ ─ ─ ─ ─ ─ ─ ─ ─ ─ ─ ─

        ←West-bound traffic                 ←West-bound
         11 55 N, 45 E                       14 25 N, 53 E
    ─ ─ ─ ─ ─ ─ ─ ─ ─ 2-NM Zone of Separation ─ ─ ─ ─ ─
         11 53 N, 45 E                       14 23 N, 53 E

        →East-bound traffic                 East-bound→
    ─ ─ ─ ─ ─ ─ ─ ─ ─ ─ ─ ─ ─ ─ ─ ─ ─ ─ ─ ─ ─ ─ ─ ─ ─ ─
         11 48 N, 45 E                       14 18 N, 53 E
```

Most ships were likely to power at high speeds to minimize their exposure in these waters. We had at least two serious hazards facing us. Although the pirates represented a very direct peril, I thought the chance of Laelia being run over by a skittish ship whose officers were not eager for a Somalia vacation was a more immediate danger. It is not unusual for a terrified individual to concentrate on one peril, but fall prey to another menace.

Most ships had their AIS transponder on and Laelia's chart

screen displayed the icons of nearby ships. We could check the CPA (closest point of approach) while the ships were still fifteen to twenty nautical miles away.

We learned that the pirates would launch fast pangas with powerful outboards from a mother ship. Several of these pangas would converge on a targeted vessel. Once the pirates had boarded the ship, it was unlikely that the navy could dislodge them.

One sailboat ahead of Laelia reported on the radio net in the morning, "This is sailing vessel Morning Star checking in, but damned if I am going to give my position on the air. There are pirates near my location...I heard gunfire earlier. Last night I saw several fast pangas in the distance. They left when a warship appeared. There was also a helicopter passing overhead later."

During the night we received a security announcement on the VHF radio in the US Coast Guard style of radio voice, with an US accent. That was reassuring because VHF has a short range (line of sight) with a reach of about twenty to thirty nautical miles, depending on the height of the antennas. It meant that we had a warship nearby. Later there was a VHF communication between a merchant ship and a warship with a British accent. Of course we lurked and listened in on any interesting radio exchanges.

We saw a plane around sunset and a warship in the wee hours of the night, but we made no radio contact with them. We reported our GMT noon positions to the UKMTO (UK Maritime Trade Organization). They seemed to be the primary coordinator for managing the corridor in the Gulf of Aden. There were navies from many countries forming the Combined Maritime Forces. We understood that there were naval ships from NATO, EU, China, India, Malaysia, Thailand, and Russia at the time.

We had been at sea for some time since the Maldives. We gave up the chance to re-provision when we diverted from Salalah. By the time Laelia was in the Gulf of Aden, we had been out of green vegetables for several days. We still had cucumbers, carrots, and apples in the refrigerator, as well as oranges and pomelos in the cockpit. There were onions, squash, and sprouting potatoes in the basket under the cockpit table. We started working on the cheese supply, our backup protein. We had been making yogurt, but hadn't needed to start growing bean sprouts just yet. Food wise we were in good shape.

Notes made during passage:

"The night is dark with only a crescent moon, but the planets are bright enough to reflect off the water with a silvery shimmer. The Southern Cross is still with us, but traverses only a short arc across the southern horizon. The Dipper is high up in the northern sky. The bioluminescence is strong; the bow wake and the waterline are lit up. The propeller, when under power, leaves a 30-foot trail of brightly lit water and occasional flashes of extra bright particles. Even more enchanting is when there happens to be a strong wind kicking up a sea of white caps. As unbelievable as it may sound, every one of the white caps is lit up like a glistening fountain. Across the dark water are hundreds of these silvery fountains bursting forth. It is like a Maxwell Parrish image in motion."

While I was off watch during the night trying to catch a little shut-eye, I heard Judy on the VHF radio.

"Titan Sea, Titan Sea, this is Laelia, Laelia, Laelia. Over."

"Laelia, this is Titan Sea. Over."

"Good evening, this is Laelia, we are the sailboat six nautical miles directly in front of your bow. Do you see us on your radar? Over."

"Let me see... Yeah, I see you loud and clear going five knots."

"I would like to request a CPA of one nautical mile." Judy sounded like a seasoned watch officer. Indeed, she had already logged many thousands of blue-water miles.

"Yes Ma'am. Titan Sea out." It was an immediate response.

I couldn't resist getting up to look at the AIS display on our chart screen. It was not quite 15 minutes when the 650-foot cargo ship, Titan Sea, overtook Laelia.

"Wow, he went by us at exactly one nautical mile on our port side," I said. A short time later, we felt the wake from Titan Sea sloshing Laelia around.

While on watch later, I saw on the screen seven ships in a very tight group. It looked like a fighting formation. There were two rows of three ships each, followed by another at the tail end. Laelia was moving along at a stately pace with the squadron of seven ships gaining fast astern. I thought it wise to move Laelia aside.

I checked the ships' names on the AIS screen. The formation, as it turned out, was a mixed group of tankers and cargo vessels, all had different European destinations. The ship at the tail end was an Indian warship. It dawned on me that it was not by chance that these ships were in such a tight formation. The Indian warship must have been an escort for the other six.

The next afternoon, we heard a frantic call on VHF 16.

"Coalition Warship, Coalition Warship, this is cargo transport Antares requesting assistance. We have suspicious fast launches heading toward us."

"This is Coalition Warship, what is your position?"

The transmission followed a protocol in a coolly methodical manner, gathering the ship's particulars with little excitement. The inquiry included the positions, the color of the speeding launches, and how many persons as well as whether any firearms were visible. "How many launches do you see?"

"There are at least four suspicious fast launches on our starboard side," the ship's master replied.

These old salts are usually tough as nails afraid of nothing. This time we could detect agitation in the master's voice, maybe colored with a tinge of fear.

"Continue your present course and maintain your best speed. A vessel will be dispatched to your location. Warship out."

Apparently the pirates were listening in on these radio transmissions, because after a short while the captain reported that the launches had turned back.

Later that night there was a repeat of the call for assistance by the same ship. The ship was much farther ahead of us, out of our radio range. We only received the information second hand from another cruiser. Apparently, in the dark, the fast launches were spotted a little too late. The last transmission from the master on that ship was: "We have been boarded."

As we were approaching Aden and nearing the end of the MSPA corridor, we had to make a decision. If we went all the way to the end of the corridor, we would then have to make a right-angle turn to head north towards the Port of Aden. On the other hand, we could just veer off course from our present heading and sail directly to Aden, and save a few miles by cutting the corner.

Of course once we got out of the corridor, we were no longer under the protection of any warships. We doubted that a warship could really protect us if the pirates were determined to capture our boat. Laelia simply could not move fast enough to get away from these fast pangas used by the pirates.

The irresistible argument for taking the short cut turned out to be the wind. We had been sailing for days with an ENE wind directly on our back on a WSW course (252 degrees) along the corridor. By veering in a more northerly direction, we would have the wind more on our starboard beam. (Most sailboats are faster on a beam reach than with the wind directly on the stern.)

As we headed more NW, Laelia pounced at the waves and dashed ahead. It was exhilarating when Laelia reached eight knots.

Uhh, how about the pirates? Well, how will the pirates find us?

Once out of the corridor, with no more shipping traffic, we turned off Tiger, our active radar reflector. Then I turned off the steaming light, a white light on the mast required when Laelia is under power. Finally, I turned off the tricolor lights with a slightly guilty conscience. The tricolor is the set of navigation lights on top of the mast of a sailing vessel. The red, green, and white lights tell other vessels our direction of movement at night. This was required for safety. We also went radio silence.

We were still slightly detectable because we had an aluminum radar reflector on the mast, but we knew it provided only a very weak reflection and was not very visible at longer distances. We turned our own radar on only intermittently to check for obstacles in our path such as another boat. In the moonless night, Laelia was almost invisible.

Notes made during passage:

"To evade being detected by pirates, we resorted to stealth. We used radar only occasionally as the only navigational aid to plow through the moonless night. I worried that the bioluminescence was in its full glory. Fortunately, despite the scintillating light show, the actual light intensity reflected from Laelia was not enough to be visible from a distance."

We notified the UKMTO by email that we had departed the Transit Corridor and received back a nice thank you and acknowledgement from the Commander of the Royal Navy.

6. The Red Sea Escapade

Arriving Port of Aden, Yemen (12 47.519 N, 44 58.794 E), 24 February 2009. Arriving Elba Reef, The Red Sea (21 59.716 N, 37 03.337 E), 21 March 2009.

Landfall in the Port of Aden
Aden, the legendary port, is a strategic sentinel at the southern entrance to the Red Sea. It had an imposing presence as we approached from the sea. After many weeks away from land, our first sight of the jagged mountain towering over us was stunning. The looming igneous rock appeared dark and powerful. There was an old fort on the hilltop guarding the harbor entrance. Although the fort was in ruins, we could imagine roaring cannons raining fireballs at approaching ships.

Close up from the shore, the mountain was not as captivating because it was barren. The volcanic rocks had no soil to support vegetation. Houses, on the sloped foothill, were of a drab earth tone. Everywhere I looked, my eyes were craving for some living color. At a few intersections, the city had planted rare small patches of grass. The bright green was dazzling and exuberant by contrast.

There was a mosque not far from the Jewish Cemetery in Aden. It was situated with tall mountains in the background. The light-colored mosque with its graceful domes and tall slender minarets, contrasted against the dark, timeless volcanic rock, was one of those irresistible photo-ops. Unfortunately, to take that picture, I would have to negotiate a busy traffic circle on foot. Considering how Yemenites drive their automobiles, I quickly gave up the idea of that particular photo.

In Yemen, there were traffic regulations on paper. However, we were told that there was no enforcement. Driving required a strong sense of fatalism. Drivers were forever honking their horns either to warn someone that he was in dire danger or simply to relieve frustration. It was a wonder there was not blood everywhere on the road.

Yemen would not have been on our list of must-see places in the world. Yet, having been there once, I would very much like to return for a longer visit someday. Laelia was anchored in the same harbor where the USS Cole was attacked in year 2000. As recently as January of this year (2009), a pipeline was blown up and, last month, two German archeologists narrowly escaped kidnapping by disenchanted tribal members. Conditions appeared to be deteriorating ever since.

We decided to make landfall in Aden for several reasons. Primarily, it was the closest port to the Red Sea for us to refuel and wait for favorable wind to sail north. We did not have great expectations of what we might find. We had heard derogatory comments from other cruisers about Aden. Even so we were sorely disappointed upon our first foray into the waterfront. The buildings were in poor condition, streets dirty, and rubble-strewn back alleys suggested long neglect. Children of various ages were running around loose late into the night. The "Sailors Club," a nightspot on the waterfront, played loud music until the wee hours.

Our impression improved after some sleep and a trip into the better parts of town. Even the waterfront had its charms. The Prince William Pier, although the locals didn't know it by that name, is a solidly built concrete dock with stairs for passengers to disembark from small boats. On shore overlooking the pier is a clock tower that is the splitting image of Big Ben, but it makes no sound and is a smaller scale version of the one in London. There is a Mosque with loudspeakers calling the faithful to prayers. Scattered shops are old and have little to offer, but the little grocery store had eggs and frozen peas in addition to other non-perishable items. A bookstore!

"You have quite a collection here," I said to the young Yemenite behind the counter.

"Well, I inherited the bookstore from my father," he said. "He was British. He collected many things. The collection of postcards here is like a picture of Aden's history." He pointed at a box of old cards.

"That's the rock arch sky-bridge over the pass." He pointed to the card I was holding, "It was destroyed when the one-lane road underneath was widened for modern traffic."

On docking the dinghy at the pier, we were claimed by a family that offered to be our driver and tour guide. It started out when Judy and I approached the concrete pier in our dinghy, scanning the barnacle-covered wall and the green alga-infested steps for a handhold and landing spot. I unintentionally made eye contact with a middle-aged Yemeni gentleman leaning on the rail. He was waiting for just such an opening and rushed down to help, and I was his fast friend forever.

"I will help you," he said as he reached out for the dinghy painter.

Truly, it would have been ungrateful and poor manners for me to refuse his offer of assistance, but I knew what was to follow.

"As-salamu alaykom," I greeted him as I threw the painter line to him.

"I am Sayeed," he introduced himself. I introduced Judy and myself and thanked him again. I was trying to figure out a way to extricate us from our benefactor politely.

"Welcome to Aden. I can provide you with a driver and a guide at very good prices," Sayeed said.

"We don't need a driver now. All we want is to walk a little after many days at sea," I replied.

He was very persistent and introduced us to his cousin, his nephew, and other relatives. They approached us in relays, but we managed to decline them all...politely of course.

The next morning, as we approached the dock in our dinghy, there was Mr. Sayeed again. I greeted him by name. He was delighted and pointed out to the other prospective guides that he and I were fast friends. I realized my mistake too late about such dockside etiquette. So we relented and engaged Abdulla, Mr.

Sayeed's nephew, as our driver and Mr. Hari, another relative, as our guide. We agreed on a daily rate that covered both their services. We would decide each evening if we would need their services for the next morning.

Hari and Abdulla took us to a local restaurant for our first meal ashore. It was clean and the food was good. Hari ordered in Arabic big pieces of goat meat cooked in curry and plenty of flat bread. We ate downstairs in the public area. There was an upstairs dining room to accommodate women unaccompanied by adult male family members.

"It's Ok for Judy to eat with us here?" I asked Hari.

"No problem...they are used to western women. And you're with her," Hari replied.

Yemen is religiously more conservative than the Maldives or Indonesia. Here the women were totally covered from head to ankle in black when outdoors. Eyes could be visible through the slit between the hijab and the veil. Some would add another headband with black mesh draping down to the waist to shield the eyes. Most would also wear black gloves to cover their hands, making concealment complete.

The reason given for such coverage was for the protection of women.

It was particularly interesting to read the heated discussions in the newspaper (in English) on whether men needed more education than women and whether women should be allowed outside the home unaccompanied. There was hope, at least there were such open discussions.

Despite these cultural differences, the Yemeni people gradually "grew" on us as we got to know them a little. We found Yemen, as a country, charming and exotic. We were amazed by the amount of antiquities we discovered simply by poking around a little. Having a good guide made a big difference.

In general, the people we met were honest, resourceful, and proud of their heritage. We saw dignity despite the obvious poverty. The Yemenis have a long history, but in modern times, they were caught in the middle of the Cold War. The civil strife between the North and the South continued after South Yemen gained independence from the British in 1967. As I write, Yemen is in the middle of a fierce proxy war between Iran and Saudi

Arabia. I fear for the good people we befriended.

The small country is situated on the SW Coast of the Arabian Peninsula with a population of about twenty-five million at the time.

"Our first election will be in April. We hope to get an honest president," Hari, our guide, said.

"The president now is not honest?" I asked.

"He spent all the money for his own people. We got nothing." Our guide was getting a little agitated.

With many of these countries, attempting democracy for the first time, the tribal connection is still deeply ingrained. Perhaps it is hardwired in the human brain. I would be surprised if anyone coming to power in Yemen didn't look after his own people first. It is unlikely that there would be the kind of leadership to address the needs of the entire country although things could change slowly.

Hari and Abdulla took us to the best Internet café at the Aden Mall where there was also a Baskin Robbins Ice Cream stand and a LuLu's Hypermarket (a supermarket). At the mall there were a number of women's dress shops selling all sorts of colorful, low-cut western gowns that seemed out of place here. Judy and I couldn't figure out who would be buying those fine, colorful, and revealing outfits. We also puzzled over the many bridal shops where white wedding gowns, not unlike those selling in the bridal shops of Los Angeles or Sydney, were on display. We puzzled over the mystery.

Finally we had to ask Hari. It turned out the Yemeni women would wear these gowns at home and at weddings. The bride would change into the white gowns at the wedding party attended by only women, all in their fine evening gowns. The groom and his friends and family, all men, would have their separate wedding celebration apart from the women. I thought it would have been quite a scoop if I could take photos of the respective wedding parties, but I didn't receive any invitation. I found out later that even taking photos of properly attired women in public places was not considered appropriate behavior.

I was taking a few photos in the busy shopping mall. A security guard approached me and informed me that photos were not allowed because there were many women around despite the fact that they were all covered from head to toe in black.

We learned that having a guide and driver was a good deal for us. Hari or Abdulla knew where everything was located in town. Even for simple chores, their knowledge was helpful. For example, the outboard repair service was tucked away in a back ally far away from the anchorage. There was no way I could ever have found the place on my own. Our little outboard was acting cranky and needed servicing. While we waited for the tank test to be completed at the shop, Abdulla's uncle, Mohamed (he went as guide when Hari was not available), showed us where we could have some tea at a corner shop.

Some flat bread was already sizzling on a pan over a drum-like stove. We sat outdoors among all the hustle and bustle of the market place. We ordered tea; it was either white or black. Judy asked if the tea could be sugar-free. A quiet shake of the head by Mohamed indicated that was not a possibility. Tea came heavily sugared. White tea had milk and black tea had mint twigs. The flat bread could be plain or with eggs cooked on it. Mohamed ordered bread with eggs and another with eggs mixed with green onions and tomatoes. The food was yummy.

Four cups of tea and two large baskets of local fresh bread with eggs was the equivalent of US $2. Food in general, for us, was not expensive if we went to places where the locals ate. A family of four could probably eat for less than two or three dollars a day if they bought their supplies at the open-air markets. Telecommunication and bus transportation were also very affordable by local standards.

On the other hand there were many beggars, especially the old. Many women begged and would accept food. During our walk, Mohamed bought fruit drinks from a vendor for himself and paid for a few extras to be given to the women beggars.

"I don't give anything to men, they can work," Mohamed said.

Judy and I made a trip out of Aden on our own. The public bus made a lunch stop at a diner in a small town. There were people begging at the open doorway of the diner. The waiter, as he was clearing various tables, gathered the leftover food and placed it on a table near the open doorway and allowed an old man to sit at the table to eat what was there. Judy and I gave the flat bread left at the end of our lunch to the women waiting at the door. Many of them appeared hungry and took the bread eagerly.

Sights of Yemen

Not far from the waterfront, Hari pointed out the Jewish Cemetery. I was surprised that there were Jews in Yemen and that the cemetery was left undisturbed. We learned that Yemen used to have as many as 46,000 Jewish citizens. In 1948-49, about 45,000 of them were airlifted to Israel by an operation code named Magic Carpet. According to the publication "Yemen Today" (02/2009) there are still about 500 Jews in the country. One village north of Sana'a housed 280 Jewish residents and was considered a tourist destination. The Yemeni Jews are famous for their silver work and carpentry. In particular, they are known for crafting the best jambiya, a fierce-looking curved dagger that bespeaks the hereditary social status of the wearer.

In the English-language newspaper we read of several murders of Jews in recent years. In the latest case, the court had found the perpetrator guilty, sentenced him to a psychiatric hospital, and ordered his family to pay restitution the equivalent of US $27,500 to the victim's family. Not surprisingly the victim's family refused to take the "blood money" and wanted "true justice"...the death penalty.

The Yemeni government in recent years offered the Jewish residents small plots of land and US $10,000 for relocation nearer to the capital where it would be safer. I didn't think that was an adequate plan. Most of the Jews are skilled artisans. Traditionally, they have a barter system worked out with local Muslim farmers who depend on their services and craftsmanship. Moving them away from each other would serve neither group well.

Considering the giant pro-Gazan rally held in the sports stadium during the recent Gaza crisis and the strong anti-Israel feelings reported by the papers, the situation was not on the mend. The irony was that the Jews in Yemen considered themselves Yemenis; they had lived there for centuries serving an important part of the local economy. Despite their often second-class status in Yemen, not all wanted to emigrate.

On one trip with Hari and Abdulla, we went to Krater, a small Arabic town just outside of Aden. It was a beehive of commercial activity. We saw a small shop where a lone camel was used at a small mill to grind sesame oil. Colorful shops with Arabic signs selling fabric, baskets, or food were all along the street. Bulk foods in sacks and boxes were piled on pickup trucks, handcarts as well as camel carts. Just to make it more interesting, there were also donkey carts darting in and out of traffic. Men in Arabic headscarves were rushing everywhere. It could have been two hundred years ago if it weren't for the automobiles and trucks clogging the roadway.

"Today, we go see the water tank," Hari announced with uncharacteristic fanfare.

"Water tank...Is that interesting?" I asked. I thought perhaps Hari was running out of sightseeing ideas.

"Yes, water tank is interesting," Hari persisted.

The water tank turned out to be a series of massive reservoirs discovered in 1854. The restoration by the British Government took 45 years. It was originally built perhaps around 427 BCE plus or minus a few hundred years. The whole system of water works was embedded in a rocky volcanic valley. We saw only three of the reservoirs, each the size of a moderately sized five- or six-story building. They were cut from solid rock. I was told that there were 18 of these ancient reservoirs with a total capacity of as much as 20 million imperial gallons, but only three were easily accessible by a footpath and steps built during the restoration. Extensive channels, bridges, and ducts were part of the storage system to divert water to the reservoir. It was indeed very impressive, considering that the ancient builders had no power machinery.

We saw out-of-town tourists wearing the jambiya, a curved knife in a fine sheath. It is an important status symbol passed on from father to son. We met a young man in a jambiya shop who showed us the different jambiyas that belonged to his great grandfather, grandfather, and father, but those were not for sale. Not many residents in Aden wore the fierce-looking knife. I was told that the wearing of the jambiya was a regional custom. Those that wore the jambiya would no doubt feel naked without their knife prominently displayed across their body. I had seen young children not much more than twelve years old proudly wearing their jambiyas. The bloodthirsty curved knife from a tribal-warrior past was now mainly decorative, but it was as important to the wearer as his pants.

Judy came across an Arabic war song in a novel, *The Lion's Game* by N. Demille:

The Death Feud:
Terrible he rode alone
With his Yemen sword for aid;
Ornament, it carried none
But the notches on the blade.

A sight no visitor could miss happened every afternoon when Yemeni men would sport bulging cheeks looking like a lopsided hamster. It was not a tumor or a growth or a swollen gum disease, but simply a cheek full of chewed khat. Khat is the leaf from the tree *Catha edulis*. About 80% of men and 50% of women in Yemen chew khat.

A newspaper reported that 30% of the Yemeni population is dependent on khat for their livelihood, either growing or selling it. The cheapest khat sells for YR100 (equivalent to fifty cents) for a small bag to be consumed in one afternoon. The chewers claim that it helps them concentrate better and feel happier. It is also considered a social lubricant because when the men, young and old, sit around to chew khat, socioeconomic distinctions are not relevant. They just sit and talk and tell stories.

Women also chew khat, but they need their male relatives to buy it for them. There are many street corners or fixed locations in the market that sellers would distribute bags of khat from the tailgate of their pickup trucks. Buyers would always open the bag to examine the quality before handing over the money. Our two bus drivers on a long intercity run bought khat at rural locations where they could get the best and freshest khat at the lowest prices. They washed the leaves and carefully kept them moist and cool. Our bus driver was actually chewing as he drove the bus.

The driver offered me a small leafy twig to chew. He laughed heartily as I accepted his offer. I tore off a handful of leaves and chewed, but didn't find it very tasty. I didn't feel any physiological effect either. The most embarrassing part was that as I chewed, I unthinkingly swallowed the leaves instead of keeping them in my cheek. *I am a failure in khat chewing.*

As long as we were in Yemen waiting for favorable sailing weather, we thought we might as well look around the country. Foreigners are required to complete a fair amount of paper work in order to travel in Yemen. We had to go to the tourist police to obtain a travel permit stating our itinerary and fill out a multitude of forms. Finally we were allowed to buy bus tickets for Sana'a. The 260-mile trip took seven hours and climbed about 2400 meters in altitude.

All along the route, there were regular military checkpoints where soldiers with automatic weapons inspected passing vehicles. They boarded the bus and examined our travel permits. At these checkpoints, there were four-wheel-drive vehicles with heavy machine guns mounted on the truck beds at the ready.

Most of the terrain is mountainous and very dry at that time of the year. We saw many areas where the land appeared to be cultivated and bordered by rock walls. Rocks were everywhere so the walled terraces served as a way to dispose of the rocks in order to reclaim the land for cultivation.

We understood that rice is the primary crop at many places. Yemenis love to eat rice. Having seen terraced rice fields in SE Asia we knew how enchanting the lush green terraced fields could be. On that particular tour, we were satisfied with the scene of a desert full of rocks. The few isolated spots where we saw some greenery all turned out to be groves of small trees of *Catha edulis*...khat. These trees grow well in arid land and a cutting could begin to produce in six months and reach full productivity in eight years, providing excellent profit. Subsistence farmers could hardly resist such profitable lure. We saw markets as we went through small towns. Oranges, tomatoes, potatoes, melons and squashes as well as many nuts and dried foods such as raisins and dates were readily available. At least some farmers were still planting food crops.

We met an elderly gentleman at a restaurant along the bus route. He was around sixty or seventy years old eating alone two tables away from us. His jacket was clean and well pressed although there were repaired threadbare spots at the elbow. He wore his aqua colored jambiya with gold inlay prominently tucked under his belt across the middle of his waist.

As he walked by our table, I greeted, "As-salaamu alaykum."

He stopped and responded. I asked in English if I could take a photo of him. He understood my gesture and nodded. He sat very tall and straight, a proud figure radiating dignity.

Antiquities of Sana'a

Sana'a, the capital of Yemen, is a big sprawling city. Our local guide informed us that Shem, the son of Noah, founded the city after the flood. Yemenis we met were proud of the knowledge that Yemen is a country with a wealth of ancient history.

Historically, just to the east of Sana'a was Marib, the center of power of the Maeen Empire predating Islam. Then came the glorious dynasty of Sheba when Yeman was united under one kingdom. Many historical landmarks were attributed to this period, including the ruins of a dam and the throne and temple of the Queen of Sheba.

Many empires and conquests had come and gone since. By the 7th century AD, Yemen came under Islam.

Much of the wealth in those days derived from the fact that Yemen was at the hub of the east-west trade route. As a result, it had a de facto monopoly over "frankincense and Myrrh...sought after by every temple of the ancient world...which ensured great wealth for the region." (The quote is from *101 Things to See and Do in Yemen*.)

The Old City in Sana'a is designated a UNESCO World Heritage Site. We noticed a big hole in the top corner of the original city gate, Bab Al Yemen, the ornate wooden gate to the Old City. Apparently a cannon ball had blasted through it during one of the many battles over the ages. All around the gate is a sea of humanity engaged in selling, buying, and bargaining.

There were foods such as honey, nuts, raisins, spices, and other items unknown to us. Shoe stores, several in a row, competed for customers. Shops selling brass handicrafts were stuffed to the rafters with wares, as were basketry shops. There were glittering jewelry shops as well as tourist shops pushing trinkets and fabric shops selling silk or cotton in bright colors.

We went into one shop where I managed to bargain and bought two headscarves for myself. It would have been disgraceful to buy without bargaining...perhaps even insulting. I ended up with two because after considerable back and forth the shopkeeper and I were at an impasse. I had to either walk away or buy at the shop's offer. I told the shopkeeper that I would buy two at my final price. That worked like a charm. Both parties were able to maintain their self-respect and the transaction finished at its logical conclusion.

We visited the Rock Palace (Dar Al-Hajjar), twelve km northwest of Sana'a. A little over four hundred years ago, one of the ruling imams built this palace on top of a rock that protrudes several hundred feet from a riverbed. Over the centuries, various imams ruling over Yemen had made additions and modifications to the structure. In 1987, the Republic of Yemen decreed the palace a historic site. Not surprisingly, it became a very popular tourist destination.

Most of the palace was open to visitors when we were there. It was an unusual palace and a fortress built intertwined on a tall rock outcropping. To begin with, there were two deep wells in the palace that reach down several hundred feet to the water table below the surface of the plain. As we ascended along the steps, we saw small caves in the rock that served as burial chambers. Small cubicles, looking like cupboards, were crafted on the exposed side of the palace walled with rock lattice openings to allow air movement through the cubicle while keeping out sunlight. These were the original air-cooled chambers for storing food. Many of the modern houses possessed these air-cooled cupboards visible from the outside. There were also guard stations within the palace.

"The guard stations have such low ceilings. It must have been uncomfortable for the guards," I said.

"No, no...the guards were not grownups. They were children about eleven years old," said our tour guide.

"Eleven-years-old guards?" I was puzzled.

"Yes, children...their job was not to fight intruders...they kept track of the iman's four wives," explained the guide.

On the south of Sana'a was the abandoned village of Bayt Baws, formerly a Jewish settlement built on a rocky ridge. We walked through the huge stone gate and looked around some of the empty buildings. One house appeared to have been converted to a mosque. According to our self-appointed twelve-year-old guide, there were only six houses that had electricity and that was the number of families living there.

In earlier times, houses and dwellings were often built on cliffs or on impregnable rocky outcrops for protection from intruders. For centuries, people had lived in precarious times, judging by their need for protection.

The town of Thula (or Thila) was one of these mighty impregnable town/fortresses. Over the centuries many ruling imans had retreated to this fortress as their last sanctuary. It was built more than 2000 years ago on the side of a steep mountain. Its inaccessibility and the many castles within made it a safe haven.

Just as we were arriving at the open-air market, loud explosions greeted us. It sounded like gunfire...not something we had expected.

Our Sana'a driver had a short conversation with a passerby.

"There are a lot of fireworks and firecrackers," said Ali. "They told me that there is a wedding today."

"That sounds interesting. Can we go see it?" I asked.

I hurried Ali to get to the town square, but we needn't have rushed. These wedding rituals apparently go on forever. Most of the crowd was in their best local costume. Men in white robes and jackets that looked very much like blazers. And, of course, adorned by a jambiya tucked in a wide belt across the middle.

Four or five musicians were providing music with mostly percussion instruments. In the middle were men doing a ritual dance with their curved jambiyas drawn. The groom and his immediate wedding party (all male) sat at the head of the square watching the dance.

A young woman approached me and wanted to know where I was from. I tried to use my best Arabic, but she insisted on speaking English. She said that she could speak six languages. Indeed her English was with very little accent and she managed some not too bad Chinese before going on to Spanish. Apparently she had learned it all by talking to tourists.

A few minutes later she came back with a bunch of fabric she wanted to sell. I realized that she was cleverer than the average hawker. After that nice conversation, it would be hard to refuse to buy something

She showed us her prospective shop. To my surprise, there was a giant boulder inside the shop. There was still clay that had not yet been removed. I was told that it was not unusual for dwellings to be excavated out of solid rock. It would take her some time before all that rock could be chipped out to accommodate a functioning shop.

Shibam was founded in the 9th century AD in the valley at an elevation of 2300 meters. A flood, in 16th Century, had destroyed much of the old city. It was well known for a grand mosque and the cave dwellings that, until recent times, had people living in them. We toured the mosque, the ruins of the Imam's palace, and caves high up on a cliff.

Shibam was often called the "Manhattan of the Desert" because of its high-rise mud-brick buildings in a walled city on the plateau. My driver advised against the area because of the damage cause by a cyclone only four months earlier in late October 2008. Possibly he was also concerned about agitation by militants. Only two weeks later bomb blasts killed several South Korean tourists and their guide in Shibam.

On top of the cliff was Kawkaban. At least two of the houses had stones that reflected light like planets in the evening. The name Kawkaban meant two planets (or two stars). The whole town would look much like the starry night scene in the evening when viewed from the valley, but we were not able to stay till dark.

There was a footpath connecting Shibam to Kawkaban. The path was only 450 meters, but almost straight up the cliff. I passed on climbing to the top of the cliff in the merciless sun. I heard that the hike down afforded fantastic views.

We went to lunch at Shibam around two o'clock, the usual lunchtime in Yemen. It was at a three-story stone house with no signs and no indication that it was a restaurant. The upstairs had several dining rooms. We were led to a large room about thirty feet long and fifteen wide with chandeliers hanging from the high ceiling. Big cushions were placed all around the perimeter with low tables in front of the cushions. The walls were decorated with pictures of various scenes from Yemen and a portrait each of the president and his wife.

It was the food that overwhelmed me. The server, probably one of the family members at the restaurant, brought a big tray. He set down two kinds of rice, plain and yellow with lots of exotic spices and fragrances. There were two kinds of potatoes, one in a brown sauce and another a spicy concoction. He then brought two kinds of meat, fried chicken and boiled goat meat. There was a Yemeni salad with cucumber, tomato, and pepper. Then a fish stew cooked on top of flat bread in a tray.

The server continued with a large deep dish of flat bread cooked with eggs and goat milk. He flopped down on the table a large basket of five or six pieces of flat bread each twelve inches in diameter. He finished with a dish of something that resembled a yellow cake, but infused with the famous Yemeni honey, which is supposed to confer longevity aside from being very tasty.

I thought maybe all this food was for everyone near our low table, but no, it was just for my guide and me. I was famished and tucked in with gusto while sitting cross-legged on the cushion. Unfortunately, Judy happened to be ill that day and didn't come on the tour.

Before I started eating, I was taught to say "bismillah," meaning "in the name of God." It is considered poor manners not to give thanks before eating or drinking, whether or not the person is a Muslim or religious. The best I could unravel was that it is not so much being religious as it is a part of Arabic culture. The language, culture, and religion are so imbedded and intertwined that it is hard to separate one from the other.

To eat Yemeni style, I could use my fingers, but only the right hand. It tended to be a little on the messy side as the rice didn't always stick together and some sauces would invariable dribble onto the table or my lap. I had done that before when we first arrived in Yemen. Now, I was seriously hungry. I decided the spoon was a much more efficient conveyance for shoveling good food. Before too long, there were only a few pieces of flatbread still lingering in the basket. It was one of the best meals I have had for many months and it cost the equivalent of five dollars for two big eaters.

Sailing the Red Sea

The news at the anchorage in Aden was abuzz that there would be a four-day weather window of south wind. That was good news, but we had to hurry if we were to take advantage of the favorable weather. We had already taken on fuel and serviced the engines soon after Laelia's arrival in Aden. But, we still had to check out with the Harbor Master, take on some fresh water, and buy the last bits of perishable food. We paid Abdulla and Hari, our driver and guide. They were honest in accounting for the time...down to the last minute. I had enough local money left to give them a nice tip. We hoisted anchor early the next morning and departed.

The Port of Aden is situated on the east lip of the entrance just outside of the Red Sea. It is about 90 NM from the Bab al Mandeb Strait (Gate of Tears in Arabic), where busy shipping traffic enters the Red Sea at its narrowest part.

We went through the "Small Strait" on the east side of the little Perim Island (or Mayyun). The Small Strait is a shortcut by only a few miles, but in shallower water and had no shipping traffic. The guidebook cautioned that the island is a sensitive military area and has a restricted perimeter. Shortly before our visit, without warning, the Yemeni Navy with guns drawn had boarded a sailboat that anchored near the island. The island's position was clearly marked on the chart and a lighthouse made its location unmistakable at night. I made doubly sure Laelia sailed past with plenty of clearance.

We soon rejoined the shipping lane, staying just on the east side (outside) of the northbound lane. The presence of large ships reassured us that the water was deep and we had no need to worry about shallow reefs. The wind was blowing hard, but happily it was from the south or southeast. From time to time it gusted to 35 knots. We first reefed the main then, an hour later, reefed again.

Eventually, Laelia was double reefed on the main and the jib. Still, we were moving at eight plus knots.

The swells went up to nine feet or more...it felt like a lot more. Laelia surfed down the big swells and made sharp sideways movements as if showing off at a surfing exhibition. The autopilot was working extra hard spinning the wheel this way and that. Each time the boat surfed, the wind waves rushed past the hull, making noises like a thunderous stampede of cattle under the boat. As time went on, the wind shifted more east, then ENE, but that was still good sailing wind as we changed course to northwest to hug the west coast of the Red Sea. We crossed the shipping lanes when there were only a few ships in our vicinity.

There was a reason for shifting towards the west. The east coast of the Red Sea is part of the territorial waters of Yemen, then is part of Saudi Arabia further north. Saudi Arabia had made it abundantly clear that cruising yachts were not welcome. Our plan was to stay on the west side of the sea where we could take refuge in anchorages of Eritrea, Sudan, or Egypt as needed.

One night, not long after Laelia entered the Red Sea, we heard over VHF Channel 16 a frail voice: "Any boat from the Vasco de Gama Rally...any boat from the rally...any boat from the rally."

We were not part of the rally so we didn't respond. Soon another rally boat answered the hail.

The frail voice said, "I just collided with an island. I damaged my bowsprit and may lose my mast. I am taking on water, but I think I can keep the boat afloat."

In the dark, it was one of those chilling messages to any mariner. Any of us could be in a similar predicament. At the time, we were sailing along at a pretty good clip with strong favorable wind, but if needed, we would divert to assist a fellow cruiser in need. The conversation continued as he provided his GPS coordinates to the responder from the rally.

We jotted down his location and realized that he was more than 140 miles to the south behind us. It was not possible for Laelia to reach him within a day or two going against the wind. The best we could do was to provide a relay of his distress call if he had difficulty reaching someone. Soon the radio signal became weak and noisy and we couldn't hear either party anymore. We were surprised by the clarity of the VHF signal from so far away, although it only lasted a few minutes.

The next morning we heard, on the Vasco de Gama marine-frequency radio net, the news that a single-handed sailboat had hit a rock not far from the entrance to the Red Sea. He had fallen asleep. Soon after the distress call over the radio, boats that came up from behind him diverted and escorted him to the nearest anchorage.

If that sailboat had been run over by a ship while the skipper was asleep, no one would ever have known about it. The boat would just have disappeared without a trace.

At least in that one instance we had clear evidence that the VHF radio did have a reach of 140 plus miles. The wind had no effect on radio waves, but I wondered if the red dust that came with the wind had enough iron in it to have an effect on electromagnetic wave propagation. Perhaps radio waves could bounce off of the dust cloud? It was a fine red dust that got on everything. It didn't take us very long to figure out why they call this the Red Sea. The water looked perfectly clear, but the red dust that blew in the wind penetrates every pore and sticks to every windward surface.

As we continued north, we checked the weather forecast and hoped that the wind would continue to be favorable, but the weather window appeared to be at an end. We had passed up several good anchorages trying to get as far north as possible with the waning southeast wind. We would not have minded a stop in Port Masawa, Eritrea. We had heard good reports from others who enjoyed their visit to Asmara, the Capital of Eritrea. With active hostilities with Ethiopia lessening, Eritrea had been encouraging tourism. Despite our desire to stop, we sailed on and passed the last available anchorage while there was still daylight.

I had hoped that we could make the next anchorage about forty miles away. Alas, we saw the wind dying as the evening wore on. By nightfall, the wind had shifted north. The swells shifted along with the wind as we furled the sails and motored against the elements. In the Red Sea the swells are less kindly. They are sharper and steeper, causing Laelia to rock violently back and forth as she plunged forward against the waves. The wind was only fifteen knots, but steep swells made the going rough. It was uncomfortable, but not causing any serious harm.

My worries were for the integrity of the boat. With each swing forward and back, the torque on the rigging was enormous. *Laelia is a sturdy boat, but how much punishment can she take?* I slowed the boat down to lessen the harshness of the motion. Going at 3.5 knots seemed tolerable. Had we decided to stop at that last anchorage, we would have been eating a nice dinner by now. It was best not to look back.

At this point even turning back was not an option because it would have been foolish to enter an unfamiliar anchorage in the dark. Most of the anchorages in that area probably have fringe coral reefs that require a watchful eye on entry. We expected no beacons and navigation lights. It requires money and a stable government to keep such infrastructure in good condition. So we settled in for a nasty night at sea and pushed on ahead.

It turned out to be one of the longest nights I could remember. During the night, the outhaul to the mainsail broke. The mainsail flapped back and forth with a lot of noise and fury. We continued on with the rhythmic hum of the engine. Now, we needed to repair the outhaul under calm conditions at an anchorage.

The next morning we dropped anchor at a short distance from

Harmil Island. It was probably the last available anchorage in Eritrea near the border with Sudan to the north. We could see gun emplacements at a distance on shore. We passed a fishing boat going out to sea. The fishermen could see Laelia's US flag at the stern. They waved and shouted, "Obama...Obama..." I waved back.

A little later, Judy spied an open panga speeding in our direction. "I think there are several men with rifles in their hands," she said as she studied the approaching fast boat through binoculars.

The fast boat got closer. We could see five men in the boat, all wearing some sort of camouflage clothing. At least three were holding rifles.

"Are they pirates?" I was muttering to myself.

"It's too late to worry about that now. They are coming straight for us," Judy replied.

"Perhaps they are soldiers...there is a naval base around here." I tried to stay positive.

The boat finally slowed down and came to a stop next to Laelia's cockpit.

I greeted them, "As-salaamu alaykum." In Arabic it literally means, "May peace be upon you," but in daily usage it's just an everyday greeting. I gave them a sheet of paper that I had copied from the guidebook, in Arabic, a request for a short stay at the anchorage due to bad weather and the need for repairs. I also wrote on the paper the boat's name and registration as well as country of origin and number of crew.

The leader of the group, a big guy with short cropped hair wearing camouflage pants and an army-green singlet top (tank top), showed bulging muscles. He spoke some English and seemed satisfied with the papers I presented him.

Judy brought out some cigarettes and packets of tea and sugar for giving away as presents. I asked the leader if that was appropriate or permitted. He didn't seem to mind so we passed the plastic bags on to his assistant. We were respectful and represented no threat. The leader asked if we needed help with the repairs.

"Shukran, we are OK," I replied, thanking him in a mixture of Arabic and English. With that they waved and left.

Our outhaul shackle pin had come loose from the boom the previous night when we were sailing in the stiff wind. As a result the mainsail was flapping around and had to be dropped completely. The repair was not a major problem. I only needed to climb out onto the end of the boom to replace the shackle in calm water when the boat was not bucking like a wild stallion. The number one rule on a boat is not to get hurt.

We had planned to make a stop farther north in Port Suakin, Sudan, to top up on diesel. In any case we would soon have to begin doing day hops in the protected inner channel along the Sudanese coast. The inner channel is protected against the swells by the presence of fringe coral reefs, but for those same reasons, it was unsafe to navigate without daylight. These one-day passages would allow only 30 to 40 miles each day because, in order to see the reefs, we needed to enter the anchorage with the sun still high in the sky. Later in the day, when the sun is low near the horizon, the reflection makes it impossible to see the reef or changes in color of the water. When the weather permitted, we preferred to sail in the open water doing night passages, making 120 miles a day. Now with contrary winds and large swells, we were happy to settle for 40 miles a day navigating the inner channels.

Things Go Bump in the Night
On that particular morning, the wind in the Red Sea was strong, but from ENE. With no obvious obstructions such as islands or reefs, we sailed in a WNW direction along the Sudanese coast in the open water. As nightfall approached, we thought it would be a safe overnight passage

The wind dropped after dark and we had to turn on one engine. During the night, while Judy was on watch, she noted on the log that the starboard engine had momentarily slowed and almost stopped before regaining power. I recalled that happened once during our first year out while we were still in Mexico. When the fuel filter was clogged, the engine RPM would drop momentarily a few times before the engine shut down completely from lack of fuel. As Judy described the anomaly before she went off watch, I thought it might have been the fuel filter again.

The first thing I did was to examine the fuel filter, but it was clean. Also, the engine RPM was doing fine by then. Judy had mentioned that the boat speed was slower. I checked the speed, compared it with the watch log, and confirmed that the boat speed was definitely one knot slower than what Judy had logged just before the event.

Mmmm, this is beginning to become a mystery. It could be that the propeller has hit something in the water. Could it be that the starboard propeller has been bent or damaged?

A bent propeller would be unbalanced and would have resulted in a lot of vibrations, but there was no unusual vibration. I turned off the starboard engine and turned on the port engine. At the same RPM, the speed was still one knot slower than before. The swells were pretty much the same and would be unlikely to change the boat speed so much. By studying speed over ground and speed over water in the log, I also ruled out any change in current.

While Judy slept, I puzzled over the problem. Perhaps there was some seaweed dragging along. I looked at the starboard stern, but saw only a trail of foam and bubbles stirred up by the propeller trailing in the water. The swirl of bubbles reflecting against the full moon was bright, making it hard to see past them. I kept looking and saw nothing at first. Then I thought I imagined a faint trail of white light beneath all those shining bubbles.

How can there be a light under the boat? Where is it coming from?

I tried harder to look past the bubbles. There was definitely something, but I couldn't be sure what. When the boat went up and down a bit with the swells, I could see, momentarily, a white band that looked like the belly of a large anaconda about four inches in diameter.

An anaconda? Here in the Red Sea?

I knew that couldn't be right...the largest snake I had seen recently was no bigger than a blade of grass. Perhaps it's the arm of a very large octopus. *Mmmm...my imagination is running wild.*

I put on my harness and tether and took along a boathook to the starboard steps at the stern. I leaned over and reached down with the boathook, but the water current from the moving boat kept pushing the boathook to the surface. By now I was determined. I turned the engine speed down and went back to the steps. Now I could reach down with the boathook and move it side to side. I felt something solid.

Hah, it's not my imagination.

With the boat moving slower and with the hook pulling up the object a little, I could see a bit better through the water. It was something white with markings that looked like diamond-shaped scales. I couldn't pull it all the way up with the boathook because the water current was still too strong. I didn't want to lose the boathook in the water either. I slowed the boat some more. Now I was finally able to pull one end of the thing out of the water. I had planned ahead and brought along a short length of utility rope and tied the exposed end of the thing to a cleat on the stern.

I would never have guessed. It turned out to be a giant hawser four or so inches in diameter. It was a section of a braided line made from several one-inch-diameter twisted strands of polypropylene twine. The checkered pattern of the braiding looked through water like scales, but not nearly as interesting as if it had been scales on a real snake.

I wanted to remove the hawser from under the boat so we wouldn't be burning diesel dragging this polypropylene tail behind us. Eventually I had to stop the boat before I could pull the hawser, four inches in diameter and about 15 feet long, from Laelia's starboard rudderpost.

Apparently, when Judy was on watch, the prop must have hit the hawser first, causing the momentary drop in the engine RPM; then the folding prop must have folded, allowing the hawser to slip past and loop itself on the rudderpost. As long as the boat was moving along, the water current kept the hawser hanging on to the rudderpost. Also, polypropylene tends to float, so the rope couldn't fall off the rudderpost easily. I suppose we were lucky that neither the propeller nor the rudder had shown any signs of damage.

I brought the wayward hawser to the deck. No doubt it used to be part of a dock-line from a tanker or container ship. The pelagic gooseneck barnacles growing on the rope were all fairly young; the hawser probably hadn't been in the water for more than a month.

I took the hawser on shore when we arrived in Port Suakin, Sudan. There were several fishermen in their lean-to shelter. "Would you like to have this rope?" I asked the fisherman I met.

"Yes, thank you. I make bed with this." The fisherman gestured swinging motions with his hands. The polypropylene fiber was certainly strong enough to fabricate a nice hammock. He seemed genuinely pleased with the unexpected gift.

Ruins of Suakin Island

For three thousand years, Suakin was a strategic port on the Red Sea and, since the rise of Islam, a waypoint for pilgrims bound for Mecca. It has the dubious distinction of being one of the last slave-trading posts in the world. Its decline accelerated in the twentieth century and it became mostly ruins when Britain moved all the shipping to Port Sudan in 1905. In part the advent of steamships required deeper harbors instead of sheltering from the wind.

The small Suakin Island is connected to the mainland by a short causeway. Locals called the island Old Suakin. "Old" it certainly was, with the entire island full of old ruins. Judy and I walked around in the ruins. Almost all the structures were constructed out of cut coral blocks about the size of a standard cinder block. The larger structures were built with twin layers of coral-block walls without mortar. In between the walls were filled with rubble rock making the walls about two feet or more in thickness. At intervals, tree branches, three to four inches in diameter were placed horizontally to provide structural strength.

Newer structures had rough-sawn planks instead of tree branches and some had plaster smoothing the interior surfaces. The newest structures also appeared to have mortar in between the coral blocks, but without the double walls. Anywhere else in the world, the ruins of Old Suakin would have become a billion-dollar waterfront tourist attraction and expensive resorts, but I suppose location is everything when it comes to real estate.

The ruins seemed to have intruded across the causeway. In the town most homes were old and not in good condition. The few eateries did not look inviting. A number of donkey carts hauled water and other heavy items intermingled with Toyota pickup trucks weaving through impatiently. The market was busy selling red onions, tomatoes, eggplants, melons, potatoes, cucumbers and squash, but little in the way of leafy greens.

A few stores sold eggs and canned goods. Vegetables were cheap, but eggs and chicken were expensive. The best buy was the pocket bread, sold from a pushcart in the open air. I caught one batch just as they brought it to the market while it was still hot...before many flies landed on it.

We didn't plan to do any sightseeing. Our interest in Sudan was pretty low, not because it was a poor country; it just seemed that everything was falling apart and little effort was spent to maintaining what was left. The adults seemed tired and worn out, appearing withdrawn and perhaps even depressed. On the other hand, one of the cruisers reported that he received first-rate treatment in the hospital in Port Sudan.

Overall, I did not sense open friendliness in the Sudanese. The fishermen at the dinghy landing were responsive enough, although I did ask them for small favors, which allowed me an excuse to give them some packs of cigarettes. That helped to break the ice and gave me an opportunity to talk to them. The giant hawser also went to one of them. These fishermen were more accustomed to meeting outsiders because they sometimes crewed on vessels that took tourists diving at outer reefs. They seemed to find my Asian face a novelty that helped to relax them. They lived in primitive shacks not far from the water's edge.

The children were more engaging than the adults. While we were on a walk, boys would come and ask me to take their photos. I would then show them their images on the camera screen. We came across a family celebrating outside their home. It was the first haircut of a one-year-old boy. I asked the grandfather if I could take a photo. He was delighted and encouraged me with the photos.

A few minutes later, a young man decided that he didn't like me taking photos of several small children about ten years old. Most of my photos of people at close range, even of children, had their consent. This young man probably worked for the police or the military, because he was very fit and looked well fed. He demanded that I erase my photos.

"You can take photos of animals, but not people or buildings," he continued to demand. "You must destroy all photos."

"I have 800 pictures on that camera chip, most of them from Yemen. I can't erase them," I replied.

The young man pointed at an older man, probably his boss, and wanted me to move over there, where I found myself outnumbered by the others standing with the boss.

Someone said, "The harbor has police boats...it is against the law to take photos of any military facilities."

I didn't think I could win any arguments with this bunch. I had to figure a way out of this. I turned the camera off and turned it on again, but this time I scrolled the images backwards. The camera obligingly indicated "no image." I didn't know if the boss could read English, but I told him: "See, no more photos...all gone." Before he could come up with something, I turned the camera off and left.

I think the young man was ashamed of what my camera might capture of the poverty in Sudan. He didn't seem to realize that what I could remember was not so easily erasable. That included his attitude. He certainly added to the sourness of how we remember Sudan. What distressed me the most was that, in the absence of the rule of law, anyone at some official capacity with a little power could make demands on a whim, with a subtle threat of violence.

The quality of a country depends very much on how it is governed. With Omar al-Bashir, who was indicted by the International Criminal Court for genocide, as the sitting president of Sudan, it was not surprising that the country was in a bad way.

Port Sudan
Judy and I took a bus trip to Port Sudan to check email at an Internet shop. The bus trip took an hour and a half, costing $1.25 each way per person. The small, ancient bus was completely full, including the folding jump seats in the center aisle. It was full by design...the bus would not leave until the last seat was filled. It was quite a mix of humanity, old and young, men and women, dressed in different degrees of shabbiness. Judy and I weren't looking too good ourselves by the time the cramped bus had sweltered in the desert sun until it was full.

On the bus there were turbans, skullcaps, and headdresses for women as well as canes and sacks of things. Thankfully there were no chickens or goats. Anyway, it was a tightly packed bus with no air-conditioning, but nobody complained. Everyone waited patiently in silent resignation. This was life in Sudan. And we were there to see the world.

We got to see the countryside along the coast between Suakin and Port Sudan, about forty miles. Along the route, the dwellings were mostly in walled compounds with low shacks inside made from odd pieces of corrugated sheet metal, scrap wood, canvas, cardboard paper, and whatever scraps of material available.

Occasionally there were also good looking houses of stone or cinder blocks in individually fenced enclosures, but those were the rare exceptions.

The Red Sea coast was mostly barren dry saltpan or desert-like barren land. Some areas along the road were enclosed by fences and appeared to be cultivated. There were tents and a few Toyota pickups that probably belonging to nomadic farmers. We saw goatherds as well as camels. Not many, but also cattle. We couldn't figure out what these animals ate because there was so little vegetation of any kind for miles around. Most of the permanent structures belonged to oil or gas storage compounds. These outfits have offshore moorings for tankers to load or unload their hold. The only trees or greenery were within the property of these big company compounds.

Port Sudan is a big city, but very scruffy. It was crowded with people. Women wore bright colored robes and headscarves. Most had their faces uncovered although some were uncovered only from below the eyebrow to just over the mouth.

The market was a cacophony of buses, minivans, tuktuks (covered golf-carts), donkey carts, and an occasional camel. One surprise was the ice cream parlor just around the corner from the Palace Hotel. The interior was decorated with many colorful lamps and cut glass, as well as mirrors on three walls. It was like being inside a giant kaleidoscope. It seemed so incongruous to find such a polychromatic gem in the drab scruffiness of the city.

Disaster Strikes

One would assume that coming into a new anchorage is difficult and is a likely time for disasters to occur. It is also true that no matter how well the guidebook describes the anchorage, it always looks different than our imagined scene.

When we arrived at a new anchorage, we usually allowed Laelia to circle around to check the depth and find a suitable spot to drop the anchor. We looked for water shallower than 40 feet, then dropped the anchor and laid out a length of chain equal to four to five times the depth of the water. Then Judy would put Laelia in reverse softly to "set" the anchor and then, at higher RPM, to test the hold. The anxiety usually goes away after anchoring.

One would rightly assume that departing an anchorage would be much easier. When we left Suakin we felt pretty good. The anchor came up without getting stuck on some old cable or odd rock. There were no unexpected delays and we got going pretty early. The soft morning light and the mist over the water made the ruins by the water's edge look mournfully photogenic.

When we first came in the harbor the guidebook had instructed us to align our course with the minarets. That brought us so very near the shore, within four or five feet of the rocks, keeping us on high alert. On the way out we should have followed the incoming electronic track, but we didn't. We didn't have the minarets as a marker any more. I was steering, keeping the rocks on the port side within sight, about four or five feet away. My thought was that as long as I kept the rocks close to the port side of Laelia, the starboard side would take care of itself. I didn't know the width of the channel, but it was wide enough to accommodate our catamaran.

"You are too close to the rocks, move over," Judy said.

"It's OK, as long as I can see the rocks, I know I am in the channel and we are safe."

"Move over, you are too close."

"Will you please stop, you are distracting me," I replied.

At the time, both of Laelia's engines were engaged. The water was mirror smooth in the early morning hours. Judy was getting very agitated. I didn't realize the close proximity to the rocks was very frightening to her. Judy kept up her complaints until I reached my limit.

"I can't stand this anymore. Would you rather do the driving?" I asked.

"If you would let me get close to the wheel," she said.

I got my camera out to take a few pictures of the ruins we were skimming by. The lighting was perfect and the sight was eerie; it was the skeletons of the old Egyptian National Bank building and other large structures, all crumpled and in complete disarray.

Judy moved Laelia to a more comfortable distance from the shore as we skirted by the ruins.

In retrospect, I had steered close to the rocky shore because I didn't know the width of the channel and I had arrived close to the shore guided by the minarets. On our way out, I automatically steered a course that was comfortable for me without analyzing why I favored the scary looking rocks. Had I been conscious of my reasons, I would have explained them to Judy before handing off the wheel. She would have been forewarned.

Suddenly, we heard a loud scraping sound coming from the bottom of the boat.

"Ugh, I think we are aground."

"Oh no, how terrible, this is the first time Laelia is aground."

On a mono-hull boat, one could make the boat heel to one side to free the keel. Laelia was a super-stable catamaran and didn't tip easily. Fortunately we were going slowly and able to stop the boat quickly after the grounding. I shut off the engine right away so it wouldn't suck in sand and mud.

When the water cleared, I ran the engine to turn the boat towards deeper water, but Laelia could not get loose. It seemed that only one rudder was stuck on some sort of rock and mud shelf.

"Laelia, Laelia, this is Cormorant." The VHF radio came to life. Our friends were drinking their morning coffee and could see Laelia stopped in the channel.

"Laelia here, we are aground," Judy answered.

"Can we help?" Harry asked.

"Well, I don't know about Howard, but I think we need help," Judy replied.

They came over in their dinghy and pushed us on the bow to turn Laelia towards deep water while we ran the engine hard. Very slowly, inch-by-inch, Laelia crunched free. Our friends went back to their breakfast as we checked the boat for leaks; there were none. With a sigh of relief we thought we could just continue on our way.

The first thing we discovered was that the boat would not go straight. In fact, all Laelia could do was make tight little circles.

Well, that's no good...we can't get very far if we just keep spinning around.

If we couldn't control the boat, we would certainly run aground again. It seemed the steering wheel would not turn...the wheel was stuck to one side. I put on my swim fins and went under the boat for a look. I discovered that the starboard rudderpost was bent far enough back that the top of the rudder was rubbing against the hull. There was no way I could unbend the solid one-and-a-half-inch stainless-steel rudderpost. Also, I had very little faith that I could get any repairs done in this harbor.

Even if I could locate a machinist in Port Sudan, the logistics of getting the machinist to Suakin would be tough. It seemed that we were on our own as far as repairs were concerned. Our friends would do anything to help us, but they had no more magic than we. There was not much hope of a fix. As is usually true, desperate moments call for outrageous measures.

What if we lower the rudderpost a little?

By lowering the steel rudderpost, the rudder would protrude more into the water and no longer rub on the hull. The problem with that solution was that the rudder was kept from slipping off the boat by a plastic collar clamped around a machined groove around the rudderpost. We would have to take the collar off to lower the rudderpost, but what was to keep the rudder from slipping all the way from the boat into the ocean?

After a few false moves that didn't work, I settled on clamps. The rudderpost ended up with a number of hose clamps wrapped tightly around the post to keep it from slipping down into the ocean. As a backup, in the event the hose clamp should slip, I added two C-clamps on the post. There was some duct tape in there also to give the hose clamps more friction. The "repair" would have made a hardware store owner proud and a boat builder blush. It was not pretty, but that was how we limped out of Suakin one morning...a few hours later than planned.

There is a lesson that would be as true on land as it is at sea. In life, at any time, we are always faced with multiple hazards, big and small. We should never be so fearful of one known hazard that we run afoul of another peril. Often, the hazard we see is less dangerous than the hazard we don't see.

It was also important that throughout the incident, we worked to get us out of trouble. There was no recrimination from either of us. I knew how I would feel had I been on the wheel when we ran aground. There was no need to make it worse by casting blame.

A skipper should never have handed over the wheel in a tight situation. At the very least, I should have continued to supervise the piloting. It was my responsibility to keep the vessel safe. It was my mistake.

It was perhaps a mixed blessing that on Laelia we didn't keep a very sharp hierarchy. Although I was nominally the skipper, Judy had no hesitation in telling me what she thought. It is often the case on a small boat that family members bring their familiar roles on board with them. Couples who have long established roles on land can be conflicted by their new roles on a small boat. It is not uncommon for couples to end up estranged after only a short time as "captain" and "crew." I remembered the reason why there were many boats for sale in San Diego.

Marooned at Elba Reef

We departed Marsa Fijab, about forty miles north of Suakin, on a weather window for sailing north. By this time of the year, around the northern two thirds of the Red Sea no wind or light north wind are all considered favorable weather windows for a passage heading north.

As Laelia made headway against the interminable swells, the hobbyhorse motion induced by the sharp waves was miserable. The boat first dove down a steep swell pointing the bow at the bottom of the ocean, then as the bow hit the upward part of the next swell, the boat would snap sharply back, pointing at the sky. With each forward and back motion, I half expected to see the mast snapping in half or getting flung off the deck.

On that particular passage, the forecast was for light wind. We didn't mind running the engine if the wind was light, but we wanted to avoid seasickness in strong contrary winds and big swells. After checking the forecast repeatedly, it seemed that there was only a thirty-hour window. In that amount of time, we could reach Elba Reef, at the northern limit of Sudan, about 120 miles away. If we continued on, it would put us in an area called Foul Bay in Egypt where I was unsure of any secure anchorage.

There was a good reason why they named it Foul Bay...it was full of reefs, shoals, and isolated rocks in water mostly not surveyed. It would be foolish to venture into that kind of territory in bad weather. By then we had some experience in reef-infested waters. It is of the utmost importance to have good light and smooth water to spot shallow reefs. The helmsperson requires absolute faith in the spotter and follows directions. Good light means sun up high behind the boat and not too much wave action. The guidebook called this "eyeball" navigation and "feel your way" through the bommies. There were no safe anchorages until

Ras Baniyas ("ras" means cape or point), another 140 miles north of Elba Reef.

It seemed prudent to head for Elba Reef and wait for the next weather window. Otherwise, we could get beat up and arrive at a new anchorage in a boiling sea of whitecaps, tired and sick. Under those conditions, a collision or grounding on a reef was more probable.

It takes self-discipline and painful memory of previous mistakes to take weather forecasts seriously. We read the directions in the guidebook and started looking for Elba Reef...an elusive atoll. Unlike many atolls ringed by scattered islands, Elba Reef is mostly submerged, with no visible bits of land.

"We are less than one nautical mile from the reef according to the GPS." Judy was studying the chart screen.

"I don't see any sign of a reef...and the water is still more than 1000 feet deep," I said.

"You think the GPS coordinates in the guidebook are wrong?" It's been spot-on so far."

"I'll re-check the waypoints I entered into the chart screen," I replied. "I double and triple checked my figures when I entered them originally, but I'll check them again."

I was reasonably sure the guidebook was accurate...authors double-check those numbers. People's lives depend on them. While I checked my entries, I also compared the GPS coordinates with the paper chart. They didn't all agree in exact detail, but the overall position was close. We also had a GPS waypoint a friend had sent us that was close also.

"The guidebook mentioned that there are three conspicuous boulders visible above the water surface," Judy said.

"Well, Elba Reef has to be here somewhere...all the numbers say so," I declared.

Judy was already scanning the horizon with the binoculars. "I see something... it looks like some tiny bumps in the horizon. They are still a little fuzzy, not really conspicuous."

The rocks, not giant boulders, were about two miles to the northeast. Judy saw them only because the sea was flat and any irregularity showed. It did restore our faith in the guidebook. Soon we saw lighter colors of the water. The depth went rapidly to 600 then 60 feet. *We were now inside the atoll.*

"Wow, look at that patch of bright green water! That is one of those scattered bommies the guidebook was talking about," I said.

"Look, here is another on the right," Judy commented as she steered the boat.

"Hey, make up your mind whether you are going between them or going around the left one," I said while watching the water on the left side of Laelia.

"I can't steer any closer to the right, there is no more room here," Judy replied, watching the water on her right.

"Well, there is not much space on the left either. There is a dark shadow sticking out a bit...not sure if it is a rock or what.it is."

A few more bommies and we started to aim for the three boulders as instructed by the guidebook while watching out for more bommies all along the way. As we got closer to the boulders, we turned east for the waypoint of the anchoring spot. It was not the thirty-foot depth described in the guidebook, but we could do forty feet with no problem and laid out all two hundred feet of anchor chain.

The water went all the way out to the horizon, but there were strips of brown, green, aqua, and dark blue scattered nearby. The obstruction and danger were all around under water.

"Look, there is a ship over there not moving, probably at anchor," I said, "It's kind of a strange place to anchor...so close to the reef."

"It's all painted white, but seems like it is listing a little," Judy said as she got out the binoculars.

"Wow, it's the wreck the guidebook talked about." Judy was looking through the binoculars. "It's painted white alright, but by the birds...it's all guano. The lower part is all rusted, the ship looks intact otherwise."

It was a sobering reminder that even the pros who do this for a living could end up high and dry. It is a sad monument to navigation errors.

Soon after we dropped anchor and topped up the fuel tank from the jerry cans, Laelia was ready to go again. We saw a fleet of six boats sailing along outside the reef. We thought they were coming into the reef anchorage, but only one Norwegian vessel appeared later in our anchorage. I was surprised that the five other boats sailed on, considering the weather forecast.

As it turned out, the forecast was accurate. By afternoon, the wind picked up to fifteen knots NW, a contrary wind, and it was over twenty knots after dark. All through the night the wind howled through the rigging and continued into the next morning. I got up during the night to check Laelia's GPS position and saw twenty-five knots NW on the anemometer. I was so very glad we had taken refuge at the reef because it would have been one wretched night out at sea on a northward passage.

We heard the next day from the Norwegian boat that did come into the anchorage that one of the five boats that continued on finally gave up and had to turn back to an anchorage not far from us, but closer to shore in a prohibited area. They were met by the Egyptian Navy and had to do a lot of extra paperwork. Lucky for them that the Egyptian Navy was very professional and treated them well.

This whole contested territory was claimed by both Egypt and Sudan. The guidebook warned of possible problems if one strayed too close to military posts. Different charts also showed different national boundaries. Much of this area could be worth billions as pristine resort dive sites or marine reserves, when and if the political tension relaxes.

All around us was water, water, and more water. There was nothing here except the sea with white caps throwing spume into the air. The northern boundaries of the reef however were clearly outlined by the pounding surf that was not there when we anchored. The reef sheltered Laelia from the swells, but not from the wind. Without waves battering the hulls, it was comfortable and cozy inside the boat even as we heard the howling of the wind in the rigging and crashing of the swells at the outer reef. Inside Laelia, it smelled heavenly as Judy made pancakes for breakfast.

The wind turbine was spinning continuously so we had lots of electricity for the inverter and the computer. Having had a good lunch and fortified by a good night's sleep, I was able to do a little writing while we were tucked in at Elba Reef waiting for the next weather window. The latest forecast indicated that it would be several days before that happened. All we needed was a twenty-four- to thirty-hour window of light wind for the next leg.

As we sat in the saloon looking out at the storm, we noticed a couple of little shore birds taking refuge on Laelia. There was nothing like fellow refugees to bring out that empathy. We debated how we could give the birds some fresh water without scaring them away. Of course we had to have a nice photo of our little friends as well.

The next morning, while checking the deck for signs of damage from the storm, I discovered one little bird with its feet in the air...dead. The other bird had left.

It was several days before the wind calmed sufficiently for us to visit the Norwegian boat not far from us. We brought them some frozen Swedish meatballs from Ikea. Their two young girls were excited. Apparently they were running low on food and the meatballs were a nice addition to their menu. They gave us some fish they had caught in exchange. We chatted some more before saying goodbye. They were the only other people around and it was good to have some social contact.

We cooked the fish that night. It was a nice change from chicken. We were running low on fresh foods. Judy had started growing bean sprouts to supplement the depleted fresh vegetable supply. We tended to carry a good supply of backup foods like canned Turkey Spam, canned tuna, and cheeses. Blocks of cheese in wax keep almost indefinitely under chilled conditions. We carried milk powder for growing yogurt and had been doing that all along for our breakfast.

Two days later, Judy had invited the family to Laelia for a pancake lunch. The girls came in the salon first while the parents were still tying up their dinghy.

"Oh good, you are alright," one of them said.

"What do you mean?" Judy asked.

"We didn't know if the fish was safe to eat," they replied earnestly.

Apparently, they had caught that fish at Elba Reef and were afraid to eat it. In tropical waters, reef fish could contain the ciguatera toxin. It is a neurotoxin that can be very debilitating, lasting for years or even decades in extreme cases. The toxin molecule happens to be extremely fat-soluble and is difficult to leach out of the body, hence the long persistence of the toxic effect. We were not affected by any toxin and made no more mention of the fish.

We waited a total of eleven days before a weather window

presented itself for passage towards the northwest. Elba Reef was an unusual experience. Except for the derelict ship, a few exposed rocks, and the occasional crashing surf from large swells, we saw nothing but water. Yet it provided Laelia with a secure anchorage and protection. After that many days, we were eager to hoist anchor and head for Port Ghalib, Egypt.

7. The Nile Flows North

Arriving Port Ghalib, Egypt (25 32.001 N, 34 38.707 E), 05 April 2009. Departing Port Said, Egypt (31 16.438 N, 32 19.757 E), 16 May 2009.

Landfall in Egypt
We were in Egypt on the Red Sea Coast. As Laelia rounded the fairway buoy to Port Ghalib, there sat a forlorn abandoned sailboat on the reef. That was an ominous welcome.

We soon learned that Port Ghalib had been newly designated Red Sea Port of Entry for all foreign yachts approaching from the south. There was a big concrete dock for arriving vessels to clear customs and immigration. Other vessels had already docked and were waiting to be processed.

"That boat on the reef had a problem with its engine and tried to sail into the port on a very windy day" said a sailor, one of the earlier arrivals.

"Did it run aground recently? Can it still be salvaged?" I asked.

"No, it was six months ago. They are still arguing on who's to pay for disposing of the derelict."

Port Ghalib was a resort development like so many others along the Red Sea Coast of Egypt, spawned by the easy credit and real estate boom. Tourists flying in to unwind at the resort could take a fast boat to dive sites and snorkel in the Red Sea or ride the glass-bottom submarine boat. They never needed to meet an Egyptian outside of the resort...a separate world from the rest of Egypt.

In addition to the hotel buffet restaurant there was a TGI Friday, an upscale western styled coffee bar, and a restaurant serving Egyptian food as well as pizza. Not far from the apartments for sale were glitzy souvenir shops. A very nice three-bedroom apartment with a view of the harbor was selling for about US $300,000. Europeans trying to escape their harsh winters think this is heaven on earth.

We hired a mechanic to replace the broken engine mounts on Laelia. He brought his grandson with him as an assistant. The old man looked frail and his grandson couldn't have been older than ten. I was skeptical of their ability to do the job, but I had no choice, they were the only ones available. To my surprise, it was like a miracle. The two of them somehow lifted the heavy diesel engine and replaced the broken mounts.

With the engine in working condition again, Laelia made a short hop to Abu Tig Marina, about 140 miles to the north of Port Ghalib, to wait for favorable weather. Abu Tig is the northernmost port on the Red Sea. From there, if we sailed east, we would enter the Gulf of Aqaba (Eilat in Hebrew) and continue on to visit Petra in Jordan. If we headed north, we would enter the Gulf of Suez and arrive at Port Suez, the southern starting point for the Suez Canal. It was a difficult choice to delay a visit to Petra, the ancient biblical city, and a World Heritage Site.

While waiting, we explored nearby towns. Upon our return from one of those trips, we got some unpleasant news. The woman on the next boat, a motor vessel from Jordan, waved for our attention. She didn't speak English, but the mime she performed was unmistakable, letting us know that a small creature with pointed ears had scurried on board Laelia by way of the boarding plank. We were stern tied to the concrete dock with two wooden planks for boarding. The rat had gained access via the plank; it could have come from anywhere or from another boat.

We didn't see any sign of the rat for several days. Perhaps it had left, but that was wishful thinking. Once a rat boarded a vessel, it would take a protracted battle to exorcise the demon.

I left small pieces of food at a few locations to detect teeth marks or other forensic evidence of the creature. The food was completely gone by morning. Having eaten, the rat left a telltale calling card. With that evidence, the battle began.

We bought rattraps. A cage type with bait was set in the cockpit. Other spring-loaded traps were placed at strategic locations. Another trap with sticky glue was placed in the galley. It took three days before I saw the rat with one foot stuck on the glue. As it struggled to free itself, a second foot became mired. The rat was caught and disposed of promptly, glue and all.

Finally, there was a weather window for departing Abu Tig Marina. The passage through the Gulf of Suez didn't have the tense drama of pirates. The major hazards were drilling platforms and abandoned oil wells. We were warned that not all of the rigs had lights. We stayed close to the shipping channel especially at night. It was a surprise to us that Egypt had such extensive oil and natural gas resources. Later we read that Egypt even had a 15-year agreement to sell natural gas to Israel. It made the news because an Egyptian militant opposition group complained that the price was set too low.

The passage from Abu Tig to Port Suez took 34 hours. We approached Port Suez in the early morning and could see on the AIS screen that northbound ships were queuing up to enter the Suez Canal. The canal is only wide enough for one-way ship traffic so the north and southbound traffic took turns at different periods during the day. We checked the traffic for a lull and scooted across the channel to tie up at the marina managed by the Suez Canal Authority (SCA).

Encounters in Port Suez
At Port Suez, the SCA sent technicians to measure the sailboats in preparation for the canal passage. The canal fees are based on these measurements. Our agent gave us instructions on the amount to tip so the measurements would be reasonable. We were also assigned canal pilots by SCA to guide each boat through to the canal mid point at Ismailia. While we waited for the schedule for small crafts to transit the canal we explored Port Suez.

We discovered that Egyptians there were friendly to foreigners. Many times we had strangers come up to us and say, "Welcome to Egypt."

On our first foray out of the harbor area, we looked for lunch, but couldn't find any eateries at the waterfront. We asked about food at a coffee shop where a group of local men were smoking sheeshas, elaborate-looking water pipes, and drinking coffee or tea. I was surprised that coffee shops didn't serve food, not even snacks.

One man gestured us to follow him across the street. He pointed to a small new Lada, a Russian made automobile, and told us to get in. I was a little hesitant, but decided that it seemed safe. He drove us about two miles into downtown and pointed at a fish restaurant before leaving. The restaurant had only a tiny storefront downstairs. All the tables and chairs were upstairs.

With great satisfaction, we learned all about Egyptian fish dinners there. The fried fish steak, prawns, and squid came with three sides of green salad, tahina, and some kind of a tasty mashed eggplant dish. There was also a big basket of flat bread, each one twelve inches across. The waiter asked if we wanted soup. Of course we said yes not knowing that it was a big bowl of fish, shrimp, squid, clams, with garlic and onions. Judy didn't want to eat all of it so I got to consume a lot more than I had planned. Each bowl of soup was a meal by itself. Luckily, it was not a tourist restaurant, the bill for this amazing lunch was surprisingly low.

After lunch, we needed to do a little walking to see if our legs could still support our heavily laden stomachs. Right around the corner was a little coffee shop where several dignified gentlemen were smoking their sheeshas. They were exactly what I thought Egyptian men would be like...friendly and gregarious.

"Assalamu alaykom," I greeted them and asked if I could take a photograph of them.

"No, but you may sit down and have some tea with us," one replied in perfect English. It was not an invitation I could politely turn down, although I was somewhat taken by surprise.

"Shukran...thank you." I said.

Something was said in Arabic and the waiter brought an extra chair for Judy and tea for both of us. Then the sheesha rig was placed in front of me. It was a lot of paraphernalia for smoking a little tobacco. It had a stand with a water bowl and many tubes. At the top was a charcoal fire, and a wad of tobacco was already in place. As I applied suction to the mouthpiece, I could see air bubbles going through the water. The airflow caused the charcoal fire to burn more of the tobacco and produced smoke going through the tubes.

I decided that a little smoke wouldn't kill me immediately. Besides, the water probably filtered out the heat to make the smoke mellow. The other men were having such a good chuckle watching me fumbling with the sheesha pipe.

At this point a well-dressed gentleman walked towards us and ask me if I could spare him a one-pound coin (about twenty cents). He explained that he was from Ethiopia, but had fallen on hard times and needed some money. The others were making unkind comments to this man.

One of my sheesha-smoking companions told me it was ok to give the man a coin. As I handed him the coin, he pulled out his wallet to put the coin away, but made it plain for me to see that he had lots of paper money in his wallet. Then I was introduced to this gentleman, who turned out to be the owner of the fish restaurant. Everyone had a good laugh, but the joke was on me. That was their sense of humor and how they entertained themselves while smoking their sheesha on a hot quiet afternoon.

When we left the sheesha shop, we saw a street vendor selling flatbread on a piece of cloth spread over the sidewalk. I thought that was a photo op. Judy waited while I took the photo. When I was finished, I discovered that Judy was having a conversation with half a dozen young Egyptian women. Some wore the headscarf and others didn't.

I stayed back so I wouldn't interrupt the exchange. While it was easy to talk to men, we seldom had any opportunity to talk to Muslim women in the Middle East.

Judy learned from these young ladies that Egypt has become more conservative over recent times. Ten years ago, women didn't wear the headscarf in Egypt. It was young women, egged on by a televangelist, who decided that they should wear the headscarf. There were women wearing burqas, the head-to-foot black robes and veils, as well as those without even a headscarf. Shoulders and knees were always covered.

I talked to Egyptians who were distressed at how the country had languished. One man I knew blamed it on the government especially the sitting president.

"When Sadat was assassinated, we voted for Mubarak, but now, more than twenty-five years later, he's still there," he lamented.

"We had so much hope when Sadat was alive."

At the time (2009) Hosni Mubarak was firmly in control and the disaffection was palpable.

We waited many days in the marina at Port Suez to transit the canal, which is regularly closed to small-boat traffic in order for warships to transit. Generally, warships don't inform the SCA of their planned passage until close to midnight and would randomly slip through with the regular commercial shipping traffic. Small boats are restricted until the warships have cleared the canal. For two consecutive days, we saw two submarines and a US submarine tender transiting the canal.

The canal passage for small boats was divided in two parts. When going north, the first leg was from Port Suez through the Bitter Lakes to Ismailia. Then, after an overnight layover, boats would continue from Ismailia to Port Said.

On small boats like Laelia, most of the canal passage was just a long boring motoring trip. Big ships and tankers passed by from time to time in the center of the canal while we stayed on the buoy line with thirty to forty feet of water under Laelia's keel. We were surprised that the SCA allowed local fishing boats in the canal. These were small rowboats with no outboards managed by one or two fishermen on board, providing the only picturesque part of the famous Canal.

Desert sand was on either side of the canal. Our friends who transited the canal on the Queen Victoria going north could see the Sinai to the east and the Nile Delta on the west. From the lowly sailboat at water level, all we saw was sand. At regular intervals we could see the guard towers and soldiers along the canal banks in the hot sun with their rifles. Occasionally there were tanks parked sporadically. It was probably against the rules to take photos of anything military. We took photos anyway and the soldiers waved back. No doubt they were bored and we were a welcomed diversion.

Our plan was to transit the canal starting at Port Suez and stopping at Ismailia where all sailboats are required to tie up overnight. Instead of continuing the next morning, we decided to stay and use Ismailia as a base for land touring in Egypt. Ismailia is at about halfway along the canal passage and had secure facilities for berthing Laelia.

A Stowaway on Laelia

Ismailia is a small town named for Pasha Ismail, Khedive of Egypt, who brought the country to the brink of bankruptcy building the Suez Canal. The French built the town and houses to accommodate workers during the construction. The colonial style mansions were elegant and all had gardens, but they now belonged to wealthy Egyptians. The major boulevard had a park along the side with grass and flowers. It was maintained regularly and free of trash. Ismailia could well be the cleanest town in Egypt.

So it was particularly galling, while berthed in Ismailia, for Laelia to acquire an unwelcome stowaway. There is nothing as disturbing as having a rat on a small sailboat. It brought on a battle royal and a dueling of wits to evict the odious pest.

It started out to be a good day. Judy and I went to an exceptional restaurant in Ismailia called George. The hushed lighting, the rich mahogany decor, and the soft music from a previous era all suggested good taste. We were not disappointed. The menu was diverse, the food superb, and at a very reasonable price by California standards.

Upon our return, we saw a cat perched on Laelia.

"What's that flea-bitten cat doing here?" I said.

"I like cats," Judy protested.

The cat seemed to have taken up residence on Laelia. That was strange...we never had a cat become so attached to Laelia. The mystery was resolved early the next morning.

"Do you hear a noise in the cockpit?" I asked. "It's different." Having lived on Laelia for several years, we knew every sound on board.

"Yeah, I think it's coming from the lazarette," Judy said.

When I went near the lazarette in the cockpit, the noise stopped. I opened the cover and noticed a lot of loose black debris.

"Wait a minute, something is chewing on the thermal insulation around the refrigeration coils," I yelled in alarm.

"It has to be a rat," Judy said as she examined the rubbery debris in the lazarette.

It dawned on me that it was a stowaway rat on board that attracted the cat. The rat couldn't gain access inside the vessel because we had locked all the hatches when we were away. The lazarette was left open to help cool the compressor for the refrigeration. Without the insulation, the refrigerator would fail and our food would spoil.

"This is war," I declared and started to remove various pieces of stored gear from the lazarette. Soon, the storage space under the seat was empty and I could see the rat at the bottom of the lazarette. It had a dark grey coat and a pink tail. I fetched a wooden oar and tried to smash the rat, but it was quick. The oar kept missing, but it was just a matter of time before the miscreant got its just deserts. I was merciless.

At the bottom of the lazarette was a drain hole in case the boat was pooped and seawater had to be drained quickly. There was a rubber clamshell beneath the hole, serving as a baffle to keep waves from shooting straight into the lazarette. The rat, by this time, had scurried into the drain hole in desperation. It was still sitting on the clamshell out of my reach, but its pink tail was within reach of the oar. I gave its tail a good whack, and instantly the rat plunged into the sea. A few moments later, I saw the creature swimming away. It gave me a woeful look. I fervently hoped I had flattened its tail.

Surviving Taxi Rides in Cairo
Judy and I departed Ismailia on an intercity bus to sightsee in Cairo. We got off the bus somewhere in the middle of Cairo with our luggage in tow.

Screech! An ancient taxi came to a halt right next to us, blocking the entire lane of busy traffic. That taxi had seen better days, with dents and peeling paint all over. Calling it disreputable would have been a high compliment, but we needed a taxi.

I stuck my head in the window and said, "Victoria Hotel?"

He said, "No problem." He waved for us to get in.

The traffic was piling up behind him.

"Ten pounds," I said. It was important to agree on a price or it could get ugly later.

"No." He gestured with both his hands twice...twenty pounds.

It was hot and we were tired from the three-hour bus ride. The cars behind us were bleating their horns. Twenty Egyptian pounds was equivalent to just under US $4. I was stressed. Besides, I didn't know the going rate in Cairo, the big city. I was guessing from Ismailia prices.

"Ok, twenty pounds," I said as Judy and I jumped in the beat-up taxi. The inside was no better with torn fabric and smudges on the ceiling.

The driver stomped on the gas paddle and took off. There was a moment of silence as he sped along the busy boulevard.

"Hotel?" he asked.

At that instant, I realized that our adventure was only just beginning. I tried to tell him the name of the hotel, but he didn't understand me.

He stopped some pedestrians along the way to ask them to translate. It took two tries before he found someone willing and able to be a Good Samaritan. I would say the name in English and they repeated the name in Arabic to the driver. I had no idea that there is an equivalent Arabic word for Victoria...it is a name. Needless to say the attempt failed.

I remembered that I had the hotel's phone number. So I dialed the number and handed the phone to the driver. That was great. Now the driver knew where he needed to go, but he also had the upper hand in a new round of negotiation.

He said, "Thirty pounds" and a lot of Arabic that I didn't understand.

My options were rather limited. I could demand to get off the taxi. Then we would be stranded at a busy road with our luggage and become prey to the next taxi driver...or worse. He won.

Taxi adventures are too numerous to tell. The black and white taxis were Russian made Ladas, most of them over twenty years old. Some had springs showing in the seats or torn fabric dangling from the interior roof. The exteriors of these taxis were no better. Don't even think about air-conditioning, just pray that the brakes and steering work.

Lost in Cairo

If riding taxis is an adventure, crossing streets in Cairo is definitely an extreme sport. There are no crosswalks or zebra stripes where cars are required to stop for pedestrians. Egyptians cross anywhere they please and at their own risk. To cross multiple lanes of fast moving traffic requires nerves of steel and cold mental agility.

Crossing a busy street in Cairo is done one lane at a time and then waiting for an opening in the flow of traffic in the next lane.

This is easier said than done, because the drivers are not in the habit of staying in orderly lanes.

You might wonder: "What about the traffic police?" Well, traffic police direct traffic. Right? Apparently their job description does not include looking after pedestrians. I observed dozens of school children filtering their way across four lanes of fast moving vehicles while the police, within ten feet of them, continued to motion the traffic to move on. It is the way of life in Cairo. The trick is to go with the flow and make no sudden moves.

One day while walking around Cairo we found ourselves in a neighborhood that tourists did not frequent. The streets were not straight and were no wider than what would fit one small automobile. With four- or five-story buildings looming overhead, it was a little dark, even in daylight hours. Most of the ground floors of these apartment buildings appeared to be garages. We saw one "garage" filled with used spare parts for trucks.

"Look what's in that garage," I said.

"I can't believe it...goats," Judy said in surprise. The door closed quickly before I could take a photo...perhaps it was not legal to keep animals in the garage.

"I think there are around twenty of them," I said.

"I wonder what else is in these garages," Judy mused.

Laundry was drying overhead on the balconies or on lines outside windows. This is city apartment living with a village feel. I imagined that the women probably talked to each other as they put out the laundry in the morning.

We guessed that neighborhoods like these were where the majority of the ordinary Cairenes lived. They were definitely friendly and considered us a curiosity. They greeted us back with a big smile as we greeted them in our awkward Arabic.

We saw a shop with an ancient treadle sewing machine and asked if we could have a Greek courtesy flag made for the boat. We needed a flag for our next port in Greece. The presumed tailor spoke no English and my Arabic didn't extend past simple greetings. Even with a picture of the Greek flag in hand, it was no help.

There were several gentlemen sitting across the narrow street drinking tea and smoking their sheesha water pipe. They asked a young man to bring someone who could speak English. While we waited, they brought chairs for us to sit and invited us to tea. Between their minimal English and our Arabic and hand gestures, we had a conversation of sorts. They wanted to know where we are from and how we liked Egypt. That all went well. They showed interest in America and exhibited no hostilities. They seemed particularly optimistic and pleased about Obama.

Soon the interpreter arrived. Unfortunately, the tailor didn't think he could make a flag. He specialized only in clothing. We thanked our hosts and got ready to move on. They wanted us to stay longer, but we said that we had to keep searching for a flag maker. That was an acceptable reason to them.

Although we felt safe, we did not like the feeling of being lost. None of the streets were straight and the lack of sunlight in the high-rise jungle didn't help to maintain our orientation. We couldn't be sure we were still walking towards the part of Cairo we knew.

In the back of my mind I realized that this was a big city and there is crime in any city that size, although the rate of violent crime is much lower than in US cities. I remembered a banner that the Singapore Government had placed all over the island nation: "Low crime does not mean no crime."

On the other hand, in a small community like the one we were visiting, everybody knew what the others were doing. It would be hard for anything to happen to us without the whole neighborhood knowing. Although we were in the middle of a big city, the atmosphere was like that of a small village. The people we had met were far from wealthy, but were friendly and seemed contented about life. The men smoked their sheesha, drank their tea, and probably talked mostly about politics. I had a comfortable feeling that the people here would not harm us. We eventually found our way back to our hotel and called it a day.

Judy and I did a self-guided walking tour of historic Cairo, but we got lost. While we were crossing a deserted area behind a mosque Judy kept walking while I stopped to take photos. I was far enough away from her and out of sight that a vendor thought she was alone. He invited her to see an art gallery nearby. Judy told him she was not interested. He was persistent, but Judy ignored him and kept walking.

"Why don't you talk to me? You come all this way to Egypt and not talk to local people?" He yelled loudly trying to intimidate Judy because she appeared to be alone. He was quite mistaken if he thought he could intimidate Judy.

I could hear his threatening tone and hurried closer. I called out to Judy, "What is going on?"

At that moment, he realized that she wasn't alone. He turned to me, put on a very sincere face and explained, "There is a beautiful craft gallery of historic..."

He literally disappeared around the corner in mid-sentence. I didn't understand why until I discovered that Judy had, quite by chance, found a tourist police stall in the deserted street. She went in to ask for directions. The vendor no doubt thought she had gone in to file a complaint about his aggressive behavior.

There was a senior Tourist Police officer in spiffy white uniform at the stall. He was in his 60's, with a flushed red face, and balding. Every inch of his white uniform was filled by his considerable girth. He didn't speak much English, but was very charming and polite. With a big smile he asked how he could help. He gave Judy detailed directions on how she could get to the mosque we were looking for.

Vendors see tourists as wealthy and they think of American as particularly easy marks. They were less demanding on the Chinese because they hadn't figured out how to scam them yet. One fellow found out that I was from California...an American.

He exclaimed, "Oh, Chinese is OK, but. Americans are better...they are rich."

During our Cairo walk, I was at the end of exploring a historic mosque at the Bab al Futuh (one of three remaining Fatimid Gates). The caretaker introduced me to the imam, who extended his hand, so we shook hands. Then the caretaker told me that the imam would like to sing for me. Although nothing was said, I knew that it would lead to a payment, but it would have been very ungracious to turn down such an offer. Fortunately, this particular imam has a very mellow voice. Although he sang very softly, his singing was tempered with authority and was mesmerizing. I didn't know the words, but enjoyed a most unusual visit to a historic mosque. I did pay the imam, and I thought it was a worthy exchange.

On that visit, Judy got very tired and decided to sit in the shade outside the mosque. She had already seen more than her share of mosques. She also hated to take her shoes on and off as required for going into a mosque. While she was sitting, vendor after vendor approached her trying to sell their wares. One vendor, with a compassionate heart, came by and taught Judy an Arabic phrase to fend off these people: "Shukran, maa salama." It meant: "Thank you, good-bye." For the remainder of our stay in Cairo, Judy got a lot of use out of that phrase.

Egyptians

Egyptians are not homogeneous. There are people from other parts of Africa and the Middle East. The majority are Sunni Muslims. Coptic Christians, at 10 to 20% of the population, are in the minority. The taller, slenderer, and darker people are from southern Egypt or Sudan.

We never heard a bad word spoken of the other religions in Egypt, but we did detect an underlying tension from Coptic Christians with regard to their second-class status. Permission is required from the central government for churches to be built or even renovated or repaired. No such permission is required for mosques. Newspapers reported that Muslims who converted to Christianity complained of difficulty in having their religious affiliation changed on their identity cards. Converts in the other direction faced no such problem.

The government in Egypt at the time was pretty heavy-handed. During the swine flu scare, the Minister of Health ordered all pigs in Egypt slaughtered, even though there had been no cases of swine flu in the country. Of course Muslims did not eat pork or have anything to do with the pork industry. Only the Coptic Christians, who raised pigs, protested the action. Most of the pigs were raised on trash heaps by the Christian zabaleens (garbage collectors). The pigs were a side business that had been profitable. Killing all the pigs put many people out of their livelihood and destroyed an entire industry.

The zabaleens collected about one third of the trash in Cairo, often using donkey carts to haul bags of trash. This service was offered in the wealthier parts of the city. The government contracted foreign collection services from Italy for selected parts of the city that had to be kept clean and looking dignified, especially near the embassies. These companies used compacting trucks that were more presentable than donkey carts. In the rest of the city there was no trash collection because the poorer residents used things until there was little residue value, leaving little profit in recycling.

Despite its many obvious problems, Cairo is a great city with immense cultural and historic riches. On clear days, the city is stunning, with blue sky and a pleasant breeze, especially along the Nile River. It is the perfect place for a leisurely stroll not far from the new high-rise hotels in the late afternoon sun. There would be young couples along the waterfront whispering to each other. Tourists could hardly resist taking photos of the traditional feluccas plying the Nile with their peculiar lateen sails. It can be an idyllic and magical place.

The modern international hotels on either side of the Nile and on the Gezira (island in Arabic) are as plush as the best money can buy. Air-conditioned big lobbies with comfortable sofas served as a welcome oasis for exhausted tourists and exuberant Saudi businessmen. Most important of all, these hotels have western style bathrooms not far from the lobby. The attendants keep the facilities spotless. We used these facilities and would buy an occasional cup of coffee or a lunch at the hotel.

For sleeping, we mostly stayed in Egyptian hotels although with mixed success. They were all in old buildings with ancient elevators creaking up and down in exposed elevator shafts.

The best hotel room we happened to stay in was in Alexandria, a couple hours of train ride to the west of Cairo. At first we were disappointed by the small size of the room, but as the bellhop swung open the louvered doors to the balcony, we were stunned by the sweeping panorama of the Alexandria Harbour. That was our first sighting of the Mediterranean Sea.

We went to a lot of tourist sites in Egypt. We thought the Cairo Museum was overwhelming with an excess of riches in antiquities, but not all well displayed. One of the most poignant artifacts was a small statue of the dwarf Seneb and his family. The artist arranged to have Senab seated with his legs crossed under him so he looked the same height as his wife sitting next to him. His arms were held across his chest so the shorter length of his forelimbs was not so obvious. Seneb's two children stood in front where his legs would have been to give the impression of a pair of legs. His face was that of a proud and intelligent man. The artist had maintained the dignity of his subjects and rendered an image of a harmonious family relationship while holding true to his artistic integrity.

If we were overwhelmed by the Cairo Museum, we loved the museum in Alexandria. We also made a symbolic pilgrimage to the new Alexandria Library as a way to mourn the loss of the ancient Library of Alexandria long ago.

Tours took us to the Great Pyramids and the Sphinx as well as the Cheops Solar Boat Museum in Giza. The finale was a leisurely Nile cruise to visit the antiquities and a tour extension to see the Grand Temple of Abu Simbel.

The Baksheesh Culture
The most unpleasant aspect of our visit in Egypt was about baksheesh, which can be loosely translated as gift, tip, or bribe.

The guards at the customs gate checked our passports and whatever we brought in or out of the dock area at Ismailia. As we went through the customs gate quite a lot, we would occasionally have short conversations with the guards.

The captain asked, "Are you going shopping?"

Judy said, "Yes, at the Metro Market."

"What are you buying?"

Judy jokingly replied, "Chocolates."

The captain said, "Oh, I like chocolates too."

On our way back, Judy offered the captain a small bar of chocolate she bought at the market.

The captain was horrified, saying, "I couldn't possibly accept a gift."

I had to keep from bursting out laughing. The thought that he couldn't accept a gift was hilarious, but I kept that thought to myself. He couldn't accept it because it was in public view even though it was only a small bar of chocolate. Judy never meant it as a bribe, but appearance was everything to the captain.

We were not allowed to buy diesel fuel at the petrol station in town because the fuel was subsidized. The proper way for foreign yachts to buy fuel was to apply for a permit to purchase tax-free fuel.

"I got fuel at the petrol station in town at about one pound a liter," said the skipper from the boat next to us.

"That sounds good to me," I said. A pound was equivalent to about twenty cents US at the time. That would make diesel about US $0.80 per gallon.

"Yeah, but it's not legal and you have to negotiate with the guards," said the skipper. He was an old hand sailing in the Red Sea and the Mediterranean.

"How is it done legally?" I asked. Whenever possible I prefer to stay within the law. It is always nice to keep a clear conscience.

"I was told you could apply for a permit at the Port Office," the skipper replied.

I trundled over to the Port Office on a hot afternoon. A rotund, unshaven man wearing a singlet (tank-top) was sitting by an electric fan in his office. He was obviously an official person to be so casual about his demeanor.

"What you want?" asked the official.

"May I please have an application for tax-free diesel?" I replied.

The official gave me a pained look and asked, "How long you plan to stay at the dock?"

"Well, I plan to leave in a few days. That's why I need the diesel."

"That's not enough time for the papers to come back," he said. "Mohamed can get you diesel at the same tax-free price and he will deliver it to your boat. He delivers fuel to all the boats around here."

"How much is the tax-free fuel?" I asked.

"Same price as always...three pounds a liter." That was three times the price of diesel in town. I didn't need a calculator to know that for every liter of diesel, one pound would go to the petrol station, probably one for Mohamed, and one for our friend for sitting in front of the fan. I didn't like it, but the diesel would be delivered to Laelia. I wouldn't have to schlep all those heavy jerry cans around. In any case, it was a lot cheaper diesel than the dollar-fifty a liter ($6/gallon) I had paid in Australia.

"How do I find Mohamed?" I asked.

"He's away now, but he will look for your boat."

Indeed, Mohamed was gone for the weekend to see his wife and kids in Cairo. With time on my hands, I thought perhaps I could get some diesel on my own. I took the five jerry cans wrapped in garbage bags. As I went out the gate, the customs guard gestured me over to his guard station. He had a crooked smile exposing his bad teeth, all very yellow.

"What's in the bag?" he asked. *He knows every well what's in the bag.*

I started to unwrap the bags.

"No, no...not here...inside!" He barked as he pointed at the guardhouse.

As I carried the bags into the guardhouse, he closed the door. It was dark in there with only light coming in from one small window. I had visions of getting mugged...I wasn't too far wrong.

"Five US dollars each can," he said

"What? Five US dollars? Forget it, I'll take the jerry cans back to the boat." I reached for the door. I didn't like being trapped inside the dark guardhouse with him.

"Wait...five pounds," he said. "For each can. That's what everybody pays."

Judy and I got a taxi at the street corner that was willing to haul the jerry cans round trip for twenty pounds that would normally cost less than ten.

We bought a little more than 25 gallons of diesel (about 95 liters) at the petrol station, but I didn't have exact change. The attendant said that he didn't have enough to give change. I knew he had the change, but he wanted a little baksheesh.

"Keep the change," I said.

Why not? Everyone else is acting like blood-sucking varmints.

I suppose I could have made a big stink to get my nine pounds change, but I was anxious to get out of there. Also, I was not exactly in a position to threaten to call the police. As I loaded the fuel into the boot, the taxi driver said that the waiting time was going to cost me ten more pounds for the trip.

Oh, why not!

Again, I was not in a position to tell him to go to hell. It was too long a walk back with 25 gallons of fuel. *Partners in crime have to look out for each other. Right?*

When we got back to the customs gate, the taxi driver was going to park on the side street, but the guards shouted for him to come right up to the gate.

What are they up to now?

To my surprise, they opened the gate so the taxi could go all the way into the driveway, 50 meters closer to the dock. Normally, they only open the gate for VIPs coming to inspect the marina.

I said to Judy, "Wow, look what 25 pounds bought us."

It wasn't until later that it dawned on me that the guards were not trying to be nice to me. It would have looked very awkward for them if I schlepped all those yellow jerry cans across the gate with all of them watching. Also, there was speculation around the dock that there was an inspection by the higher ups.

I calculated that this bit of illegal fuel ended up being US $1.25 per gallon instead of $0.80 per gallon at the pump or $2.4 per gallon from Mohamed. After paying all the baksheesh to the guards, the taxi driver, and the petro station attendant, I had saved a little, but had to do all the work. The baksheesh was just like paying taxes, but directly to the citizens.

People who provided services often would ask for baksheesh by saying, "Do you have a present for me?" If I gave him five pounds, he would look at me sadly and ask for ten. If I gave ten, he would ask for twenty. I learned to say "No." After some protests, he would ask if I had a cap or a t-shirt for him. One of them even asked for some sweets for his children before leaving. It seems that there is never a stopping point.

Tipping is practiced in many parts of the world, but generally it is mutually satisfactory. It was different in Egypt. It seemed that there was not a sense of fairness or limit. Unless I was prepared, it could be difficult thinking of a face-saving reason why I didn't want to pay someone anymore. I could say, "You don't deserve any more." That would start an argument that I didn't need or want.

One time a little girl came up to Judy. The girl was about 10 years of age, well groomed, looking bright in her stiffly starched school uniform. At first Judy understood that the girl wanted to practice her English.

"Well...you can practice your English with me," Judy replied. It was not the kind of request she could refuse.

"May I have a pen?" The girl asked.

"I don't have a pen on me."

"How about your sunglasses?" The girl pointed at the sunglasses Judy was wearing.

"No, I need my sunglasses." Judy realized that the girl was simply asking for a handout. She was not poor; she just thought Judy was a good mark for something...anything. We were saddened by that experience, more so than by our encounters with adults.

Often, a guard at a temple or monument would offer tourists to take a photo of them together. This was before the selfie craze using the smart phone. We had taken photos for tourists with their own cameras and had accepted the same courtesy from others. With the guards, it was invariably followed by a request for money...not much, but most people found it unpleasant. We learned to turn down the offer politely since we didn't generally want photos of ourselves.

Having been in Egypt for a while, we became acquainted with this baksheesh custom. We were always on our guard. When someone offered us a favor, I had to run it through some part of my brain to decide if we should accept or decline. We had, for example, received an offer from a well-dressed gentleman to help us cross the Cairo traffic when we were a little slow. It took us a few extra seconds to realize and accept a genuine offer of help.

Not everyone in Cairo wanted a handout. There was the vendor who had taught Judy the phrase "Shukhran, maa salama," meaning "Thank you, goodbye" to help her ward off aggressive hawkers and touts. These were of course glimpses of behavior that led us to hope the rest of Cairo was not all obsessed with extorting money.

They didn't just treat foreigners with the demand for baksheesh. Once we were at the long distance bus station ready to board the bus. There was a delay. An Egyptian workman had a bundle of building material that he wanted to load on the bus as his luggage. The bus driver thought it was too big although the bundle was lighter than most suitcases. Before long, the foreman of the bus crew arrived. He took out his tape measure. At that moment, the workman slipped a wad of cash to the foreman. As soon as I saw the money changing hands, I knew that everything was resolved and the delay would soon be over. The foreman took his time measuring the bundle and when he was finished he nodded to one of the crews to load the bundle on the bus. It was all done with many people watching, and no one batted an eye.

Canal Transit

We were required to have pilots on board during the canal transit. The Suez Canal Authority (SCA) paid the pilots from canal fees assessed from all vessels based on their tonnage. We were told by the SCA as well as by our canal agent that it was traditional to tip the pilot a recommended amount at the end of the transit. The guidebook also warned that the pilots would try to negotiate additional baksheesh.

During the transit from Ismailia to Port Said, our pilot was talking on the VHF radio in Arabic with the guard tower. Then he told me that he needed to have some cigarettes. I thought he wanted to smoke, but he indicated that he needed to give a whole cartoon of cigarettes to the guards or the guards would stop the whole convoy.

I was rather offended by such a lame, blatant lie. I doubted very much that the guards would stop the convoy in the middle of the canal so publicly. So I told our pilot I had only one pack of cigarettes (the one pack that was visible on the table). He said that wasn't enough, but that he could buy the cigarettes from the market and all I had to do was to pay him. I replied that, if he had already promised a whole cartoon of cigarettes, it would be best for him to buy them from the market, but I wouldn't pay for it. He went on and on, but I had tuned him out by that time.

Laelia had a problem during this second leg of the Suez Canal transit. She was acting exceptionally sluggish under power. It seemed that barnacles must have fouled both of Laelia's propellers while she was berthed at the dock in Ismailia. Unfortunately, we couldn't stop in the canal to clean the propeller. The pilot was unhappy about Laelia's slow progress. I wasn't happy about the fouled propeller either, but there wasn't anything I could do while still in the canal.

As we approached Port Said harbor, I knew the pilot would ask for more baksheesh. The guidebook had warned that there would be demands of money for the pilot boat.

I told the pilot, "I'll drop you off at the public dock. You don't need the pilot boat."

He replied, "There is no fee for the pilot boat."

As we approached the dock where I was to drop him off, he pointed to the boat that was coming to pick him up.

"Only four packs of cigarettes will be enough for the pilot boat," he said.

"I don't have four packs of cigarettes," I said.

"I have to give baksheesh to the pilot boat," he replied.

With all the distraction arguing about the baksheesh, we almost ran right into a ferry that was crossing the harbor in front of us.

At this point, his greed was putting us in harm's way; he was not even doing his job. The pilot boat was trying to come next to Laelia. My patience was running low. I brought out the envelope I had prepared ahead of time with what I considered an appropriate tip for the pilot. I showed him his name on the front of the envelope.

"This is for you. If you want to give part of it to the pilot boat, that is fine with me."

He looked at me with an injured look. "You don't think I am a good pilot?"

I almost told him to get lost. But to lose my temper was not acceptable. Losing control is an admission of defeat.

"You are a fine pilot," I said. I also wanted to tell him that he was a greedy human being with absolutely no dignity.

I am pretty sure I was right, but saying all that would have done no good to anyone.

I wanted to see the world and I am discovering that the world is sometimes a little different...what a surprise. Or perhaps the world really isn't terribly different. I am just seeing it exposed.

Baksheesh is ingrained in the Egyptian culture—at least at the level of the people we dealt with. I kept hoping that the phenomenon was mainly restricted to the tourist interface and not a culture that permeated through the entire country. How could corruption ever be overcome if everyone tolerated bribes as an accepted way of life? There is no doubt in my mind that corruption exists in every country, but it would become less common if the practice were deemed unacceptable. There is plenty of corruption in the United States, but usually practiced under cover for fear of exposure.

Greed is a part of human nature, but it can be held in check by the fear of public condemnation. It's even better if greed is held in check by a person's internal compass, acquired at an early age.

It would have been desirable to get a good night's sleep and clean the propellers before departing Port Said, except for my argument with the canal pilot over baksheesh. He was angry as he left. I wasn't sure if he would seek reprisals, but I was not waiting around in Egyptian waters to find out. We were on his turf. An hour before sundown, Laelia departed Egypt forever, heading for the next harbor in the Mediterranean.

8. It's All Greek to Me

Arriving Kouremenos Bay, Crete, Greece (35 12.780 N, 026 16.413 E), 20 May 2009. At sea, near Cape Maleas, Greece (36 26.03 N, 023 12.40 E), 24 May 2010. The period of time included a surgical interlude in California.

Slow Boat to Crete
As soon as Laelia departed Port Said, Egypt, we were in the Mediterranean Sea heading for Crete as our first landfall. In the following days, we discovered that the mild Mediterranean climate, celebrated by travel posters, was not totally accurate. The sea was often petulant with quick tempests and short sharp swells coming from every direction. One of our friends was even hit by a water-funnel while sailing in the Aegean.

We discovered that windward landmasses, instead of providing protective barriers against howling storms, often accelerated the gusts as the cool air masses raced down rugged slopes and canyons. Meteorologists called them katabatic winds. We shouldn't be surprised by harsh winds, for Homer had long ago forewarned of these treacherous conditions.

Laelia's propeller problem hadn't gone away. I had thought of diving under the boat at sea to scrape off the barnacles, but decided against the idea. The waves were large, causing the boat to heave and roll. If I got conked on the head as the boat bounced up and down, a concussion was a possibility. Even a small injury at sea can be a serious problem. In the worst case, if I was knocked unconscious while under the boat, my body might not ever surface.

I shut the engines off to avoid overheating them from spinning the propeller uselessly. Not using the engine was not a serious problem while we had southerly wind. As the wind shifted to its prevailing northwest direction, we had wind on the nose. With adverse wind and inefficient auxiliary power, I had no choice except to sail. After all, Laelia is a sailboat.

It was a lot of work tacking back and forth, sailing to windward. The saying "gentlemen never sail to windward" hit home. Not being a "gentleman" was not a big deal, but all that tacking was serious labor. For boats with more crew, the tacking could be done smartly and quickly. On Laelia, because there was usually only one of us on watch while the other slept, sailing upwind was laborious and inefficient. Fortunately we only had to make long sweeping tacks, each lasting hours. We also had squalls and had to tack in blinding rain driven by shifting winds.

On the other hand, it was nice to give the boat a good wash with fresh rainwater. By that time Laelia hadn't had a good bath for several months. The harsh rain cleansed off most of the red dust and caked-on salt crystals that covered the boat. Sailing in a cold, lashing rain is never fun, but that is part and parcel of sailing life.

We aimed for the very first decent anchorage on the easternmost point of Crete. It took four full days before we set anchor in Kouremenos Bay, Crete.

It is a big bay and Laelia was the only boat anchored. The wind was blowing thirty knots and gusting much more, but the anchor held. By evening we saw small, brightly painted fishing boats with Greek flags returning to the marina. *We are in Greece.* We had a good night's sleep and were oblivious to the shrieking wind as it pierced through the rigging. The wind continued to blow unabated late the next morning. Whitecaps were all over the bay, but Laelia was protected from large swells.

It was my first chance to clean the propellers since Laelia's quick departure from Egypt. When I went under the boat, the propellers looked like they had white terrycloth towels wrapped around them. Multiple layers of fine white barnacles were growing happily on the propeller blades and the hub. I scraped and scraped with a putty knife to get rid of the thick growth. While I was in the water I inspected the rest of the boat bottom. There was growth on spots where the bottom paint had peeled off when we ran aground on a reef in Sudan. Otherwise, the bottom was very clean.

We waited several days for the wind to calm, but it continued to blow. The weather report forecast lighter winds, but we saw no change in wind strength in the Bay.

We discovered later that Kouremenos was among the top windsurfing hot spots in the world. There was an international windsurfing competition in the Bay later that summer. We read in the local paper about the Kourmenos Bay "...the Meltemi (the local wind) increases its power through the local thermal and a funneling effect that gives the ground wind an additional 2 Beaufort [about 10 to 15 mph more]. This makes Kouremenos Bay one of the most wind-certain spots in the whole of Europe. This is also why the largest wind farms in Greece are in the surrounding area of Palaikastro."

Good grief! I sure know how to pick a calm anchorage.

We probably could have waited in vain another few months for the wind to moderate. Despite the gale Laelia departed the windy bay and rounded the lighthouse (Cape Sidero, or Ak Sidheros) at the northeast point of Crete and headed west for the little harbor of Sitia. The Greek Pilot Guide indicated that we could check into the EU at Sitia. The harbor is a large square enclosure of protected water for small boats...all Med-tied. The boats were anchored at the bow and tied to the concrete quay by the stern.

We thought Med-tying despicable. First we picked a spot that had an opening on the concrete quay full of boats. Then we motored the boat away from the quay, stopped the boat, dropped the anchor, and backed up. We did all this on faith that the anchor would hold as we backed towards the quay. All we had to do was back to the wall without hitting boats on either side and let the fenders grind and mash.

It all seemed very simple as long as the boat backed straight. In calm weather, it was no big deal to thread the boat between others already docked at the quay. But, if the wind is blowing sideways, then there is trouble aplenty because sailboats move and turn when the wind blows. Well, the wind was blowing from the side and Laelia could not back into the only narrow space available.

"Try tying up at on the north mole," someone on the dock said.

"That sounds like a great idea," I responded.

As we were retrieving our anchor, we discovered that another boat had let out almost 200 feet of anchor chain out in the middle of the pond. We knew because our anchor had pulled up his anchor chain. The chain weighed more than 300 lbs. My attempt to flip our anchor to dump his chain was futile. The anchor was designed to stay with whatever it had hooked and not flip over easily.

Plenty of bystanders were offering suggestions. I thought the best way was to let the weight of the chain to do the work. I tied a rope to the opposite fin of our anchor and secured it to a cleat; as I released the tension on Laelia's anchor, the weight of the chain turned the anchor to one side and dropped the three-hundred-pound chain back in the water. After we were freed from the chain, we side-tied to the mole near the entrance. By then we were totally exhausted.

Sipping Raki in Sitia
On Sunday morning we heard church bells pealing from the little town of Sitia.

"Hey, this is something different," I said.

"It's the church bell...today is Sunday," Judy said loudly.

We had gotten used to hearing the call to prayers at five in the morning and several more times during the day, and the sermon on Friday afternoons. Surprisingly, depending on the muezzin, the call to prayer can be soothing by its regularity.

The town of Sitia climbs steeply from the waterfront up the hillside with crowded clusters of homes. Various colors are present, but a big, orange-red church dome dominates the view. The sound of bells ringing reached every nook in the little harbor town. The houses clustered together with little free space in between. The streets are narrow. Most of the houses are of heavy stone. In the sunshine, the town gleamed. The harbor was filled with brightly painted little fishing boats. It was Sunday, fishermen stayed home.

After the long passage through the Red Sea, we were enjoying all the colors dazzling our eyes. There were trees not covered with dust, and even flowers. The Cretans love their flowers and plants. There were potted plants on many balconies and by doorways. The flowers were mostly geraniums or zinnias, but set against the whitewashed walls and the wrought iron balconies, they were striking to our hungry eyes. We frequently saw long established bougainvillea climbing up buildings and trellises bringing a riot of colors to an entire side of a building. The painted walls, the daringly painted window trims, together with these breathtaking splashes of bougainvillea were feasts to our eyes having been deprived of bright colors for months.

In Crete, the amateur plant taxonomist has a distinct advantage. Even blindfolded, the taxonomist in the dark of night walking in any direction can identify the first tree he or she stumbles upon as an *Olea europaea*, an olive tree. There must be millions of olive trees in town and out of town. We took a bus trip to the neighboring town of Agios Nikolaos (Saint Nicholas) to check out the marina and make docking arrangements. On the way, we saw olive orchards extending themselves over hills and valleys as far as the eye could see. In the eastern part of Crete, olive trees are everywhere.

Friends who had helped with a harvest told us that it took four of them a good part of a week to harvest 16 trees. Assuming that it took four actual days, after subtracting the time for talking and drinking wine in between, it would be about 1 person-day per tree. For a million trees, it would take ten thousand people about 100 days to complete the harvest.

On the bus trip, we also saw flowers along the highway, mostly oleanders and scotch broom with bright pink, white, and yellow flowers. All these colors, with silvery-green olive groves in the background, were delightful. We probably seemed a little strange to be making such a fuss over a few plants, but it was definitely a "mental health" moment for us.

Along the route we saw signs marking archeological digs in progress. Some were open for tours. There were frequent miniature churches about the size of dollhouses along the road. These were small memorials, probably built by families, for those who had died from road accidents. Some memorials still had flowers placed in front of them and others had candles inside them. There was also a large War Memorial of fallen soldiers in the town center to remind everyone of those who had fought in the not too distant past. The Cretans are a very religious people. Indeed we saw churches just about everywhere dotting the landscape. Most of them are Greek Orthodox Churches.

When we first arrived in Crete, we were constantly reminded of the differences in culture from the countries we had encountered in the Red Sea. One very glaring difference was how people dressed. Young women in particular, many of them tourists from European countries, had no hesitation in exposing ample skin for all to see. Their tank tops with only frugal amounts of fabric strained to restrain their considerable assets. But, it was only the tourists who would allow their unblemished skin to roast to an excruciating, medium-rare pink in the Mediterranean sun.

Far less pleasant were men equally unabashed about their skin exposure at the beaches and on their boats. My mind was overwhelmed by the images of rather rotund men with serious overhangs of beer-nurtured bellies. For reasons I couldn't fathom, they all elected to wear tiny little bikini swim trunks. With the overhang drooping, the swim trunks disappeared from view almost entirely. All that remained were these hairy, hulking apparitions wearing sunglasses.

Sitia had tourist facilities and plenty of tabernas (little restaurants or taverns) that were not overrun by tourists. The locals lived as they always have. They come to the tabernas to drink strong coffee, play backgammon, and talk politics. They were mostly older men; not many women were among the crowd at these gatherings.

Late in the afternoon, we watched fisherman repairing their nets getting ready for the next trip out to sea. Life here is laid back with little tension. The locals go about their business unconcerned by tourists. Not even the recent worldwide real estate boom had spoiled the comfortable pace.

Cretans consume considerable alcohol, but there was very little public drunkenness that we could observe. They drink with friends and family. We learned about the local drinks from cruising friends who had lived in Crete for some years. Ouzo is a strong drink with an anise flavor. It is to be drunk very cold, preferably diluted with ice-cold water. As water was added, the drink turned cloudy. We were admonished not to use plastic glasses for this drink. Our friend's beautifully clear plastic glasses were etched to a permanent milky hue from ouzo. This can be alarming to those who value their stomach lining. But, chemists would say that it is only the anise oil in the ouzo that etches the plastic.

There was a distinctly Cretan drink called Raki that is very different from the Turkish drink by the same name. It was fermented from the pomace, grapes after they had been pressed for wine, and distilled. It was usually made at home and consumed by friends and family. Some were excellent. The alcohol content was variable and could be as much as 70%. When the home brewed raki was ready to drink, there would usually be a big party where family and friends would gather to sample the new brew.

Wines are made at home. Many tabernas would have home made wines in addition to the more expensive bottled wines from the wineries.

"I have a wine made by my grandfather," the waitress, a family member, said.

"Of course, I would like to drink the wine made by your grandfather," I replied.

The wine was poured from a tap off a small barrel, served in half-liter aluminum pitchers, and drunk chilled. It was sometimes listed on the menu as "village wine," or simply red or white wine. These were very pleasant drinks. I never tasted a bad wine in Crete.

Judy had a nice chat with the Greek Coast Guard (or Port Police) and got a recommendation for an inexpensive little restaurant by the waterfront. Their specialty was "mezes."

Mezes are traditional appetizers of fried dumpling or savory morsels. Many of them are fried with feta cheese as fillings. Such items go well with home-brewed wine and followed with some raki at the end of the meal. After a meal like that, I tried not to dinghy back to the boat too soon or do anything requiring a clear head.

Crete is full of flowers, olive trees, and "tabernas." The island has retained much of its old-world charm. We loved the tranquility. The land is permeated with ancient history of the Minoan civilization. There appeared to be a museum in every town. In fact, I was certain that if I pushed a shovel into the ground at random, I would discover some ancient artifact...perhaps even the ring of King Minos. Alas, the ring had already been found, but the story took a circuitous turn, revealing the greed and deception in the hearts of man.

Note: The relative position of Crete has been moved approximately 120 miles (two inches on this page) to the west in order for the map to fit on one page.

Wandering through Greece

From Crete, we sailed north to Corfu in the Ionian Sea not far from the Albanian border, because our friends from London were vacationing on the Island. On the way, Laelia stopped at Katakolon, from where we rode a train to the original Olympia. We also stopped at Ithaca, Odysseus's home island.

While in Corfu, we invited our friends, Mike and Fiona, whom we had met many years before in Singapore, to a day cruise on board Laelia. It was one of those marvelously clear days with blue sky, sunshine, and a mild sailing breeze. We sailed from the anchorage (39 45.969 N, 019 56.994 E) for lunch and a short cruise.

Soon after we finished with the picnic lunch on board, the temperature suddenly dropped, followed by dark clouds, thunder, and lightning. *Where is the mild Mediterranean climate?* The rain poured down so hard that there was no visibility. Perhaps there was also fog mixed in with the rain, but there was no way to tell. We couldn't see anything past Laelia's bow. We had experienced "whiteouts" like that skiing in the mountains, but not at sea.

The conditions were ripe for a serious mishap, but both Judy and I maintained our composure...no panic. It was a time to rely on Laelia's instruments. Our guests were amazed that the radar and the GPS worked so well. We followed our outbound track on the chart screen all the way back to the protected little harbor. It was an unexpected little adventure.

After departing Corfu, our goal was to see the Corinth Canal at the narrow isthmus connecting the Peloponnesus Peninsula to the Greek mainland. On the way, Laelia berthed in many little harbors and we visited new places. The first island was Kefalonia, where the story of Captain Corelli's Mandolin took place. Laelia anchored at two separate harbors on the Island. Agia Effimia is near the filming location of the movie Captain Correlli's Mandolin, but the anchorage was difficult due to sea grass. Fiskardo was where we were able to locate a mechanic to replace Laelia's worn cone-drive in the transmission.

On the way east to the Corinth Canal, we visited towns in the Gulf of Patras and the Gulf of Corinth. Particularly notable was Missolonghi, the Sacred City where Greeks were massacred fighting for independence from the Ottoman Empire. Lord Byron died from a fever in Missolonghi. The Greeks revere him to this day for his role in their fight for independence.

We visited Delphi, but the oracle was not in. I was surprised there wasn't an oracle to foretell our fate for a fee.

The four-mile long Corinth Canal was expensive per mile traveled, but primarily tourists used the Canal nowadays. It is not wide enough for modern ships. It is nominally seventy feet wide, but we were constantly worried that Laelia, a mere twenty-five feet in girth, would scrape the rocks that had fallen off the almost vertical 300-foot high walls on both sides.

After exiting the Corinth Canal, we put Laelia in the boatyard on Aegina Island in the Saronic Gulf while we toured Athens. We had hoped to take Laelia to more of the islands, but many of the volcanic islands in the Aegean Sea have very deep water, making anchoring difficult. We decided that it was easier to keep Laelia in the boatyard and take a ferry. At various times, there was labor unrest in Athens, but when the ferries were not on strike, we toured the islands in the Aegean Sea.

An Inferno in the Boatyard

The worst nightmare for a boat owner is a fast spreading fire in the boatyard. Marine fiberglass, the material most boats are made from nowadays, is highly flammable. In a crowded boatyard, vessels are packed closely together in rows. With a little wind, the fire would jump from one boat to the next and incinerate an entire yard to rubble.

A short time after completing the Corinth Canal transit, Laelia was hauled out on Aegina Island not far from Athens. Supports were placed to secure the catamaran on land at the Planaco Yard for the winter season. After the usual hubbub of a haul-out, we let out a sigh of relief and kicked back for a respite. With the boat safely secured, we could now fly back to California.

It was a few minutes after five in the afternoon and all the workers had just left the yard for the day. I saw a wisp of smoke rising up in the air not far from us. I thought it prudent to take a look.

There was no one around and I didn't see any more smoke. I walked around to admire the different boats in the yard. There were two large wooden vessels, each about fifty meters in length, with three tall masts each. They were handsome, traditional vessels. Wooden boats are always good to look at, but expensive to maintain.

There is no smoke...it's probably just my imagination.

We had a long day already bringing Laelia for the haul-out. As I admired the long sleek lines of the traditional vessels one more time before leaving, I saw something moving in the pilothouse.

Oh, good grief! It looks like fire flickering inside the pilothouse high up on the deck.

"Fire!" I yelled. There was no one around to hear me. *How do you say "fire" in Greek?*

By this time, the smoke was rising from the bridge deck. I ran to the guardhouse by the front gate. There was usually a guard at the gate. The guard was on the phone. I pointed in the direction of the vessel. By that time there was more smoke. The guard nodded that he knew.

We might need to evacuate. As I rushed back to Laelia, I was out of breath and there was a sharp pain in my chest. I had to slow down.

I thought about what essentials to take with us in case we needed to flee the fire. On land, it was impossible to move Laelia on short notice. We would have to abandon Laelia, but there was time to rescue our passports, medicines, and the camera...and our credit cards.

"There is a boat on fire," I blurted out as soon as I climbed on the boat.

"What fire?" Judy was surprised.

She came out to the cockpit to look. By this time the fire was already fully visible with tongues of orange glow licking at the air. There was smoke, but it was not yet heavy.

"Where is the fire department?" I wondered aloud.

About fifteen minutes later, we heard sounds of a siren. Several vehicles with faded red paint arrived. These were more like utility vehicles.

"These fire trucks look like they are from the museum," I said in disbelief.

The firemen were in assorted clothing...probably volunteers rushed to the fire from whatever they were doing. They had a few hoses they were attempting to connect together to reach the hydrant, but the hoses were far too short. The hydrant was nowhere in sight. The boatyard stored their hoses at separate stations...one hose section at each station. So the firemen were running around trying to find segments of hoses. Some of the hoses appeared to be in locked cabinets. No one seemed to know where the keys were kept.

The pilothouse was now completely engulfed in flames. The wind was picking up, but away from Laelia. Instead of fleeing, we watched the confused scene from Laelia's deck. We could feel the heat from the fire. I got a bucket of water ready in case the heat became too intense for Laelia's hull.

I got my camera out. First I took photos from Laelia, but I only had a partial view of the burning ship. I went closer to the fire, staying behind the keel of another boat to shield me from the heat. I could smell the smoke in the air and feel the heat radiating.

One of the security guards rushed over to me. "No photos, no photos."

"OK, ok no photos," I replied as I put the lens cap back on. I had quite few photos already.

A fire is definitely a photo opportunity. As soon as I got back to Laelia, I took out the memory chip from the camera and replaced it with a new chip, just in case they came after my camera chip.

By this time the fire had spread to the deck at the base of the mast. Embers were flying in the air fanned by the wind. Apparently, the volunteer fireman had given up on the fire hose. Instead they had a garden hose connected to the water faucet near the ship. There was not enough pressure form the garden hose. The water reached only to the side of the hull. The fire was another twenty feet above.

A tall ladder was placed next to the ship and one of the volunteers climbed up close to put water on the deck. I could feel the heat more than one hundred feet away. He didn't have any protective clothing or goggles that fireman normally would wear. He was brave, but he didn't have asbestos for skin. Soon he had to retreat from that searing heat.

There were sudden loud sounds of explosion and puffs of black smoke in the air.

"It's probably the portable propane tanks exploding," Judy said.

Most sailing vessels carry propane for cooking and heating and gasoline or diesel for auxiliary engines. A ship that size would carry a considerable amount of fuel.

We heard people yelling. Then we realized that the masts had tilted towards where the firemen stood and some of their vehicles. These were tall heavy metal masts and could squash anything in the way as they come down. They could definitely kill. People scrambled and vehicles screeched. The sky was black from the smoke.

A mast came down with a loud crash and a cloud of dust and smoke, but no casualties.

"What are they doing?" I was surprised to see the fireman jumping in their vehicles again.

"Looks like they are leaving," Judy observed.

"They can't leave, we'll lose the whole boatyard," I said.

"They weren't getting anywhere with the fire anyway."

I found out from one of the yard workers that there was a call from the residential area on the hillside. The flying embers had created a roof fire at a home. The volunteers considered homes a higher priority than boats. I suppose the homes could be their neighbors' or their own.

About an hour later, the firemen returned. This time they had with them a pumper truck and started pumping water from the sea not far from the fire. The fire had engulfed the entire ship by this time. The other wooden ship next to the fire was also ablaze. Embers were landing on boats farther down wind. Workers were using garden hoses to cool the hulls that were already bubbling from the heat. The garden hoses were effective on the small pleasure boats that were low enough for the hoses.

The seawater from the pumper was effective in keeping the fire from spreading to other boats. It was too late to save the two big wooden ships. The firemen were letting the ships burn themselves out. The fire raged on late into the night. I could hear the pump running as I fell asleep. By morning, there were piles of blackened wood and the smell of wet smoldering charcoal.

A Medical Event

We traveled between Athens and Aegina Island where Laelia was "on the hard" in the yard. On one trip, we were rushing to catch a ferry. We were a little late and had to hurry. Judy was walking along a few steps ahead of me. I tried to catch up to her.

My, she is walking abnormally fast today.

Usually Judy complained that I walked too fast so I had to slow down and not leave her too far behind.

"My legs are not as long as yours, so I can't walk as fast. You'll just have to slow down," she would say.

Today, she is moving right along. What happened? Her legs aren't any longer.

By then, I was some distance behind her huffing and puffing, breathing hard. I couldn't catch up. That had never happened before.

I felt a little unease in my chest. It wasn't pain, but I knew not to push myself any harder. Wiping the sweat off my brow to keep the trickle of liquid from getting into my eyes, I stopped a moment to catch my breath.

This is not right. There is something wrong. Don't push it...

Turned out, Judy was racing ahead to keep the crew at the ferry from pulling the gangplank away...and she was successful. We both got on the ferry just before it departed from the dock.

"How come you were dragging so far behind? You look tired...is there something wrong with you?" Judy was giving me the third degree.

"Well, I think it's time for another stent when we get back," I said.

"Oh no, are you sure you can wait that long? It's a long flight back."

"Yeah, I think so. It's too complicated to end up at an emergency room here. I'll take some extra full strength aspirin morning and evening and take it easy on activity. I already have my annual appointment with the cardiologist when we get back."

"That appointment is not until a couple weeks later in August," Judy pointed out. "I'll have to call to move the appointment up."

"We'll need to allow extra time at the airport so we won't have to rush." I was thinking ahead. Air travel these days could easily drive sane people unhinged and precipitate heart attacks in healthy people.

We were staying at my brother's home in California, but, when we returned, they were just leaving for Alaska. We told them nothing because we didn't want to alarm them. Judy called the cardiologist's office. She knew what to say to move the appointment forward.

"We'll do an angiogram and take it from there." My cardiologist sounded confident. "If a stent is necessary, we can put one in at the same time."

That was what I had expected. It was good that I made it back without any mishaps on the way. But life has a way of throwing well-made plans off track and awry.

"The angiogram showed a lot more blockage," the cardiologist said. "It will require more than a few stents. You'll need bypass surgery." Whoa...that's an open chest procedure. I could see myself all flayed out and bloody.

"We'll have to keep you in the hospital until the surgery," the cardiologist continued.

Hmmm...he's worried that I'll have a heart attack and drop dead suddenly.

There wasn't much I could do. I had to wait for all the anticoagulants in me to be metabolized before they could do the cutting. So I waited. I was impatient, but glad that I was on home turf and had doctors who knew my condition thoroughly. The surgeon told me that he had done many hundreds of these bypasses. I suppose that's good.

Most hospitals have volunteers that come around to patients with serious procedures to cheer them up. On the night before my surgery, a young man in a Raggedy-Andy costume came to ask how I was doing. He was prepared to rescue me from a deep depression. As it turned out, the three of us had a fun conversation about sailboats and adventures at sea.

"You are very unusual. You both seem so happy," he said. "Most people are very worried about their surgery."

"We are happy because we are here in the hospital instead of some deserted island or on the airplane," I said. "Had we been at sea, with a heart condition, many days from shore, we would definitely be unhappy."

Heart attacks at sea can happen. More than a year after my bypass surgery, one of our friends, an Australian, died at sea. His wife made a valiant effort to save him to no avail. There had to be an autopsy as a legal requirement in the Caribbean Islands.

"I want to know the results. I want to know if there was any way I could have saved him." She knew she had done everything she could, but she was fearful that she hadn't done enough. Tragedies at sea like this also put a heavy toll on the survivor.

My bypass surgery went well. We arrived back in Spain in January, took language lessons in Cadiz, and traveled by rail to Seville, Granada, and Barcelona. We then explored Italy before returning to Greece in May 2010.

Launching Laelia
The City-State of Aegina was a strategic naval power and a center of trade in ancient times. Its island location in the Saronic Gulf, twelve miles SW of Athens, allowed it control over the waterways between Athens, the Peloponnesus Peninsula, and many of the surrounding islands.

Aegina, according to Herodotus, had contributed to the historic naval battle of Salamis where the Greeks defeated the Persians in 480 BC. During the beginning of the Peloponnesian Wars the Island was invaded and sacked by armies led by Athens. After that it was invaded by a succession of conquerors. In modern times, Aegina had the distinction of minting the first coin in Greece. It was also the first capital of Greece after independence from the Ottoman Empire.

Nowadays the little island is invaded by nothing more than vicious hordes of summer tourists from Athens and other parts of Europe. The waterfront of Aegina Town was completely occupied by tabernas with tables extending to all of the sidewalk areas. Sitting at these outdoor dining tables, we watched power launches and sailboats jostling for space to tie up at the concrete pier.

In early May, we returned to the Planaco boatyard on the north side of Aegina Island. It was a daunting task trying to get Laelia seaworthy again. She had accumulated not just dust and sand on deck (probably blown all the way from Africa), but bird droppings mixed with crystals of salt deposited from sea spray during the winter months. We uncovered items that had been wrapped for storage and put back sails that had been taken down. The anchor chain had to be inspected to make sure it was serviceable and marked with colored electrical ties every 30 feet. Then, Laelia was washed and coated with layers of anti-fouling paint.

We tested the electronics, the anemometer, the depth sounder, the radar, and the wind-driven generator, but amazingly they all worked. There was a collective sigh of relief from both of us. Next, the dinghy was pumped up to see it was still airtight. I had drained the fuel tank of the 2.5-horse outboard before leaving. I fully expected the outboard to be in good condition since I had covered it up carefully to protect the outboard from the elements almost a year earlier.

"I don't believe this...the fuel leaks out as soon as I pour it in," I grumbled.

'Guess who just showed up?" Judy sounded cheerful.

It was the mechanic...as if by plan, at that exact moment, he showed up in his beat-up Opel.

The other miracle was that he fixed the leaky carburetor and tested the outboard on the spot, at no charge. Well…. he did bring me the bill for servicing Laelia's auxiliary diesel engines.

As it turned out, the mechanic was an American. He had emigrated from Greece while a young teenager and worked in Long Island, NY, for much of his adult life. His wife wanted to come back to Greece to her home island. He learned to speak Greek as well as a native, but I think he missed talking to Americans. He was still traveling on an American passport.

Laelia was becoming more shipshape, but we had a rudder still sitting on the ground. It couldn't be put back on the boat until Laelia was lifted up to have enough ground clearance to insert the rudder stock from under the boat. The rudder was taken out to repair damages incurred when we ran aground on a reef in Sudan during the Red Sea passage. There were more chores, including servicing the heads and the holding tanks. These sanitation items were not required for navigation, but they were necessary for living aboard. We also drained the fresh water tanks and refilled them with a little added Clorox. Little by little Laelia was getting ready to go to sea again.

The boatyard had good security, but very poor facilities for living aboard. It would have been hard to live on the boat without a good shower and working bathroom. It was early May and still low season with few tourists on the resort island.

We managed to find an apartment at a pretty good price a few miles from the boatyard. It had a large swimming pool and a small walled yard. The owners kept five tortoises that were native to these islands in their yard. There was otherwise not a noticeable wildlife population. We were told that the local animal hospital would provide low cost accommodations to volunteers (mostly foreign students) in exchange for work at the hospital.

We rented a tiny little car that looked like it had its stern half chopped off. It was just a square box with some kind of engine...old and rattling, even on smooth roads. We knew how to drive a stick shift from many decades ago. Of course the windows went up or down only with a hand crank. We thought it was a Kia or a Hyundai... red, mobile, and frugal on fuel.

One fine Sunday, we toured the little island. On the northwest cape of Aegina, there was only a single column remaining from a once beautiful temple to Apollo. In the interior of the island, high up on a hilltop, there was a very well preserved temple to the Goddess of Aphaia. It looked a lot like the Parthenon on top of the Acropolis in Athens, but was much smaller. Most of the columns were still intact.

The island had many pistachio trees. There were stores selling nothing but pistachio products such as oil, paste, candy, and nuts. We bought a bottle of pistachio honey for the manager at the hotel we used many times in Athens, and some snacks for ourselves.

A Greek who had retired from the sea after many years in the merchant marine owned our apartment. His wife was British. Every year, she celebrated her arrival in Aegina with a party. We were invited to her thirtieth annual party. There were many British expatriates and Greeks there. The British lived permanently in Aegina, but returned north regularly to visit. The food was good and more wine and beer appeared in front of me before my glass was even half empty.

Greek Bureaucracy

Finally Laelia was ready to launch, and we had to check out of the island with the Port Police. Normally it is just paper work and a small fee, but Greece had instituted a scheme called a Transit Log that required fees to be paid every three months for the use of their territorial waterways. It was a cruising permit, but it seemed wrong to have to pay this fee when the boat had sat in the yard for many months. The Port Captain showed me in his rulebook the paragraph that talked about the fee, but "it was all Greek to me." I certainly felt the disadvantage of not knowing the language.

The Port Captain informed me that I owed other taxes. He would not sign off on the port clearance until we paid all our bills. He was on the phone speaking in Greek for more than forty-five minutes. He recalculated the length of the boat, trying to round the number up to 13 meters. No matter how many times he punched the calculator, it still came up with 12.8 meters (42 feet).

Then he insisted that I go with him, by riding on the back of his scooter, to the tax office. Apparently he had been on the phone with that office already as they continued the conversation. They spoke in Greek, but would not inform me what they were talking about. It was quite rude.

As their discussion got more heated, the Port Captain asked me how much fuel was on the boat. I was puzzled and a little slow in answering, trying to figure out the significance of that question. Showing much impatience, he then asked me how many horsepower the engine had. At that moment, my survival instinct must have kicked in to add a little extra smarts in my thinking.

I told him, "It's a sailboat."

He didn't like that answer and kept asking about the motor. By then I knew for certain that having even a plastic toy motor on my boat would be ruinous. After some moments, the Port Captain got very angry and left in a huff.

The lady who was still there at the tax office asked me in English what kind of boat it was. She also showed me the tax schedule that showed a tax rate of 300 euros per meter for motorized vessels 13 meters and over in length. (I could only guess that the Port Captain was arguing that 12.8 meters should count as over 13 because it was a catamaran, and any engine would make it a motorized vessel.)

"It's a sailboat. " I stuck to my response.

"I believe you, but I need proof," she said, very sincerely.

The US Coast Guard documentation gave the length, but described the vessel only as "recreational" and said nothing about sail or power. Finally, in desperation, I pulled out a boat card (it's like a business card) with a picture of Laelia on it. I showed her that the vessel had a mast and a boom with sails on them.

"OK, that is all the proof I need," she said. "You don't need to pay the 3900 euros." I let out a sigh of relief, but that was not the end of the nightmare.

When I returned after walking the two miles without my scooter ride, I was considering mayhem. The Port Captain then told me that my transit log had expired and there would be a fine of thirty euros per day. I was to pay the customs office before he could give me the departure clearance. At this point I considered simply leaving Greece without any port clearance, but the Port Police could show up at the boatyard to stop the launching and confiscate Laelia.

Thirty euros a day for 180 days was simply extortion. Apparently, the Port Captain had already talked to the customs office. The officer was friendly and told me that it was the job of the Port Police to explain the rules to visitors and to file the transit log at customs when the boat was laid up, but the Port Police didn't know what they were doing. He signed off and stamped the papers without bothering with the fines.

By the time I went back to the boatyard, Laelia was already up in the lift waiting to be launched. I had to quickly assemble the rudder and do my part of the launching.

Our Greek friends later told us that the motorboat tax had recently been passed by the Greek Parliament, but not yet activated. In any case it would not apply to sailboats. All told, it took a little under six hours to check out of Aegina Island. We had met plenty of port captains in many countries. We encountered a Greek Port Police Office in every little harbor, big and small. Some were friendly, some officious, but none quite so greedy and malicious. This was our most traumatic experience with officialdom anywhere in the world.

Escape from Greece

Originally, we had planned to sail to more islands, but decided that we had had enough encounters with Greek port captains. The rules were never very clear and appeared to be interpreted erratically at the whim of local bullies. We had a very sour taste of things Greek as we departed.

The Customs Officer had given Laelia five days to clear out of Greek territorial waters. During this period we were not allowed to check into any marinas, but could anchor off the coast.

Laelia made an overnight stop at Russian Bay on the west side of Poros Island, about fifteen NM from Aegina. The next morning, we sailed by the town of Poros. On the southwest side of town there is a moderate sized bay between the east shore of the Peloponnesus Peninsula and Poros Island. The deeper water in this bay formed a narrow channel curving right along the town center of Poros, with all the tabernas and their outdoor tables under colorful umbrellas.

We were very envious because our Spartan breakfast had already worn off. Laelia was very close to shore and we could see the gelaterias and the beautiful produce displayed in the markets. Other boats were tied up at the quay. We were tempted to stop for an hour or two, but knowing that another Port Police office was right there at the waterfront, we decided to give it a pass.

When we went past Poros, it was bathed in warm sunshine with not a cloud in the blue sky. As Laelia put Poros behind us, we could see dark clouds gathering over the island. Ominous storm clouds appeared "out of the blue." They were hanging low with shades of gray to charcoal black. Then we saw spikes of lightning spearing the town repeatedly.

We hurried along, checking the wind direction and hoping that the maelstrom would not catch up with us. Soon, one crack of lightning struck vertically down and hit the water about a hundred yards behind us. In front of us was still bright sunshine and blue sky. There was no good explanation of the sudden tempest. I could certainly understand why mariners of old believed that ill-tempered gods were casting thunderbolts about.

We were beginning to learn more about the climate along the Peloponnesus Coast. These are high mountains with precipitous drop-offs to the sea. There are plenty of opportunities for the movement of air up and down the mountain. The clear blue skies in the morning could easily turn into dark looming clouds caused by the updraft as the sun warmed the mountain tops.

We enjoyed the many anchorages along this coast, but the best part was meeting friends new and old. We pulled into a small harbor called Ermioni for fuel that we had not managed to fill upon our rushed departure from Aegina.

As we drove our dinghy to shore, we saw a cruising couple waving and yelling at us from the dock. They had recognized Laelia from a distance. They were Tessa and Tony of s/v Little

Round Top and June and Jeff of s/v Concerto. We had last met them in Crete. It was a happy reunion, one of those memorable moments that we will always treasure. We left Greece on a happy note after all.

Final Challenge in Greece

On our final passage in Greek waters, we had a favorable wind as we headed south hugging the East Coast of Peloponnesus Peninsula. Late in the day, we were approaching the southeasternmost point of land, Cape Maleas, known for its erratic weather and treacherous seas. The Cape had earned its notoriety over the millennia. This was where Odysseus almost reached home in Ithaca, but met ill winds and wandered for ten more years.

We approached the Cape with trepidation not knowing how seriously the foul conditions warned of in the guidebook would affect Laelia. We couldn't find a convenient anchorage near the point of land for the night. As a result, we were approaching the fearsome Cape Maleas in pitch darkness as the full moon dropped behind the mountain ridge early in the evening.

Our biggest worry was shipping traffic, which could mow Laelia down at high speed. The traffic was dense at the Cape as ships from all directions converged to take the shortest path around the point of land. Collision was a possibility and ships had been rammed in the past.

We had Polaris at our backs and the Big Dipper (Ursa Major) on our starboard stern. It was too dark to see any details on land. The mountain ridge sloping down to the Cape presented a silhouette looking like a giant whale with the Cape Maleas Lighthouse as its left eye. It knowingly winked at us every ten seconds. I took that as a nod of approval as Laelia slipped past the Island of Kythira into the Ionian Sea.

It was here that Laelia crossed our previous track on our way to Corfu one year before. That meant we had circumnavigated the Peloponnesus Peninsula. More importantly, we were now out of Greek waters.

9. Knights of Malta

Arriving at Grand Harbour Marina, Malta (35 53.314 N, 014 31.121 E), 28 May 2010. Depart Grand Harbour Marina, 27 June 2010.

Approach to Malta
We were now in the Ionian Sea and in front of us was open water all the way to Malta. It took four days to arrive in Maltese waters

The fortifications on the approach to the Grand Harbour were impressive. This was our first sighting of the famous Fort St. Elmo. It would have been daunting to attack Grand Harbour from the sea while batteries of booming cannons were sending big cast-iron balls hurtling from St. Elmo. I could imagine the scene when the Turkish armada of the great Sultan Suleiman the Magnificent was determined to annihilate the Knights of the Order of St John in 1565. To conquer the Island, the Sultan needed to seize the harbor to shelter his fleet from the winter storm. Even in modern times, Mikhail Gorbachev and George H. W Bush had to postpone their 1989 shipboard meeting near Malta due to bad weather. It was dubbed the "seasick summit."

Fort St. Elmo, situated between two natural harbors had to be taken. The Sultan had a powerful force of 138 ships and a numerical advantage of 38,000 men with the expectation of taking St. Elmo in less than a week. "The horizon was filled with white sails emblazoned with the Sultan's red crescent" (from The *Maltese Islands* by Charles Owen) as the bombardment began.

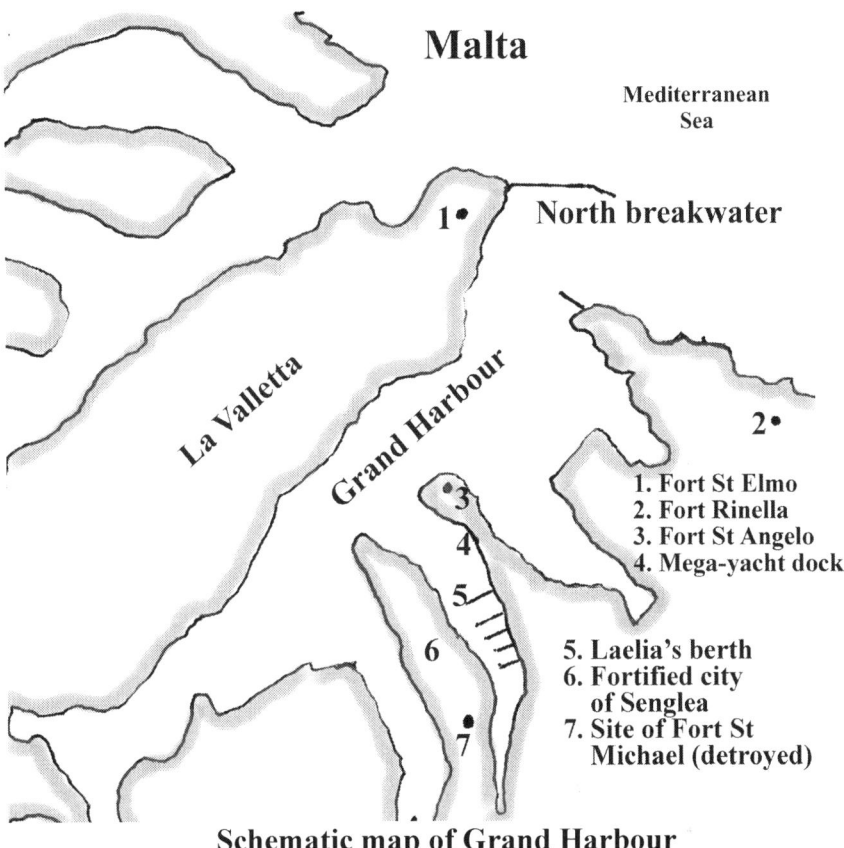

Schematic map of Grand Harbour

To everyone's surprise, 100 knights with 500 men, resisted the siege by holding out at St. Elmo for five long weeks. To be fair, there were another 500 knights and a few thousand soldiers serving as replacements, as the original defenders perished from the constant and relentless bombardment.

As St. Elmo fell, the remaining knights holed up in Senglea, a fortified city, across the harbor under the protection of Fort St. Angelo and Fort St. Michael. Laelia was docked, between St. Angelo and Senglea, in the midst of all that history. Fort St. Michael was blasted to smithereens long ago by the Sultan's artillery from higher ground overlooking the marina. However, despite the superior force, the Turkish expedition was never able to conquer Malta.

The high ground, from where Forts St. Angelo and St. Michael were bombarded, was fortified after the Great Siege. Nowadays cannons are used there only for ceremonial purposes. We heard the loud booming concussion of the cannon every day at noon. That was at one time a nautical tradition, so ships in the harbor could set their chronometers for navigation. The midday cannon firing is now a quaint anachronism, but we rather liked it.

We were a little mystified one night a little after 2100 hours when we heard the cannon at the Battery firing five loud explosions.

What is going on? Are we under attack? Is there a fire or some disaster? It took some time for us to learn that there was a wedding in progress at the battery. Indeed the fort appeared, from a distance, to be all lit up. There was a party. The cannons were maintained by a volunteer organization and will accept a fee to fire the cannons for special occasions. *Well, that's not a bad way to raise club money to support an archaic tradition.* Judy and I toured the battery the next day and watched the ceremonial midday cannon firing. We could even see Laelia at dock in the distance under the smoking muzzle of the cannon.

Laelia was docked in Grand Harbour Marina not far away from the mega-yachts at the water's edge of Fort St. Angelo. It is the homeport for the Maltese Falcon. Laelia had shared an anchorage off the Island of Corfu with the famous yacht a year earlier. It was built in 2006 and has three freestanding masts with no wires and lines around the mast to make the sailboat look messy. Each mast has six yards, like on a square-rigger. The masts rotate to adjust to the wind direction. We remember the Maltese Falcon best shimmering in the moonlight at night. The Falcon at 289 feet (88m) in length is the third largest private yacht in the world, after Eos and Athena (excluding clippers and tall ships). It has six cabins and can accommodate twelve guests. It would sell at the time for around $100 million, but could be chartered for a mere $600,000/week. A crew of 16 would help cruise at 15 knots and bring the Falcon to a maximum speed of 20 knots with a good wind.

All the way across the Pacific, the Indian Ocean, and the Red Sea, every country had required a clearance from the previous port for checking in and clearing customs...except Malta, where the

Capitanerie di Porto didn't even want to see a port clearance from Greece. *Perhaps it's all Greek to him too.* We could have departed Aegina Island without bothering to check out. It triggered a sense of rage in me, recalling my humiliation at the hands of that bully on Aegina Island. We later learned that many boats familiar with local sailing customs routinely depart Greece without checking out.

Historical Malta
We came to Malta knowing little of the country, but we found ourselves immersed in its fascinating history. It was impossible to walk the streets and see the sights without absorbing events going back thousands of years. The history was rich and glorious. The legacy was of knights and battles and also of mysterious temples made from giant stones going back to the Neolithic Age

In 60 AD when St. Paul was on his way to Rome to answer charges against him, his ship was wrecked in a storm off the shores of Malta. Local residents saved him and nursed him to health. <http://www.visitmalta.com/en/st-paul-in-malta> Legend has it that, while picking up some firewood at a campfire, Paul was bitten by a snake. It was a miracle that he showed no ill effects from the snake venom. (Apparently there are no poisonous snakes on Malta now, but it is not clear if there were such venomous reptiles 2000 years ago.) The word spread and locals flocked to Paul's gospel. The Maltese became Christians and have been ever since that event. They lived side by side for two hundred years with Islamic Arabs from 870 AD. The Maltese are still devout Christians; the Norman Conquest (1090) firmly established Catholicism as the primary religion. I saw elderly people crossing themselves as they sat down on the bus or as the bus went past a church.

Of course with the way some of these buses were driven, one would quickly develop a need to pray. Appropriately, the bus interior was plastered with religious aphorisms and displays galore of crucifixes and rosaries. Every fort, every neighborhood, or any item of significance is named for a saint for protection.

The Maltese are clearly a tenacious people. The deep religious faith among the population is no doubt a contributory factor and had sustained them over the centuries. The country is comprised of two small islands, Malta and Gozo, situated in the middle of the Mediterranean and occupying a strategic location for the control of sea routes from Europe to North Africa and from the Suez Canal to Gibraltar. The Maltese have seen many conquerors and invaders over the millennia. At various times, the islands had been sold repeatedly. Somehow the Maltese outlasted and survived all their masters and rulers. As a result many Maltese are multilingual speaking Maltese, English, and Italian. We were even able to detect the Arabic incorporated in the Maltese language.

The modern history of Malta began in 1530 with the arrival of the Knights of the Order of St. John. These knights and fighting friars were originally an order of monks with the primary aim of dispensing aid and particularly medical aid to pilgrims in the Holy Land. Before long, it became obvious what the pilgrims really needed was armed assistance. Also, as they occupied hostile territory, they had a need to defend themselves and their property. As monks took up arms and fighting knights from Christian countries arrived to join their ranks, the medics became the Knights of St John, but their primary purpose remained medical assistance. Even to this day, many ambulance groups still use the eight-pointed Maltese cross as their emblem and some are named St John.

There were Neolithic antiquities dating back more than 5000 years on Malta and Gozo Islands. These megalithic structures had been buried for millennia and, now unearthed, remained in good condition. The prehistoric people and their culture were shrouded in mystery regarding who they were and why they disappeared so abruptly.

We were very lucky to get two tickets (obtained online several weeks in advance) to see the Hal Saflieni Hypogeum, a World Heritage Site on the island of Malta. It is an elaborate three-story subterranean sculpture carved from solid limestone by people with only bone and stone tools. The exhibit allowed only 80 visitors a day to limit the exposure of carbon dioxide in the limestone structure. The Hypogeum was most likely a sacred sanctuary when it was first carved and was extended and deepened over the centuries, but used by later Bronze Age inhabitants as a necropolis.

Sights of Malta

In Fort Rinella, we saw the 100–ton gun. It is a rifled muzzle-loader capable of sending a one-ton shell three miles. It was in 1878 that the decision was made to build the fort housing the gun. At that time, the Italian Navy had made plans to arm four of their armor-clad warships with the Armstrong 100-ton guns. To make sure the Grand Harbour at Malta would not be at the mercy of any navy, the British needed four guns of at least the same range.

One-hundred-ton gun at Fort Rinella

The fort, with dual underground hydraulic loading rail systems for quenching and loading the gun, was completed in 1884. If everything worked according to plan, the gun could fire one shell per minute. The gun was never fired except during practice, but became obsolete soon after.

We toured the underground tunnels used as bomb shelters during the Second World War. The Maltese lived in these tunnels sometimes for days at a time. There was even a birthing cubicle at the end of a tunnel. For their tenacious bravery, the entire population was awarded the George Cross. The George Cross is displayed on their National Flag.

To make up for the lack of colors in their buildings, the Maltese love flags. We saw flagpoles on not just government buildings, but also on commercial buildings and even churches. The flagpoles can be vertical and some are like bow sprits on sailboats. On feast days with giant flags billowing in the wind, the bright colors were surprisingly exhilarating.

The Maltese also love fireworks. Cannons are fired for special occasions, but fireworks are going off almost every week it seemed. One night after dark, we noticed bright lights not far from our boat. *Fireworks this close to flammable fiberglass boats in the harbor?* We rushed on deck to take a better look. It turned out to be a large motor yacht caught on fire not more than 30 meters from us. A small tender was trying to tow it. For a moment it was up wind from Laelia. This could be serious. The smoke was intense and embers were flying in the wind. I went and got our five-gallon jerry can of water to prepare to douse any embers landing on Laelia.

Conflagration over Water

Fire in a marina is a very dangerous matter. Every vessel carries some fuel. Large yachts carry thousands of gallons. In most boats there are also propane tanks used for the galley. It would take only one boat spilling its complement of fuel on the water to spread fire to dozens of others. Fiberglass is a flammable resin. It is not inconceivable for a fire to incinerate every single boat in the marina in short order. At that particular moment, it was still possible for us to put out any small fires caused by embers, so it was not time for evacuation as a life saving measure. Just the same, Laelia was at the end of a long dock, I made a quick mental note on how long it would take us to run to the safety of shore.

We could hear the sirens from the fire engines. They arrived in the northeast bank of the marina not far from Fort St. Angelo, but the fire was too far from the shore for them to apply water with their hoses. There must have been some communication between the towboat and the fire brigade. We saw the tender towing the flaming boat towards the fire engines waiting on shore.

I muttered under my breadth, "No, no not there...that is where the mega-yachts are berthed."

It was not about how many hundreds of millions the mega-yachts are worth. I was worried about the tens of thousands of gallons of fuel stored in each of those monsters. If one of them caught on fire in the marina, we might as well evacuate immediately. Before too long, someone must have had the same thought. The towboat soon changed course and headed out to the main channel where there were no vessels in the immediate vicinity.

Soon the fire started to diminish as the flaming boat was reduced to its waterline. It probably took no more than thirty or forty minutes from when we first saw the fire. By morning there remained only some oil slick and charred debris floating on the water.

Gozo and Comino Islands

There was a small resort island, Comino, located between the two primary islands, Malta and Gozo. Before we left for Tunisia, we thought we would stop by Comino and Gozo Islands. To our horror, we discovered several hundred runabouts in the harbor. We were barely able to squeeze Laelia past the entrance of Nikalaw Bay on the north side of Comino Island on a scorching-hot holiday weekend. We stayed and tried to make the best of an uncomfortable situation.

All of a sudden, I saw Judy jumping on the stern deck whistling and waving.

That woman must have lost her mind.

"What are you doing?" I asked.

"I saw a logo on that little motorboat." She said in between waving and whistling. *That makes no sense to me whatsoever.*

"What logo?" *I can't imagine a logo to make her jump like that.*

"I think it's an ice cream boat," she said.

"Oh...that's going to be pricey." *Any ice cream that gets delivered all the way to an out-of-the-way anchorage has to be expensive.*

"I don't care. It's ice cream." She sounded determined.

The motorboat had Magnum ice cream bars...expensive little treats, but very tasty. It was just right for a hot Sunday afternoon.

We continued on to Gozo to see the 5000-year-old megalithic temple, a UNESCO World Heritage Site. These temple builders lasted thousands of years, but disappeared suddenly.

10. The Mediterranean Sea

Arriving Yasmine Hammamet, Tunisia (36 22.362 N, 10 32.800 E), 09 July 2010. Arriving Gibraltar (36 08.904 N, 005 21.196 W), 18 September 2010. Time included a trip to Yorkshire, England.

Yasmine Hammamet
We secured Laelia in a marina in Tunisia so we could fly to England to visit our daughter and her husband. Why Tunisia? It is in North Africa, not far from Malta where we were at the time. The new marina in Tunisia cost only half as much as in Malta. That was a good enough reason for us already.

It was also important for Laelia to get out of EU for tax reasons, and to avoid overstaying our 18-month limit. The EU rules were murky and the enforcement erratic; it was best to play it safe. Who knew when we might meet up with another megalomaniac port captain? The chance to visit Carthage was another good incentive.

Tunisia is an interesting country with probably the most liberal legislation on women's rights and religion among Islamic countries. At the time, it was stable and reasonably prosperous, but with a very weak press. It had a highly educated population. They have elections, but under one-party rule. Political dissent was not encouraged. The 74-year old ruling president had been in office for 23 years. The absence of real democracy was the primary weakness in this otherwise very admirable country.

Yasmine is about forty miles south of Tunis on the East Coast of Tunisia in a "Tourist Zone" where there were no mosques. We didn't hear the call to prayers until we went into Hammamet. Tourism provides an important fraction of the national tax revenue.

Yasmine itself is a beach town with hotels and lots of tourists. It is known for its jasmine and hence the name. Alcohol was freely available in hotels and restaurants. Summer is blue sky from horizon to horizon day after day. Clouds are rare.

The harbor had a fleet of "sailing" pirate ships that provided day tours with BBQ and swimming as part of the package. Loud speakers fortified their music on board. It was amazing to watch a couple hundred half-naked, beer-drenched, sunburnt western tourists on these pirate ships singing and cheering. The scene sorely tested my idea of refined public behavior, but they were having fun. Among them were many Muslim women conspicuous by their more conservative clothing on these tours.

There was a lot of antiquity in Tunisia. We toured the archaeological site of Carthage, the seat of power of the Punic Empire that ruled not only North Africa, but also a good part of the land around the Mediterranean. From Carthage, Hannibal brought elephants across the sea for his expedition across the Alps by way of Cartegena, Spain.

Laelia docked at Yasmine for an entire month. During that time, we explored Tunisia and flew to England and back. With our objectives accomplished, we were ready to move on. We waited for a weather window with westerly winds and departed for Sicily with a stop at Pantalleria Island, the source of much of the world's supply of capers. We kept Laelia at the anchorage for two nights to rest up and to figure out why Laelia was losing so much transmission fluid.

Invasion of Sicily

It was a misty Friday morning on the 13th of August 2010 and the atmosphere was a little on the gloomy side, but not particularly alarming. Laelia had arrived the day before on a puff of steady west wind at Mazara del Vallo's outer anchorage late in the afternoon. Mazara is on the western point of Sicily. The bay, large enough to accommodate more than several dozens of anchored vessels, is shallow with mostly ten to twelve feet of water.

We saw only two sailboats anchored and one of them left before dark while the other departed before we finished our breakfast of muesli and yogurt. Laelia was alone in this huge anchorage. *Why did they leave? What do they know that we don't know?*

We wanted to visit Sicily, but we never meant to invade the island. All we wanted to do was to check in with the local authorities. We wanted to document that Laelia had arrived in Sicily (EU Territory) from Tunisia (non-EU). I thought it was important to establish a paper trail in order to satisfy the EU tax laws regarding temporary importation of boats. In other countries checking-in usually involved an inspection by the Health Department (quarantine) followed by Immigration and Customs. Of course the Greeks have their port police and port captains in every little harbor. In Italy the authority is called Capitanerie di Porto and has control of the harbor.

We made landfall in Mazara for several reasons. It has an anchorage and is the most convenient of the ten ports of entry to Sicily from our departure point in Tunisia. It is also the base of the biggest fleet of fishing trawlers in Italy. With that many trawlers plus a shipyard, there are bound to be many good mechanics in town.

Yes, Laelia had a mechanical problem. The port sail drive (transmission) seemed to be losing transmission fluid faster than was appropriate. After I gave the engine a good two-hour work out as we approached the harbor, the sail drive promptly lost half a pint of fluid. For a transmission that had never needed any transmission fluid top up in the previous six years, that was alarming.

One might think that it isn't a big deal to add some transmission fluid every few hours, as some people do with their automobiles. Surely I could just keep adding fluid to the transmission, but what if Laelia needed her propulsion for more than two or three hours in the middle of a storm? The engine had all sorts of dire warnings, like not to open the plugs on a hot sail drive on penalty of severe burns from spurting oil.

In any case, I was against pouring fluid in a dark engine compartment while the boat was bouncing in a raging storm. The worst part was that I didn't know how or why the transmission fluid was disappearing, so I imagined all sorts of terrible causes that all seemed to cost money...lots of it. Thinking ahead, I knew Laelia would need both of her engines if we were ever to get home by way of the Panama Canal. The canal authorities require boats to move at a minimum speed during the daylong transit.

In order to get ashore and find a mechanic, we needed to check in and take care of the "formalities" first. We asked people at the marina clubhouse, "Where is the Capitanerie di Porto?" All three of them pointed to a new looking building across the harbor.

We drove our dinghy across the harbor and docked at the only landing accessible to the building. As we climbed ashore, two burly guards promptly confronted Judy and me.

"No, no, not allowed...forbidden military." They gestured wildly, followed by more Italian. *Yikes! Are we in trouble again?*

I had almost gotten myself arrested for taking a photo of a "police action" in the Rome train station some months previously when we were traveling as tourists. Now I had visions of being put in a military jail for invasion by sea of a forbidden military installation in Sicily. *Only this time I won't have Judy to bail me out because she is going to be in jail with me...ha ha.*

The guards marched us to the building. Well, we didn't exactly march; the guards politely asked us to follow them.

They took us through internal security barriers looking for someone who could speak English. A little later, a young officer in a spiffy white naval uniform approached us. We explained that we needed to do the check in formalities. He was very polite and explained that there was not too much in the way of paperwork. A little later his commander appeared and gave us a form to fill out. I did the form and added a crew list, certified by Laelia's official boat stamp and the Captain's signature...well, my signature. Then the pertinent data was entered into an official logbook. That was it. We were done checking in.

I thought I needed a scrap of paper to show in case some other Capitanerie di Porto asked, or if we happened to be stopped by the Coast Guard cutter in Italian waters. The commander obligingly had the completed form with his signature on it photocopied. They were being very patient in humoring my requests. While I was doing the paperwork, Judy asked the young lieutenant about finding a mechanic. Between the commander and the lieutenant, they recommended a mechanic whom they claimed to be the best in the area. Our misadventure was turning into a boon. The lieutenant even offered to call the mechanic for us.

While we waited for the call to get through, the commander produced a cup of espresso for me. I was about to decline, but thought better of it. I drank the sugar-saturated espresso and thanked him for the excellent Italian coffee. I was telling the truth...the coffee was excellent. Trust the Italians to eat and drink well, but they should lay off the sugar.

The lieutenant not only made an appointment with the mechanic for us, but also, on his own initiative, convinced the dock master at the marina to give Laelia accommodation at the dock, on a busy holiday weekend, if we wanted it. He thought the anchorage would be very rough overnight and perhaps for a few more days. Indeed the wind had shifted from west to south and occasionally SE. That is the direction of the Sirocco from the Sahara Desert.

I didn't think a south wind by itself would be a problem. However, I wasn't too sure what the swells would be like, since the anchorage was open to the south with a considerable fetch to allow the wind plenty of distance to pile up big swells. A swell of a meter or so in deep water can become a big roller when it hits the shoals.

The Italian Waters Pilot had indicated that the anchorage was good only in settled weather. With all that in mind I didn't turn down the offer, but knowing that any marina berth in Sicily would not come cheap. As it turned out, having the boat at the dock allowed the mechanic to come and go at his unpredictable schedule and expedite the repairs. It was also nice to celebrate our 47th anniversary a couple of days later without getting all wet riding the dinghy ashore and then returning by dinghy in the dark.

We were lucky to have stumbled upon the Capitaniere di Porto by ignorance, but amply rewarded by the kind of help of which we could only dream. The lieutenant certainly went above and beyond the call of duty to give us a helping hand. On his way to escort us out into the yard, he understood that we still had our dinghy tied up at their dock.

"That's not very good," he said. "You could be in the way of our operations."

"Sorry," I said lamely.

"It's no problem...you two don't look like terrorists."

As it turned out, the mechanic was two hours late. He was more interested in helping us move Laelia from the anchorage to the marina dock than anything else. He and his assistant had decided that the fluid leak was at the clutch linkage. They decided to put a new gasket at the clutch push rod and installed the whole thing the next morning.

By then it was the Saturday of a five-day holiday. I thought it was very decent of them to get the job done so quickly and on a holiday weekend. They seemed like excellent mechanics, although there was no hope of them ever being "on time" or keeping a schedule. They did an excellent job and even cleaned up the engine compartment. We had some beer together after the job was completed. They were particularly interested in the big isolation transformer on Laelia.

At the marina, it seemed like every boat was hauling and loading groceries and bottled water for the holiday getaway. There were shopping carts upon shopping carts trundling up and down the dock. We decided to take a walk into town to find a Vodafone shop to buy a new 3G SIM card. We needed the card to check email. Unfortunately because of the long holiday weekend the stores had abbreviated hours on Friday or were simply closed all day.

We saw a bunch of people in suits and fine dresses coming out of a church. Then there was the bride and groom having their official photos taken under the giant Ficus trees in front of the church. I looked around to see if there was a reception with free food and drinks. It was getting to be lunchtime. Alas, there was no reception and no food in sight.

The town came really alive after dark. By eight-thirty at night, all 200 plus outdoor seats in one Ristorante were fully occupied. There was a row of six or seven of these sprawling restaurants on the waterfront. They call themselves Ristorante-pizzeria. There was a buffet antipasto table with thirty or so dishes and a multipage menu for the rest of the offerings.

The key to the excellent food here was the freshness of the ingredients. Eggplants were cooked in so many different ways it was hard to keep track of them. Then there were the zucchinis grilled or cooked in olive oil with a touch of lemon juice. Of course artichokes in various forms appeared in dishes on the antipasto table.

The pizzas came in two sizes. We ordered a large, against the waiter's advice, and the two of us could not finish the 25-inch by 14-inch oval shaped pizza. We ate the leftover for lunch the next day. We tried to figure out why the pizza tasted so good. It was just cheese, tomatoes, and some unknown vegetables. We decide it was the very good cheese and the fresh tomatoes cooked into the cheese that made it special.

I ordered a carafe of wine, but forgot to specify "piccolo" (small). Good wine is not to be wasted so I managed to empty the carafe. It was a beautiful night with almost a half moon so it was appropriate to stroll back to the boat slowly. I did scramble aboard Laelia unassisted.

Mazara del Vallo had been a good stop for us, but the town

itself was not very prosperous, we could tell by the number of buildings that were unused and the number of storefronts that were vacant. The huge fishing trawler fleet appeared idle in the harbor. We saw only smaller fishing boats plying the waters. It was well known that the fish stock in the Mediterranean had been dwindling. The fishing industry, a mainstay of the town's economy, appeared to be on the decline. On the other hand, there were lots of signs indicating that the town has not given up and was reinventing itself.

There was regular entertainment at the town square next to the ruin of the Norman arch. One late afternoon we were surprised to see hundreds of chairs set up in front of a podium. While buying a gelato cone, I had a chance to speak to an elderly Italian gentleman. He spoke excellent English and told me that he had lived in New York for many years and had come back to Sicily to retire. He said there would be a Town Hall meeting at the square.

"There are many problems to discuss," he said. The town, with many retirees, was apparently going through a transformation from a fishing economy to other new endeavors. One of the new ventures was no doubt tourism.

The town square was also a venue for stage play performances. We again stumbled into the big seating area one night and stayed for a while to watch the drama, but not knowing Italian, we found the dialogue a little less than captivating.

The night before our departure from Mazara we anchored Laelia in the outer harbor so we could make an early start. Around four in the morning as we were about to raise the anchor, we saw fireworks right over our heads. It was the finale of some musical performance. The fireworks were being launched from the breakwater of the outer harbor. Some small amount of the fireworks debris landed on Laelia, but none caused any damage. That was not a bad sent off...with fireworks!

Trapani

Each time someone asked, "What do you like most about the journey?" Judy would reply, "I like arriving."

The reality is that arriving is good only after the boat is secured and the paperwork finished. For me, arrival at a new port is always full of anxieties. The channels are narrow and hazards abound.

Crowded anchorages and poor substrate for anchoring are never pleasant. The worst part is dealing with immigration, customs, and port captains.

Passages at sea, especially long ones, are generally safer. There is always a certain natural rhythm of life at sea. Even when there was a storm, there were definite procedures for battening down and dealing with adverse conditions. Coming into port meant sinking back into herd conformity and artificial constraints. Perhaps those were the things I was trying to escape...I couldn't be certain.

Laelia arrived in Trapani, on the NW point of Sicily, after an uneventful fifty-mile northward jaunt from Mazara del Vallo. The wind was light for most of the trip. As we approached Trapani Harbor, the wind picked up and the sea got angry and became rough. The wind didn't abate in the harbor as we had hoped.

There were quite a few mooring balls that had been placed in the anchorage for the America's Cup trials back in 2005. We had "fun" trying to catch one of these big red balls about the size of a large trashcan. Just as we got close to one, it would get away before we could tie a line to it.

"How come no one else is tied to these moorings?" Judy was wondering aloud.

"Well...there are two other boats not far away, but they are both anchored," I said.

"The guidebook says the moorings are free," Judy said.

"Well, if they are free, it probably means there is no money to maintain them."

We worried a lot. Normally, moorings need to be inspected once a year. If the moorings hadn't been maintained since their installation, five years is a long time. There might have been a lot of corrosion or broken links.

A woman was at the back steps of Laelia. She swam over from one of the anchored boats.

"We were tied to a different mooring. This morning it dragged more than 100 meters," she said. "That's why we are anchored."

I thanked her and told Judy to get ready to do some anchoring. Just then, I saw a fast cutter in the anchorage, a Guardia Costeria vessel, approaching Laelia. It had the red diagonal stripe across the bow. It appeared to be the international insignia for the Coast Guard.

"That mooring is not safe," said the young man in English with a heavy Italian accent.

Sure enough, it had not been maintained. This was regrettable. Had they charged a fee, there would have been funds to maintain the moorings. It would have been worth paying a reasonable fee.

Anchoring was difficult because of the strong wind. The boat was being blown around faster than the anchor chain could be paid out so it was difficult to get the anchor to bite into the mud. We had to use the engine to slow the movement. We got the boat anchored far enough away from the other boats, but a little too close to the mooring balls. When the wind clocked around, Laelia's anchor rode could get wrapped around one of the moorings. That would have been a pain in the neck. Not only were these moorings not safe to use, they actually laid waste to a large portion of the anchorage.

It was hard to believe, but we had to anchor five more times as the Coast Guard wanted us to move again, and then the Harbor Master had a different idea where we should anchor. A little later, another boat anchored too close to us, but didn't care. Then there was a ship that needed to turn around. We finally went all the way across on the far side of the harbor. It was inconvenient, but we were not in anyone's way.

From the anchorage, we could see the ancient city of Erice perched at the top of a steep mountain. The guidebook said that on a clear day, one could see North Africa from Erice. (We didn't need to see North Africa...we had been there already.) We went across Trapani a short distance by bus then took the cable car to rise more than 2000 feet straight up. Erice is an ancient all-stone village. Even the streets are all paved with cobblestones. The Romans, Vandals, Arabs, and Spaniards ruled the town over the centuries, but it survived them all. It is a worthy antiquity and a destination.

Despite all those ancient sights and vistas around, the first place Judy and I ended up in Erice was in a restaurant. We had a good lunch, the most memorable part was the Prosciutto di Parma, thinly sliced, over rock melon. One could easily become addicted to that kind of gourmet eating. In the town there was also the Pasticceria del Convento where nuns sold delicious pastries made from their own kitchen.

Leapfrogging through the Mediterranean

Although we toured the Mediterranean countries extensively, much of it was while Laelia was laid up in the yard in Greece. We started with a Spanish language school in Cadiz, Spain, in January after my bypass operation in California. That was when we discovered that the Mediterranean winter is seriously cold.

We also got a lesson in Spanish eating habits. A small cup of espresso and two thin pieces of toast just wasn't an adequate breakfast for us. Even the mid-morning coffee break, with more of the same, didn't help. Tapas are great...I never knew pig cheeks could taste so good. On the other hand, anything cooked in squid ink just didn't have visual appeal.

We went on to Seville, Granada, and Barcelona. We stayed a whole month in Florence, Italy, living in the basement of a building that was the home of an executioner during the time of the Inquisitions. From there we hopped over to Rome where I almost got arrested for taking a photo of a police action. I suppose police everywhere are touchy about being watched and recorded.

We also visited Lucca and Pisa and went on by train to Cinque Terre. In Venice, we explored the canals by vaporetto. We discovered Split, Croatia, across the Adriatic Sea from Venice. Split was originally built as the retirement palace of the Roman Emperor Diocletian. As a change of pace we flew to Istanbul and visited the Bosporus on a tour ship, but got only a peek of the Black Sea. Then we returned to Greece where we spent much time in Athens and Aegina Island.

By the time we departed Trapani aboard Laelia, we were satisfied as tourists. We began to anticipate the Atlantic crossing. Our minds were set on Gibraltar as the starting point of the adventure. Our first stop was in Sardinia, less than two hundred nautical miles away from Trapani. Not knowing local conditions, we emailed ahead to reserve a space in the Villasimius Marina. Upon arrival, we saw a beautiful shallow bay that could have served as a free anchorage just in front of the marina entrance.

"We can just anchor in this bay tonight and save some money," I said.

"It looks like a good anchorage, but we have a reservation and they are holding the berth open for us," Judy objected.

"Well, I suppose we should honor our commitment to the

reservation," I agreed reluctantly.

As it turned out, it was a very well kept marina with good facilities although they only had med-ties that I disliked. During the night we heard a lot of noise and commotion in the marina. When I got up to investigate, I discovered that a storm was blowing. Across from Laelia, the wind had unfurled a sailboat's jib that was beating itself to death with snapping sharp noises.

Not far away, more people were shouting as they towed a Hallberg-Rassy into the marina. Apparently, the skipper had sent a distress call. His boat was hitting the bottom as each swell rolled in during the storm. This is a problem that could plague shallow anchorages when the swells are large. It seemed that we dodged a bad storm in an overly shallow anchorage.

An unanticipated benefit, while docked at the marina, was that we got to tour Sardinia for a couple of days. Despite the obvious wealth visible in the marina, most of what we saw on the island was agriculture. The economy didn't seem to be robust or thriving. The country stores and the village cafes didn't have that sunny and upbeat ambiance and the ordinary people seemed to be just surviving. I could only suspect that there was a large wealth disparity on the Island, as we have seen elsewhere.

Laelia departed Villasimius Marina early in the morning, heading WSW in the Gulf of Cagliari, with clear sky and light wind. We soon passed, to our starboard side, an ancient watchtower (Torre di Capo Boi) on a promontory. It was an early warning lookout for attacks from the sea. Life was precarious in these parts with frequent raids.

For most of the day, our primary concern had been about dodging fishing floats. I was amazed that there was still any fish life left, considering the high concentration of fishing activity. It was just after sunset when Judy noticed on the radar that we had a fast vessel in Laelia's track. We changed course to avoid getting run over, but the vessel also altered course to stay in our track. After a few attempts, we slowed Laelia down. We could see with the binoculars that it was a grey-colored cutter.

"We are a sailing vessel named Laelia, Lima, Alpha, Echo, Lima, India, Alpha. It is USA flagged vessel. You are following too close. Please respond in English. Over." Judy spoke slowly and clearly.

There was no response. We could now see that it was not a Coastie...no red stripe across the bow. Instead, it was from the Ministry of Finance. We had heard about the several ministries that collected taxes in Italy. *It's a revenue cutter. At least it's not a pirate, but the practical distinction might not be so clear.*

Finally, there was a voice in English on the radio: "Documents, passports, and boat information..."

"Copies, Ok?" Judy replied. There was no response. In any case, I wasn't about to pass any original documents over the water. *What would I do if the passports fell in the sea?* There was someone on the bow of the cutter with a long handled fish landing net. I always had copies of all those documents at the ready so it was easy to put them in a ziplock bag and drop them into the net. At that moment the cutter was behind Laelia, within about six feet, matching our speed at two knots.

"Where are you from and where are you going?" The voice needed more information.

"We have been to Villasimius, Trapani, and Masara de Vallo and we are heading for Cala Portocolom, Majorca," Judy answered.

At that point the landing net was extended at their bow again with the returned papers.

"Buena Sera." A parting salutation was extended over the radio. Soon the cutter sped away and we could hear the voice accosting a British boat. We continued on and stopped in Majorca and other ports along the mainland coast of Spain.

Our final leg was supposed to be a three-night passage to Gibraltar, but we had a little storm along the way that was not in the forecast. It was a lightning storm throughout the night. Laelia sailed through squall after squall with strong shifting winds. Then the lightning crackled overhead. It was mostly lateral strikes from cloud to cloud. The blindingly bright electric discharges flashed zigzag across the sky. The discharges came one after another or several at the same time. Occasionally I could see flashes of bright red light.

It took me some moments before I realized that I saw red because I had closed my eyes unknowingly by reflex now and then. What I saw was the red color of blood flowing through my eyelids. I only heard dull rumblings that passed for thunder. After the lightning, the torrential rain treated Laelia with a nice fresh water wash.

The strong wind made the boat sail faster than planned and would have made us enter Gibraltar Bay late in the evening on the third night. We normally preferred not to enter harbors in the dark, and especially not harbors with heavy shipping traffic. So we anchored near a little beach about fifteen nautical miles north of Gibraltar. We had a good dinner and a comfortable night's sleep while the tail end of the storm played itself out.

The next morning, we timed the tide so that we wouldn't have to fight the current on our way into Gibraltar. The Atlantic constantly flows into the Mediterranean to replace the evaporated water, and the east-flowing current can be very strong at certain hours of the tidal cycle.

The final obstacles before making landfall at Gibraltar were the fishing nets strung crisscross Laelia's path. Apparently the fishing was very good due to schools of tuna transiting the Strait of Gibraltar. The nets were strung many hundreds of meters across the water with only small floats, about three inches in diameter, at the surface. Even with binoculars, these nets were not visible until we were almost on top of them.

The fisherman got very agitated telling us where to go. We certainly didn't want to run over their fishing nets, as they would wrap around boat appendages under water. It could result in hours of delay and most likely a swim under the boat so early in the cold morning.

The passage wasn't all unpleasantness. Just before we entered the Gibraltar Bay, a big school of dolphins came by to say welcome. We hope they don't tangle with those nets. I imagine they don't like the fishing nets either.

Soon, we secured Laelia to the concrete dock at the Marina Bay Marina, surrounded by a Mexican restaurant, the casino, and O'Reilly's Irish Pub.

11. The Rock and the Canary

Departing Gibraltar (36 08.904 N, 005 21.196 W), 14 October 2010. Arriving Santa Cruz de La Palma, Canaries Islands (28 40.711 N, 17 46.025 W), 21 October 2010.

The Rock of Gibraltar

On Sunday, it was raining in torrents. Every direction I looked it was drippy wet. The Rock over us was all shrouded in fast moving clouds. As the west wind whipped through the channel, the soggy flags and banners in the rigging were snapping and crackling. It was a cold, bone-chilling rain.

According to our original plan, we would have departed Gibraltar for the Canary Islands the day before, but the weather window was not open. At the moment, there was a fierce North Atlantic storm raging some one hundred nautical miles west of us. By tonight, in the open ocean the wind was expected to be over 35 knots and gusting up to 45 plus.

We had been caught in such unpleasant weather before, but we would never intentionally venture out in such conditions. We knew from experience that it would be miserable to be seasick. It was especially no fun when both of us were rushing to reach for the same bucket. The interminable motion wore on every muscle of the body and the constant retching dissipated even more energy.

The low-pressure systems associated with these storms were counter clockwise spirals in the northern hemisphere. The wind generated by this storm, as it approached the coast here, was from the SW, an adverse wind for sailing to the Canary Islands. The synoptic chart regarding the weather forecast showed little sign of any dominating high-pressure system in the Atlantic. That meant we would be waiting much longer for the elusive weather window.

The "Rock" of Gibraltar is a giant limestone outcrop 411 meters high pushed up eons ago by the colliding African and the European plates. In geological time, Gibraltar and Morocco were joined. The Rock of Gibraltar and Jebel Musa in Morocco represent the twin pillars of Hercules. Jebel means "mountain," we were told, and in Spanish Jebel became Gibel. A Muslim named Tarik discovered the Rock, thus the name Gibel Tarik meaning Tarik's rock. As time went by, Gibel Tarik became Gibraltar.

Gibraltar is a good place to provision for the long passage. At the Morrison's Supermarket, just about any food can be bought...well, almost any food. The irony is that it is impossible to refill our propane bottle in Gibraltar or in Spain. According to locals, there was an accident involving gas bottles some years ago, so a Spanish law was passed against refilling any foreign bottles. All the cooking on board Laelia depended on propane. Fortunately we had heard of that law and refilled our main bottle in Sicily. However, our smaller backup bottle was now empty. Most likely it would be the same situation in the Canary Islands, a Spanish-speaking island.

We went up the Rock and toured the many caves and tunnels. We were careful with the thieving monkeys that greeted us. Most tourists learn about them the hard way, but we knew about monkeys in general and were on our guard. It would have been interesting to attend a concert in the cave. The acoustics would probably have been lively. There were chairs already in place in the concert cave, but no performance was scheduled. Alas, no notes from inside the Rock.

We toured the Botanical Garden and ate at the Mexican restaurant on our dock. We taught our Australian friends all about Mexican food; the two-for-one fajita on Tuesday nights was a big hit. Eating out helped to conserve our limited propane reserve for the Atlantic passage on Laelia.

There were many boats on the dock in Gibraltar getting ready for the Atlantic passage. It was a good sociable gathering. We had parties on the larger boats where we reacquainted ourselves with old friends and met other cruisers for the first time. Life was good, although expensive.

On the marina dock, most discussions were about weather.

The most frequently asked question was, "Is the hurricane season in the Caribbean finished for this year?"

"I don't think the Atlantic cruising season starts until after the first of December," said an old sailor from England.

"I don't know...there have been serious storms as late as Christmas," said a tall sailor with a deep frown.

The truth is that there are inherent risks when one is on the water, particularly in the North Atlantic. There is no absolute safety in an ocean passage. The difference between a successful passage and a disaster is often determined by the weather.

The fury of an Atlantic storm had sunk many ships over the centuries. I had read about the fierce winter storms, but I didn't realize that, between June and November, many Caribbean hurricanes could still carry quite a punch as they trailed off into the Atlantic Ocean.

For Laelia, an Atlantic crossing was unavoidable if we wanted to get back to California. Gibraltar was the jumping off point from the European mainland for the Caribbean, with possible stops in the Canary Islands and the Cape Verde Islands.

Aside from preparing the boat to endure harsh punishments, we studied the weather pattern for the best time and track across the Atlantic. We received almost daily email updates from our friend, Bruce, about the Atlantic weather.

Provisioning for Four

We had prospective crew for the Atlantic passage starting at the Canary Islands. That was something new for us on Laelia. Floyd and Mildred knew how to sail and they owned their own boat in Florida. Floyd in particular wanted to experience an Atlantic crossing.

With more than just the two of us to stand watch at night, we would be less sleep-deprived. Also, with experienced sailors as crew, we could be bolder on Laelia's sail plan. We could fly the spinnaker more often, perhaps even at night. On the other hand, with more people on board, extra provisions were required.

Gibraltar is culturally diverse, but with a strong British

influence. The big Morrison's Supermarket (formerly Safeway) was very convenient. We thought it would be a good idea to buy as much as possible of the non-perishable food we needed here. We didn't know what would be available in the Canary Islands.

We learned, as we made a shopping list, that provisioning for four people was vastly different than for just the two of us. It was surprisingly difficult to scale up the provisions. This crossing was expected to be around twenty days, but depending on the wind and sailing conditions, it could take as many as thirty days.

How do you feed four people for an entire month?

Not only the amount of food seemed staggering, but we also had a problem of freezer and refrigerator space. We couldn't just bring a goat or a couple of hens on Laelia, as did the sailing ships of old.

I also had to consider the eating preferences of our crew. Although we called this couple "crew" they were not really paid crew. Floyd and Mildred were sailing friends we used to run around with in Ventura, California. Now they would be guests on board Laelia, our home. They lived on their own boat, but wanted to join us on a long passage. They had wanted to cross the Atlantic with the ARC Rally several times, but had for one reason or another dropped out. Floyd was making a living as a boat-delivery captain. He needed to add an Atlantic crossing to his resume in order to do trans-Atlantic deliveries.

I was looking forward to having more help on the foredeck with managing the sails. With more people, we could share many of the chores such as setting the spinnaker, cooking, and standing night watch.

We realized there would be adjustments to fit four people in a space of not much more than a small living room for almost a month. As we would have done with guests even for a meal on land, we asked them what sorts of foods they didn't eat.

We got back an email:

Hi Howard & Judy,
Regarding foods, we thought best to show a list of what we would try to include on passages either with our own boat or delivery boats. If any of these are not available in Gibraltar we can purchase and carry them with us. Usually, Mildred will

make yogurt and bread if the oven is available. Regarding meat, we eat most anything but not very much. No allergies that we know of. I like to fish and would bring my line and lures if that is okay but understand if you prefer no blood (fish only) on the aft steps. We are very easy going with food except try to avoid most "junk" type food. Does this sound okay.

Breakfast: yogurt, milk in a box, powder, yeast covered w/ dried berries, almonds, walnuts, oatmeal not instant, peanut butter no trans fats, bread, wheat flour, wheat germ, yeast, flax seeds.

Lunch/Dinner: Brown rice, black beans, wheat pasta, canned tomatoes/spices
Drinks: Tea, Cranberry juice
Hugs,
Floyd and Mildred

It seemed they had acquired more than a little of the healthy eating preferences in the last six years while we were away. Eating less meat did make the provisioning easier. We didn't normally eat big pieces of steaks and chops anyway; mostly it would be stir-fried chicken and beef when available. I could cut the meat supply by 25% for each of us, which would save lots of space in the freezer. It would save some money too.

There was nothing on their list that we couldn't eat except that Judy is allergic to walnuts. They seemed to have a preference for beans and brown rice. Well, we could adapt our eating somewhat and buy more beans. Brown rice was a little harder to come by, but we found some eventually when we crossed the border to shop in Spain. We normally used instant oatmeal when available to save time and propane. With more people to share the cooking, it wouldn't be too much of a problem to give up instant oatmeal and spend more time in front of a hot stove.

From their derogatory comments about bread in a subsequent email, we learned that they couldn't eat white bread or any bread with preservatives. But, if Mildred wanted to bake bread, we would have no problems. I could eat fresh baked bread with delight, although I had little admiration for such narrow eating preferences. I kept that thought to myself.

I had been hungry without food for days at a time as a child in

Hong Kong and I had witnessed starvation close up involving entire refugee families. In the back of my mind, only privileged people in rich countries can be so picky about what they are willing to eat, absent allergies and other medical reasons. My unkind thoughts about spoiled rich people were suppressed because these were friends. Personally I have always been thankful that I had any food to eat at all. Judy always says that I was on a "see-food" diet.

For provisioning, it was much easier to stock flour than bread. Even bread with preservatives couldn't survive thirty days in any sort of tropical heat without getting a nice coat of Aspergillus mold. Flour would take up much less space and Morrison's sold flour in convenient one-kilo vacuum-sealed bags. I thought the provisioning was coming along well.

My email reply to Floyd and Mildred:

Fishing is not a problem. Yes, fish blood on the back steps is fine. I don't mind helping with the cleaning up. I have a sharp fillet knife and some lines and lures that I bought in Mexico, but you might want to bring your own favorite lure.

What kind of flour does Mildred use for bread? Is regular flour OK? For long passages it is difficult to carry much store-bought bread so I will get some flat bread as back up, Indian Roti. They are kind of like tortillas, but softer when at room temperature. You can make fish tacos with them. Mostly we use flat bread for lunch as we only made fresh bread when we ran out of food once upon a time in Fiji. By the way, the oven is small and a little dodgy, but worked the last time we used it.

We have a yogurt maker and have been eating staples such as pasta, couscous, and Basmati rice. We have not done many beans from scratch, but I do have a pressure cooker to help conserve propane. Do you also do dry red beans or pinto beans and such?

Peanut butter is hard to come by here. They mainly have the hydrogenated kind. Drinks such as coffee are available, but cranberry juice can be a storage problem for 30 days.
Howard and Judy

As we made multiple trips to Morrison's, we ended up with ten kilos of bread flour, both whole-meal and seed flour, plus dry yeast in packets. We also bought assorted beans, red, white, pinto, and lentils. We found black beans much later. We even found regular brown rice and Uncle Ben's 10-minute brown rice. Of course we bought long-cook oatmeal and milk powder for making yogurt. There was more...including a frozen turkey breast and a pumpkin for Thanksgiving...and we had to haul all that on board Laelia.

In Gibraltar, taxis are not available when there is a cruise ship at the dock. The cruise-ship tourists are more-profitable prey. We knew our way and had walked to the market. After our big shopping spree, we were unable to face hauling all that weight for several miles walking back to Laelia and I didn't want to get caught stealing a shopping cart. Instead, I got clever beyond my years.

I approached a reasonably well-dressed gentleman, a perfect stranger, who seemed self-confident, "Sir, would you be willing to give us a ride?"

"Uh...where do you want to go?" He seemed a little surprised and perhaps nonplussed.

"Just a few miles to the marina. I would be happy to pay what I normally pay for the taxi, but today there is no taxi."

"Well, I have a car and I'm willing to help, but you'll have to wait for me to finish my shopping for just a few things." He could see the piles of purchase in my cart.

Judy and I got a very nice ride back to the boat in a brand new Mercedes sedan with all our provisions. He wasn't shy about accepting the euros I offered. Perhaps we were the earliest unofficial Uber clients.

Santa Cruz de la Palma

Before departing Gibraltar, I wrote an email to our daughter who was about to sail across the Atlantic on a sixty-meter tall ship.

> *Maureen: We'll see you when we can in the Caribbean. Have a good Atlantic Crossing. Looks like there is a weather window beginning today...it worries me how quickly the weather forecast changes in less than 24 hours. We'll depart tomorrow morning two hours after Gibraltar high water for Santa Cruz de La Palma in the Canaries. It should be a 6 to 7 day trip with very light winds. Off to get things ready! Mom and Dad*

Our departure from Gibraltar was uneventful. Friends came to take photos of Laelia with Judy at the helm as we departed. "Good sailing...bon voyage," they shouted as I pushed Laelia off the dock. Although infrequent, there was the possibility of rogue waves in the Gibraltar Strait, but we encountered none. We did experience a strong current in our favor. Catching the tidal flow was a big help.

The main problem we encountered was the many fishing nets on the African coast. Some nets were many miles off shore. They were low at the water surface with no lights or pennants. As the sky dimmed by evening, it was hard to spot the nets. Laelia had actually "jumped" over one such net. We were lucky because Laelia's keels must have pushed the net under the water allowing the propeller and rudder to go over the net before the net slowly refloated to the surface.

One of our friends wasn't so lucky and had to spend several hours cutting his boat free again. We had good wind and sailed south along the west coast of Africa. As we arrived at the Canary Islands, there was still enough of the weather window remaining to allow Laelia to continue on to Santa Cruz de la Palma.

The Island, La Palma, is the most NW of the Canaries. It is also the most wooded of the archipelago. The porous volcanic rock holds water and provides ground water for lush vegetation to grow. The tall steep mountains soar into the clouds from the sea almost vertically. The vegetation provides ground cover on the mountain that looks bright and inviting on sunny days, but dark and foreboding under inclement conditions.

There is a certain mysterious feel with these mountains. They are, after all, the world's biggest volcanic caldera with two active volcanoes on the south side of the island. The SW side of the volcanic slope apparently overhangs the supporting base of the island. There are fears that, if the fault on the overhang gives way, there could be a massive landslide with the potential of causing a devastating tsunami on the East Coast of North America.

The islanders call their land "La Isla Bonita" (the pretty island). In my view, this is not only a beautiful island, but also an inspirational island. It's still unspoiled by tourists. The locals we met all made sure we knew that they welcomed us and they liked visitors, but they did not want tourism to overrun their island.

When we first approached the island from the sea, we saw a

town with houses that climbed vertically up the slopes. We saw white, brown, yellow, earth-tone pink, and even a few green or blue structures. This is a confident and happy people not afraid of bright colors. The skyline also had that bright and well-scrubbed look. Perhaps it was the rain or just a reflection of our own upbeat mood, the town dazzled with cheerfulness.

This colorful town, Santa Cruz de la Palma, with the backdrop of dark wooded mountains topped by swirling clouds at the peak, was very picturesque. The city center was a gem. The century-old cobblestone street was off-limits to vehicles. The buildings from the 15th century were all in good repair. Many of the balconies were made of hardwood that looked like new, and the contrasting color scheme continued. There were also balconies festooned with exuberant flowers and hanging plants.

"You know...there is something missing," I said.

"I noticed that too...and I figured it out," Judy replied. "There is not a single trace of graffiti anywhere."

"Hey, you're right. There are no beggars or any sign of homelessness either."

The drivers here screeched to a halt when we even approached near a zebra-striped crosswalk.

"I haven't seen such polite drivers since New Zealand," Judy commented.

Their behavior told me a lot about how the local people felt about themselves. They impressed me as a people who took pride in their land and their way of life.

We walked and took the city bus to see the island. For two euros, the bus took us on a four-hour trip around the north side of the island. We saw green jungles and volcanic rocks as the bus careened around narrow mountain switchbacks and on rocky ledges.

There were numerous banana plantations on terraces that had been hand built by stacking volcanic stone after stone and rock over rock. Especially on the SE side where the caldera was not enclosed, there was mile after mile of banana, up and down the slopes. We have never seen so many banana plants all in one place.

Unfortunately for the island's economy, we understood that the bureaucrats at the EU decreed that bananas all had to be of a minimum size to be sold in the EU. Didn't they know that bananas come in different varieties and sizes? We tried the bananas from La Palma. These bananas were smaller, but had an outstanding flavor, taste, and texture.

We were taking shelter from a sudden downpour in a little restaurant with four or five tables in the little bar. The heavy walls of stone were about two feet thick with massive hand-hewn timber in the ceiling. It was very quaint and cozy.

We had hot coffee and a cold local beer to fend off the moisture. Since it was getting late in the afternoon, we also ordered a few tapas. The one that caught our eyes and taste buds was the goat cheese (queso de cabra) with red and green mojo sauce and honey. It happened to be a young cheese with a very mild taste. We were hooked. We found more goat cheese in the market and ate some almost daily. We also bought a small round of it for the long passage.

After our crew arrived in Santa Cruz de la Palma in the Canaries, we all stayed together on Laelia for four days before departure. While at the dock with shore power available, Judy made use of her waffle iron and made waffles topped with a peach Zanzibar sauce. It was quite a hit. We mainly cooked with shore power to conserve our propane for the Atlantic passage, since we couldn't refill our propane tanks in the Canaries either.

During this time, our crew, Mildred, cooked once. She cooked black beans and made a beet salad. It was tasty. I cooked once...a sweet and sour chicken dish with brown rice mixed with black beans. Everyone seemed happy with the dinners.

We ate out twice. Both of our crew ate pizza with meat toppings. Once we went to a traditional Canary Island restaurant next to the Cathedral in the mountains. Mildred ordered chicken and Floyd an omelet. I had grilled rabbit and Judy ate pork loin. As far as I could see, our crew's eating habits were not all that different than ours. Like Judy, they were not adventurous eaters, but they were certainly not vegetarians. Otherwise, I would need to revamp our meal plans and re-assess Laelia's provisions.

Santa Cruz de la Palma was a good place to provision, but we didn't know that while we were still in Gibraltar. There was the *Hiper Dino Super Mercado,* a supermarket. For fresh foods, there was a popular farmer's market. We made additional acquisitions of perishables including fruits, onions, avocados, and more rounds of *queso de cabra*.

Those were fun times; we did some boat work and a little sightseeing. Floyd winched me up the mast top while Judy belayed me, using the backup halyard, for extra safety. The wind indicator and anemometer on the mast top had lost three of its four screws and was about to fall off. It was not easy doing anything sixty-five feet over the water with the mast swaying in every direction. All I could do was to tape the wind vane support securely with duct tape. The wires for the active radar reflector, nicknamed Tiger, were also secured with more tape. I checked the shrouds to make sure there were no burrs on the wire. (Shrouds are the stainless steel wires holding the mast up, presence of burrs would indicate problems...wires about to fail.)

We invited cruisers from other boats to join us in some drinks and snacks. I discovered that Floyd no longer indulged in any alcohol, not even beer, but that was certainly not a problem although he seemed to want to hide that fact. Generally speaking, the worst problem is a crew unable to forgo alcohol on a passage. As a rule we never indulge in alcoholic drinks until after anchoring or docking. Judy prefers to celebrate with chocolates.

There were cruisers from all walks of life and from different countries. Elmer was a single hander. He learned to sail as a boy scout in South Africa, later he earned a degree in marine engineering in England. He had worked on ships. He retired many years ago and had already circumnavigated the world at least twice, maybe more, but he had lost count. At 85, his plans were to continue sailing on his beloved sailboat...period. There was also an American couple from California. The husband retired from working as an agent for the DEA (the Drug Enforcement Agency). We enjoyed their company except when he went on a political rant.

John, an Englishman, owned a pub back home. His brother looked after the pub while John went sailing.

"How is the pub doing with you away?" I asked.

"I don't know. I haven't heard anything from him in a long time," John replied.

"What's that?" He pointed at the fruit hammock.

"That's a persimmon...it's not ripe yet," I told him.

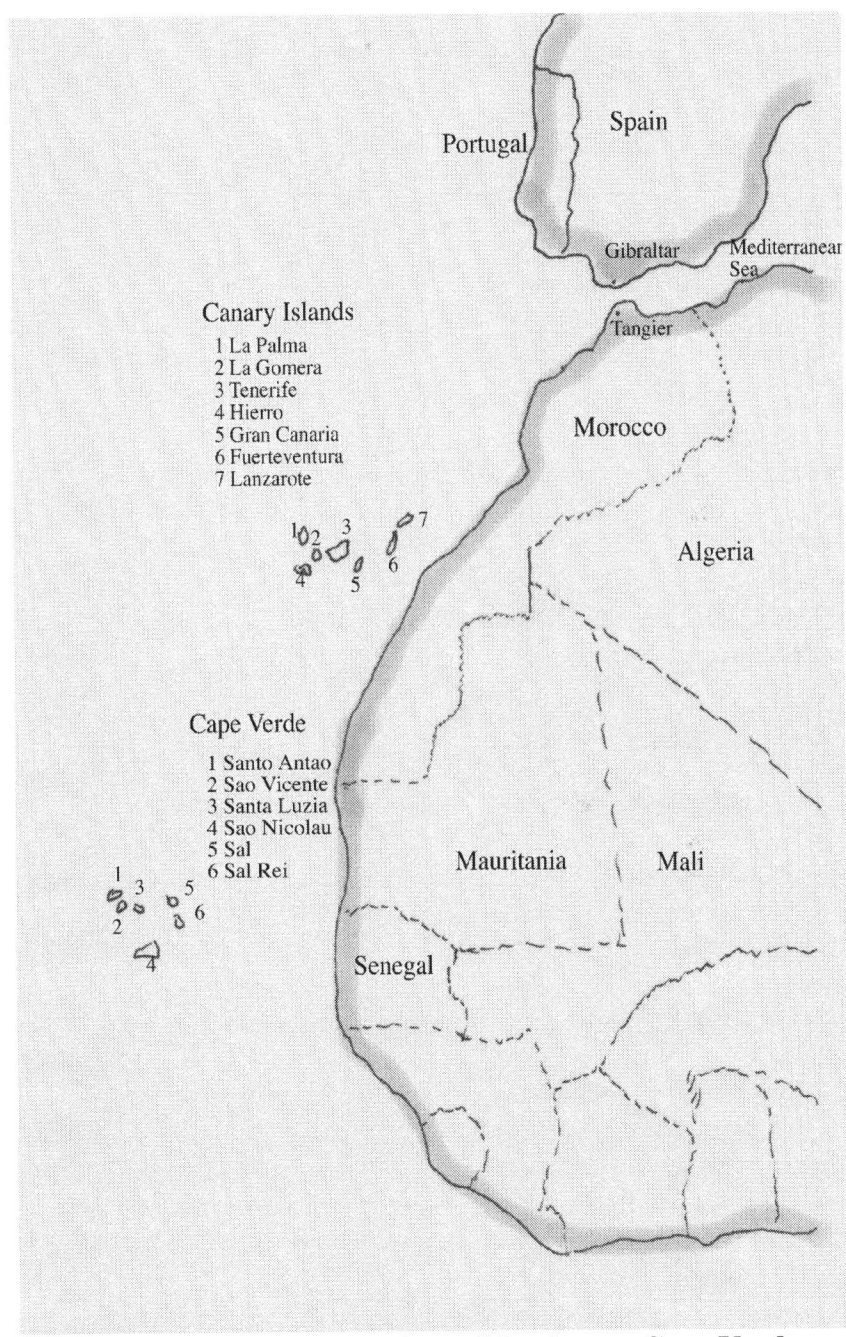

West African Coast from Gibraltar to Cape Verde

"I have never seen one of those. What does it taste like?"

"It's sweet, but tastes terrible when it's not ripe...very astringent," I told him.

"I don't know what you mean by astringent," he said. "What does that taste like?"

"Well, it's hard to describe the feeling...it puts hair on you teeth and makes your mouth pucker," I said.

"That doesn't tell me how it tastes." John just wouldn't let up.

"Can I taste it?" John said.

"You're right...the only way to find out is to taste it. But, you'll hate me afterwards," I warned him.

"No, I won't hate you, I want to taste it," he insisted.

"OK, you asked for it." I cut a small piece for him.

"Ohhh...it's not good." John made a face and spit out the small piece of persimmon and said, "Now I know what astringent means."

In the evenings Judy, Mildred, Floyd, and I played mahjong and a board game called Sequence. These games aren't any good with just two people. So that was another advantage of having crew.

12. An Impromptu Port of Call

Departing Santa Cruz de la Palma, Canary Islands (28 40.711 N, 17 46.025 W), 07 November 2010. Diverted on 12 November, and arrived at Mindelo, Sao Vicente, Cabo Verde (16 53.178 N, 024 59.445 W), Sunday, 14 November 2010.

Timing the Weather
We received an email message from our weather guru:

October 31, 2010
To: Judy & Howard Wang
From: Bruce
After the 10th, the trip west from the Cape to the Windward Islands looks O.K. with wet troughs every other day. Winds will hold as E 15-25 knots and wave height at six feet. The troublesome part is the upper atmosphere trough continues to deepen with the trough line in the middle of the Atlantic. That should continue to make the eastern Atlantic squally and the western Atlantic stable.
Best regards,
Bruce

The eastern Atlantic was where we were and squally was not what we wanted. Bruce also sent news that hurricane Tomas was gaining new strength. Tomas started as a tropical storm on 29 October and elevated to a Category-1 hurricane on the 30th for two days and seemed to be gaining again.

Based on water temperature data, Bruce thought Tomas was

likely to be the last tropical storm of the season. In any event, except for Tomas, there were no new reports of tropical depressions forming. That was encouraging. After all Tomas had been around for some time already. It was not likely to go on for another three weeks, the minimum time it would take for Laelia to sail to the Caribbean. In my mind, with hurricanes becoming less of a threat, all we needed was a weather window of favorable winds at the Canaries.

Some may think that we were pushing our luck, with hurricane Tomas having just dumped a load of rainwater on Haiti and now swirling around Cuba with increased vigor. Closer to home, well closer to our boat...there was a low-pressure system making a frontal passage south of the Canaries. Bruce, a specialist in Atlantic weather, warned that we should expect plenty of rain and strong winds. We didn't mind getting wet and the wind would mean a faster passage. At least that was the thinking while I was still sitting in the relative comforts of the marina.

We were receiving daily updates of Atlantic weather forecast from Bruce. In one he wrote:

Nov. 9 to 11. Significant deterioration of weather in the Canaries. Strong wind with rain....It looks unpleasant......

It appeared that, if we didn't depart the Canaries by the 6th or 7th, we would have to wait another week at least. Although we had already decided not to stop there, the Cape Verde Islands could serve as a fallback safe haven in the unlikely chance that the weather in the Atlantic turned foul. In any event the immediate wind direction was favorable for departing the Canaries.

It was the night before Laelia's departure on 7 November 2010 from Santa Cruz de la Palma, Canary Islands, not far from the west coast of Africa. The sky was dark and overcast with not a star or moon. The wind was heavy, laden with moisture.

Laelia was well provisioned, sitting low in the water, with little of the waterline showing. The water tanks were full and fuel tanks at the high mark. We were ready to make the jump "across the pond" to the Caribbean. It would be a 2800-NM passage, taking perhaps twenty to twenty-five days.

The plan was to sail south or SW until a few hundred nautical miles from Cabo Verde (Cape Verde). From that point on, we would steer a course west or southwest to just beneath latitude twenty degrees north until the Caribbean. We would make landfall somewhere between Martinique, Antigua, or Saint Martin depending on the wind.

Departing from the Canaries
On a blustery Sunday morning, at 1125 UTC, we departed the Marina de la Palma in the Canaries. Cruisers from at least three other boats came to help us with the dock lines and saw us off. The weather forecast from our weather guru indicated strong winds in a favorable direction as we were in between two fronts. We were all looking forward to a fast trip all the way to the Caribbean, sailing the traditional route by going south, then west. By that route, we expected to avoid the occasional fierce north Atlantic winter storms and to be within range of the usually consistent NE trade winds.

It was an exciting time, with adventure in our hearts as Laelia sliced through the blue water of the Atlantic for 2800 nautical miles. The quality of life on board depends very much on the sea state. Even if the wind is favorable, rough swells and confused seas are always uncomfortable. Luckily there was no outright seasickness on Laelia, but the constant movement of the boat was wearing on everyone.

It usually takes about three days before we get our "sea legs." The night watch also disrupts our sleep pattern, contributing little to the sense of wellbeing. Often the early part of a passage is just standing watch, eating, sleeping, and then repeating that routine again the next day. Mentally, I always reassure myself that things will be better. All the chores such as cooking and running the boat still have to be done. That is when a lot of foods precooked before departure and quick-cook items become desirable.

This is not like being on an ocean cruise with gourmet dining. There is no service...we are it. Life is frugal, as water, electricity, and fuel all need to be conserved. Mostly it is about endurance during the first few days...surviving one day at a time. One has to have faith and believe that things will be better soon. Life does get better on the passage invariably, but getting past that initial acclimatization at sea takes perseverance and grit.

One Day at a Time

Day 1: We were 95 NM from Santa Cruz de la Palma at 0600, Monday 08 November 2010. All was well aboard. We had a good day. Weather forecast from our weather guru, Bruce, was for strong wind and rough seas and that was what we had. Using only the jib, we were sailing at six knots. The seas were about 3 meters at 12 seconds...it had been lumpy and not the most comfortable, but tolerable. Last night dinner was chicken with onions and carrots in oyster sauce to accompany black beans and brown rice. I made yogurt for breakfast to go with the oat cereal.

Day 2: The day began with a clear sky in the morning, but clouds gathered as the day wore on. By noon angry dark clouds were swirling overhead. We prepared for a drenching, but received only a few drops of rain as a warning. Mercifully, Mother Nature spared us any harsher punishments for intruding into her realm.

Ugly, lumpy waves pounded Laelia incessantly. The boat yawed, pitched, lurched, and rolled side to side. It was difficult to move around without constantly gripping for handholds. Every muscle fought to readjust to the rapidly tilting horizon and changing gravitational force as the boat was picked up by the waves and dropped unceremoniously.

Surprisingly all of the crew held on without complaint...rather stoic. I was the only one admitting to feeling queasy. The nausea started while I was typing on the keyboard before dawn. I had a nasty feeling that my stomach would like to evert itself, and that feeling lasted until halfway through dinner. I was not sure eating was the commonly recommended cure for seasickness, but it worked for me. The queasiness went away.

Dinner was somewhat simplified, due to "Chef" Howard's biliousness. We had Uncle Ben's 10-minute brown rice mixed with pre-cooked black beans to complement chicken and zucchinis cooked in hoisin sauce. Black beans were a new addition to the diet aboard Laelia. Boiled chicken breast had always been a staple for sandwiches and could be used for dinner to shortcut preparation time. In fact we had chicken avocado sandwiches for lunch with genuine Dijon mustard brought by Mildred from France.

It was an uneventful day with only one ship sighted nine nautical miles away, and one brightly painted red and white fishing trawler gliding away over the horizon late in the afternoon. One lost bird took refuge in the cockpit and left a messy calling card. Alas, a few hours later the bird was discovered flat on the trampoline, wet and cold. It was recycled into the ocean... a burial at sea without much pomp. It was a reminder of our own fragility and mortality.

We charged the house batteries around sunset in preparation for the long night. The wind turbine worked mightily, but was not able to supply all the electronics and refrigeration. A sliver of a moon, a brilliant yellow crescent, followed the sun over the horizon within a few hours.

We had a four-on-and-four-off watch schedule with two teams. Mildred and Floyd were one team and Judy and I the other. Within the team one person could take turns napping. It seemed to be working adequately, although Floyd was doing the major share of their four-hour watch. He mentioned to me privately his doubts about his wife's ability to stand night watch on her own. The watch schedule was decided with that consideration in mind.

It was a deep dark sky with brilliant starlight. At midnight when I came up for my watch, Orion was already halfway up in the sky, but other constellations were partially obscured by dark clouds. The wind had intensified to twenty-five knots with gusts up to thirty.

Laelia sailed with only the jib at six knots, hour after hour. The jib sheet felt like a steel cable to the touch as it pulled the boat along. The boat creaked and groaned. Then there were the loud crashes as waves hit the hull and the occasional slamming under the bridge deck. In the cockpit, the sound of rushing water was punctuated with the crackling of the wind-whipped US flag at the stern.

Surprisingly, there was little in the way of bioluminescence. There were isolated globes of light in the dark water behind the stern, but no brightly lit trails of luminescence like those in the Pacific or the Red Sea.

Occasionally Laelia would surf down a big swell at nine or ten knots. There was no mistaking the event; it sounded like a herd of wild horses stampeding under the boat. Of interest was the occasional spell of silence. This did not occur very often, but when it did happen it commanded attention. It was as if the boat was suspended in mid-space with no apparent motion...not a lurch and not a quiver. Time stood still, silence reigned for a few seconds. It was always a very pleasant occasion, although fleeting.

Day 3: We were 395 NM from SC de La Palma.. The day began with the appearance of a faint white glow on the misty horizon about 15 degrees to starboard. What could it be? There were no islands with city lights within hundreds of miles in that direction.

Perhaps a fishing boat was using lights to attract fish?

We had seen fishermen do that in Indonesia. Upon checking the chart plotter screen for the AIS data, it seemed that a ship was some 18 NM away in that exact compass bearing. It was a 948-foot tanker named LNG Delta, listed as "not under command," and it was heading SW at 1.4 knots. That was barely drifting for these big guys. From past experience, I knew to stay well clear of "not-under-command" vessels. That ship could be having engine problems.

Our crew, Floyd and Mildred, went off shift at 0800 without eating breakfast, although I had just prepared it for all four of us. Instead, they cooked a beautiful breakfast at around 1100 hours. I looked hungrily at all the dry fruits and nuts Mildred put into the oatmeal with fresh fruit on the side. It was approaching lunchtime for Judy and myself. Mildred did offer a bowl of the leftover oatmeal they couldn't finish to Judy, who ate some, but let me gobble up the remainder.

I didn't think it was a good idea to run two separate shifts in the galley. Labor was limited on a small boat. If our energies were spent inefficiently, we would be stressed. Even propane for cooking needed to be conserved. Provisions were in common, although Judy and I had bought almost all of them. It could become a problem if we continued to have separate menus. Also, it had already created a problem of when to have lunch. They had just eaten breakfast, but I was ready for lunch.

"Mildred, that was delicious. But, please fix breakfast at an earlier hour in the future. If you cook, please do it for the entire boat," I said. "I can set up a schedule for sharing the cooking chores."

Mildred ignored me and didn't say a word. I looked at her in confusion.

"We'll discuss this and get back to you," Floyd said.

"Ok, I'll fix lunch today at two o'clock instead of at the change of shift."

The menu was chicken-avocado sandwich with Dijon mustard again. Our avocados were becoming ripe...we needed to eat a lot of avocados. Our menu was by necessity determined by what would spoil if not eaten soon.

The strong wind continued and waves were big, but becoming more regular. Dinner was Asian noodles with chicken, onion, and green beans cooked in oyster sauce and served at 1930 hours. It was quite a hit; at least that was what I was told.

Life aboard was becoming more like the usual passages of sleeping, eating, and standing watch. In reality it was quite boring, but we dared not ask for more excitement. Judy and I knew to be careful of what we wished for. We had learned from experience that a boring ocean passage was infinitely preferable to exciting ones.

Day 4: Thursday, 11 Nov 2010: Tales of difficult crew and tyrannical captain are legend. I just didn't think it would happen to us on our little Laelia. Our problem this time was not about nasty weather or unforgiving seas, but was about the most unfathomable aspect of any endeavor...behavior of human beings.

The day began at midnight as Judy and I came on shift to a misty overcast sky. There were a few lightning flashes on the distant horizon with no thunder. Later, the humidity and haze lifted and stars brightened the sky. The barometer was heading higher.

Mildred prepared breakfast. As I had requested, it was for all four of us at 0745 hours. It began with a dish of fresh pears and bananas. Mildred also prepared a hot course of oatmeal cooked with dry cranberries and flavored with honey and topped with nuts for added protein. It was a super deluxe breakfast that took some amount of time to prepare. We all complimented her on the great meal. It was truly a better breakfast than what comes out of many restaurant kitchens.

We had passed latitude 23 27 N, the Tropic of Cancer. Officially, we were now in the tropics. It did feel warmer as the sun climbed higher. The waves were now under two meters and more orderly. The wind dropped to an acceptable 12 to 15 ENE. Without the constant pounding by the lumpy waves and the incessant noise, it was more comfortable. Everyone was more energetic and seemed happier.

Floyd finally decided to do some fishing. He brought out the lure that he had purchased in La Palma and towed it behind the boat on a tuna cord. Laelia had, by that time, already put a few hundred nautical miles under her keels from the Canary Islands and was in the blue water of the Atlantic. There were not as many fish in deep water unless a school was passing through. We saw a tern flying low over the water. That gave us hope that there might be some fish nearby.

We saw flying fish, but not as many as in the Pacific. It was common to find a few of them on the deck in the morning. After only five or six hours, Floyd seemed to have given up and took the lure out of the water. I thought that he was a little too hasty in giving up if he was counting on fish for his meals. From my own experience, it took considerably more persistence to catch any fish, especially in deep water. I would have left the lure in the water for days until there was a fish on the line.

Lunch at noon was chicken and avocado salad spiked with apples. Traditionally chicken salad has celery in it, but celery doesn't store as well as apple in the refrigerator. Also, we were a little short of pre-cooked chicken by now, but had plenty of ripe avocados. It sounded like a strange mixture, but it wasn't half bad. Usually Judy would tell me immediately if my concoctions were not up to standard. Nobody complained, although Mildred didn't appear for lunch at all.

As if being in the tropics signaled something to our provisions, we found the half loaf of pumpkin seed bread that had not been refrigerated had turned moldy. It got tossed overboard. Then, some of the sweet potatoes were discovered to have rotted.

After lunch the wind from dead astern had dropped and Laelia was dawdling at around three knots. We decided to set the spinnaker. It took us a while to untangle the lines. Eventually, the spinnaker flew open as the sock peeled up.

Immediately Laelia came to life at five-plus knots. For quite some time, the wind increased to between fifteen and seventeen knots. We read and napped while Laelia surged ahead at better than six knots. Before sunset the wind was becoming stronger, so we decided to dowse the spinnaker.

The Trouble Begins
Day 5 began at midnight with light wind and calm sea. Laelia lurched along slowly in eight to twelve knots of east wind. Despite the discomforts during the beginning of this passage, we enjoyed the fast pace of sailing. By now we were accustomed to, and expected a much faster boat speed. It was especially exhilarating when we had the bright red-white-and-blue spinnaker flying over the bow. We could hardly wait to set the spinnaker upon daybreak at change of shift. Once filled, the spinnaker immediately powered Laelia at over six knots.

After some prompting by Floyd, Mildred prepared breakfast again in the morning, but she was not happy about it. It was oatmeal cooked with honey and dry fruit topped with nuts and bran complemented with a plate of cut fresh fruit. It was not only very healthy, but a truly tasty breakfast.

Surprisingly, Mildred also volunteered to prepare dinner for that day. She had soaked the black beans the night before and did the cooking in a pressure cooker during her afternoon watch. For dinner we ate the black beans flavored with a bottled tomato salsa. There was also a sliced beetroot salad. The supermarkets in the Canaries sell cooked beetroots vacuum-packed in plastic. With a little vinegar and mustard, the sliced beets became a credible salad to complement the bean soup. Mildred even prepared a small dish of chopped raw onions that was consumed by me only. It turned out that she thought I liked onions and that I had mentioned that we had lots of onions on board.

"Thank you for fixing the onions for me. The raw onion goes well with black beans and I like it a lot," I said. "What do you and Floyd eat during passages?"

"We haven't done any long passages. On short passages we brought prepared sandwiches," she replied.

"Well, that sounds convenient."

"When Floyd was on his delivering trip, he would have hired crew with him. They brought their own provisions and ate separately." Mildred volunteered the information.

"What did Floyd eat on these trips?" I really wanted to know their eating habits on passages.

"On those trips, he ate just peanut butter and bread or sardines and bread."

"That's all?" I was a little surprised by the Spartan diet.

"That's all he brought with him, but I never went on these long delivery trips," she said.

It was a pleasant conversation. I began to understand her lack of experience in passage making, despite the fact that they lived aboard their sailboat for many years. I suppose even Floyd didn't have any experience in passages lasting twenty to thirty days. I thought any misgivings regarding the meal schedule were resolved and settled.

Then I remembered that Judy had asked if I wanted her to make pancakes some morning. I thought I would check to see if our crew both liked pancakes for breakfast. I didn't receive an answer right away, but the answer came soon enough. Less than an hour later, Mildred came back with considerable determination.

"I don't really like pancakes," she said.

"Ok, thanks for telling me. We don't have to have pancakes." My question about pancakes seemed to have triggered an avalanche of buried resentment or perhaps suggested an alternate strategy in her mind.

"We don't like to eat what you cook," she said abruptly.

"Well, what don't you like about my cooking? Perhaps I can make adjustments," I responded.

"I cannot tell you," she said

Puzzled by that answer, I asked her, "Why can't you tell me?"

I received no reply. It was a complete mystery to me because, although Mildred ate normal amounts, her husband, Floyd, had been eating with gusto and had second and third helpings. He had actually displaced me as the vacuum-cleaner person who would finish all the leftover food on the table.

I was unable to find out what it was that they didn't like about the meals. I got a hint later when Judy told me that Mildred had complained to her that the brown rice I cooked was not the kind of brown rice they were used to eating. Obviously, that couldn't be the only reason, considering that they ate all kinds of stuff while we were still at the dock in the Canary Islands.

"I will cook what I like to cook and only when I feel like cooking," Mildred declared and continued, "I apologize for not coming to lunch. I hope you don't take it personally."

"No, I don't take it personally. But, if anyone cooks or prepares a meal using the galley and provisions, then the meal is for all four of us. I also required that meals be at approximately fixed times so everyone can plan their sleeping around the watch schedule and meal times." I wanted to make the basic rules clear to her. I was willing to accommodate the needs of my guests and to negotiate with her, but I could not allow her to dictate the basic running of the vessel.

In my mind such simple discipline was obvious and unavoidable on a small boat like Laelia. It would have been silly to have everyone cooking and preparing meals on their own at odd times. I considered it not only a waste of labor, but it would deplete the propane supply and water for washing pots and pans.

Worse yet, we would all be competing for the same provisions. Judy and I had bought almost all the provisions on board. At the time the provisions Mildred and Floyd had brought with them were nearly all gone. She clearly had no clue on provisioning for a long passage.

I offered Mildred a role in the meal planning so the food would be more to her liking. I also let her know that she was welcome to cook as often as she would like. The requirements remained that the meal times must have a fixed schedule and that there would be only one shift in the galley.

Her answer was immediate: "I only cook for two people and at whatever time I feel like eating."

To such a non-negotiable demand, my only answer was, "Absolutely not." After all, we were crossing an ocean. Some modicum of discipline was necessary for our safety and survival. It was not like sharing a holiday apartment without a care in the world.

I had thought having crew meant less work for me instead of more. I was puzzled. These were friends, they were guests on board in my home, but she was taking over...not just the provisions and the galley. Even on a cruise ship with paid clients, there would be schedules and menus. Floyd knew what was happening, but stayed aloof.

"You are a tyrant, a dictator, just like the Communists, forcing me to eat food I cannot eat and on a schedule" Mildred was crying and shouting.

That was the last time I heard whole sentences from her; from that moment on, she uttered only monosyllables or a mixture of sobs and vitriol. She sulked and completely stopped eating with the rest of us.

I noted missing avocados and disappearing black beans from the refrigerator. Her husband asked me quietly not to make a fuss over the missing food. Although Floyd continued to eat my cooking at lunch and dinner, remained civil, and sailed the boat with me conscientiously, the tension on board was heavy and unpleasant. Floyd was not talking much and offered no explanation.

We were living in a very small confined space. By necessity we had to be closer than most families on land. Eating and working as a team should have been automatic...so I thought. Floyd and Mildred didn't seem to realize they were guests in our home. There was no reason to treat us with such disdain. Even on land, it would have been odd and rude to stay three or four weeks in a friend's home using their provisions but cooking and eating separately at a schedule contrary to household activities.

Mildred continued to sulk, acting sullen, and was not eating with us. I discussed with Floyd my concerns over her situation. I was worried about her mental state.

"I don't think she will do anything self-destructive," Floyd said.

That was only slightly reassuring to me. It seemed clear that the problem was not going away. She seemed to have no interest in helping to modify the menu to her liking, but dwelled on demands that I could not possibly accept. I was not certain that the situation on board was even safe, with everyone under the gnawing strain of such painful tension.

"How can we tolerate this depressing condition for another three weeks?" I asked Judy when we were alone.

"You know I never wanted any crew," Judy said.

"Neither did I, but they were friends and really, really wanted to come on a long passage."

I decided that there was only one solution, and a narrow window of opportunity was approaching. It was our only way out.

I said to Floyd, "We are now about 250 NM from Cape Verde and are still up wind from the Cape for another ten hours. A stop at the island can be done easily. Would you consider getting dropped off at the Cape?"

I wasn't sure Floyd would agree, but while Mildred was sobbing and shouting insults earlier, I had a hunch that perhaps she just wanted to be let off the boat. I was worried that she would do something stupid like jumping overboard during the night.

"I will discuss it with Mildred," said Floyd.

A bit later Floyd said, "Drop us off at Cape Verde." He gave no explanation. I didn't have to convince Floyd that he needed to end a passage he had set his heart on for many years.

About 200 NM north of Cape Verde on 12 November 2010, 0748 UTC, we changed course, diverting to Port Mindelo, Sao Vicente Island in the Cape Verde Islands.

Judy was on the SSB radio net later that day, as was her usual role, to report Laelia's position to the Net Controller. On long passages, sailing vessels often organize an informal radio net at scheduled times on a specific frequency. It was often with people we had never met as well as with people we knew from previous ports. They were reassuring voices on the radio with first names and their boat names. (In US waters we also used our radio call signs.) Judy would exchange weather information and share events of interest if any. The net provides considerable camaraderie as well as a sense of being in touch.

At the time, the net we were reporting to was called the Rum Runner's Net. Judy reported that we were diverting to Cape Verde to drop off crew. She couldn't elaborate much because our crew was sitting across the table from her. Usually a vessel would only divert to an unplanned destination if forced by bad weather, equipment failure, injury, or serious illness.

Diverting to Cape Verde to drop off crew turned out not to be such an unusual occurrence. We didn't know it at the time, but found out later from several other boats that they had had similar experiences. It seemed that whatever personal problems individuals have on land are accentuated and greatly amplified at sea. At sea is not a place for therapy...it's more like a stress test.

Even after the decision to divert to Cape Verde, morale on board was not good. There was no conversation anymore and I was no longer doing any writing each day. Mildred was still sulking and not eating with us. Floyd did what work needed to be done, but he was no longer staying up for the entire four hours during their night watch.

When I was off watch, instead of sleeping, I worried. I would get up on deck at night frequently when it was not my shift. On at least one occasion, I discovered that Floyd was sleeping on the settee and his wife, Mildred, was sitting with her head on her arms at the table, also asleep. It was acceptable for one of them to be sleeping, but not both.

The autopilot was steering the boat, but by then we were closing in on the Cape Verde Islands. I expected to encounter more fishing boats and cargo ships as we approached populated islands. Keeping a good watch was more important than ever for our safety.

On Sunday morning, 14 November, we approached Port Mindelo on Sao Vicente Island. It took several days to clear Laelia into the country because we arrived on a Sunday followed by a "Police Holiday." No port police or customs were available to check us in (and do the paperwork on the crew change) until Tuesday morning.

It was with a great feeling of relief that we bid our crew goodbye. We have not heard from either of them since that moment.

What went wrong?

Judy and I had spent more than reasonable effort and money trying to make this passage a pleasant one for our friends. Not the least of our efforts was trying to buy provisions that they said they would eat. Yet, very little of it was appreciated.

Much of our cruising experience across the oceans had been to adapt to local conditions as we went from country to country. Our "crew," Mildred, seemed to have little interest in adapting.

It dawned on me that perhaps the food was only a pretext, hence the rigid, non-negotiable demands. Mildred's real goal may well have been to force me to drop them off. It was my assessment that she had a fear of being far away from land.

They had planned to cross the Atlantic several years earlier with the ARC (Atlantic Rally for Cruisers), but had dropped out without explanation. They had many other opportunities to make the passage on their own boat, but seemed reluctant to do so.

Had Mildred told me that she was fearful and would like to be dropped off, I would have, in all decency, done exactly that. Yet she chose to throw a tantrum and sulked to manipulate her way to the same outcome. Instead of admitting her fears, she put the blame on the food, the tyrannical captain, or any convenient scapegoat. Unless she owns up and confronts her fears, she will never be able to exorcise that demon.

13. Dashing Across the Atlantic

Departing Mindelo, Cabo Verde (16 53.178 N, 024 59.445 W), 16 November 2010. Arriving Antigua (17 00.223 N, 061 45.624 W), 04 December 2010.

Departing Cabo Verde
Laelia was underway soon after our crew departed on Tuesday. We left Mindelo Marina, Cape Verde Islands driven by a stiff wind funneled between the two islands of Sao Vicente and Ilha Santo Antao. White caps were everywhere. Laelia responded to the fresh breeze like a young colt. We were flying...at least that was how it felt, although Laelia was only sailing at six knots. Perhaps it was because a heavy burden was lifted. Had our crew stayed for the next few weeks, it would have been sheer agony on a small boat with no exit...for all four of us. Ever since Floyd and Mildred left at 0700 hours for the airport, the song "Oh, What a Beautiful Morning" kept reverberating in my mind.

It was good to be underway again. We continued to receive weather forecasts from Bruce by email via the SSB radio. It seemed that the wind would be generally ten to fifteen knots except for occasional calms.

Notes written at sea:

Bon Dia:
The sea looks dark in the dim light at early dawn with dense clouds overhead. It was an uneventful night. Wind had been light with

swells from the north on the beam; it was neither fast nor the most comfortable. Yet we had put almost 100 NM behind us in approximately 20 hours. As I write, a glorious red sun just popped up on the horizon on Laelia's port stern. The whole world has now acquired a rosy tinge. It is time to put up the spinnaker.
Laelia at sea (16 47 N, 026 38 W)

Life soon settled into a routine of sleeping, standing watch, and eating. In between, we read and kept the boat moving along. The boat chores were becoming a regular routine. The boat was well provisioned. We started out on the eggplants cooked with onions and minced steak. That went well with the ten-minute brown rice at dinner.

The moon, high overhead, was not full, but so bright it cast a strong shadow underfoot. Venus still appeared bright, but Orion was only faintly recognizable in the sky. A few isolated cumulus clouds made the sky look pale blue by contrast. The wind was mild and felt humid. I scanned the horizon, but found no lights of any sort. It is always reassuring not to find another vessel nearby, be it boat or ship. On a long offshore passage, vessel traffic is our main hazard.

Early in the morning mist, we spotted a sailboat about a hundred yards on the port bow.

"Holy cow! Look over there, a sailboat near us," I shouted.

"It looks like Elmer's boat. It's got the double foresail and the blue UV cover," Judy said.

"He doesn't have his masthead light on. We were so close, but didn't see him all night." I was not happy about that. Any boat with no light on at night is a serious navigation hazard.

We knew Elmer from the marina at La Palma. He had sailed many days ahead of us to Cape Verde Islands. It was quite a coincidence to find his boat here. Judy hailed the boat on the VHF radio, but received no answer. Single-handed boaters often turn their radios off when they sleep, but forget to turn them back on. He could be asleep still. We looked for the boat on the radar screen while it was still within sight, but it was not visible on the radar. I wasn't sure if he even had a radar reflector. As much as we love to see another sailboat, we wanted to stay clear of its path.

We tried every way possible to pass him and to steer a different course so we wouldn't meet up with him again the next night. Single-handers need to sleep some time. It would have been safer for Elmer to sleep in the daytime when other boats and ships were more likely to see him. At night he should stand watch and keep his masthead light on. A good radar reflector would also improve his "visibility."

At Elmer's age, he might not have cared if he got run over by a ship. I wasn't sure about his exact state of mind, but I had no intention of colliding with him in the dark of night. We liked Elmer, but didn't appreciate his cavalier attitude about our safety. We observed navigation and safety rules consistently and had every intention of arriving home again.

Judy checked in with the Rum-Runners Radio Net at 0900 UTC. Despite our again-bent whip antenna, the radio transmission was reasonably clear on 6.516 MHz USB (upper side band). Later she talked over the radio on 8.131 MHz to an Australian boat just starting out on the Atlantic passage at the Canary Islands. It seemed we were among the earlier boats to cross the Atlantic this season; the boats following us were eager to know our weather conditions and sea state.

We had the spinnaker flying by 0930 UTC this morning after the radio net. The wind was light at around ten knots NE. The boat rolled with every NNE swell as we persisted on heading west. With such light wind, the spinnaker would spill air as the boat rolled, and would refill suddenly with a loud pop.

To keep the sail from ripping apart, I turned the boat more southward so as to put the swell more on the stern. It was not until late afternoon that we came under some dark clouds with stronger winds of fifteen to eighteen knots. Then we were able to sail due west for a couple of hours at seven plus knots. With stronger wind, the air didn't spill from the sail despite the rolling motion.

Before sunset, the sock was pulled down on the spinnaker and the whole mess dropped on the foredeck. We then unfurled the jib to sail WNW on the opposite tack. In this way, we hoped to zigzag along between the 16th and 17th parallels.

Earlier, in bright sunshine, we finished lunch with an over-ripe papaya as dessert. In the Pacific they were called pawpaws. I devoured my half with the assistance of a spoon. Judy turned hers into a gourmet experience. She sectioned the papaya evenly with a knife before drenching all the pieces with freshly squeezed lime juice. She actually ate the papaya on a plate!

We received a report:

Weather OUTLOOK:
At 17N 35W TO 17N 50W
On 11/25 to 11/26, No sig wx. Swell NNW 6 ft building to 8 ft. 12s period. On 11/27 through 12/04, No sig. wx.
NOTE: Your sailing position is in very low speed winds to your north and higher speed easterly winds with a lot of convective activity to your south. Over all I believe you're O.K. for the most comfortable ride.
Remember the elephant graveyard stories, there apparently is a polar front graveyard [frontolysis] to your west. 50W to the Windward Islands appears to be where the polar fronts from the U.S. die. There are showers associated with these fronts as they become stationary and then modify themselves out of existence.
Regards,
Bruce the Forecaster

Reply from Laelia to Forecaster:

Thank you for the weather outlook. Sounds like a few showers are on the way ahead. That will be nice to wash off some of the accumulated salt on the boat. Hopefully convection activities such as thunder and lightning will not accompany the moisture... We set the spinnaker after lunch when the swells calmed. Laelia sailed along at five knots in light wind of ten knots true. It was a quiet afternoon in lazy sunshine. There has been no more excitement other than a few collisions with some flying fish.

Judy had a conversation in the afternoon on 8 MHz with a boat still back a few hundred NM south of the Canaries. They were the envy of all of us with their whale and dolphin sightings...

They entertained themselves the rest of the afternoon with more excitement. All of a sudden their spinnaker halyard parted. Next thing they saw was their spinnaker floating alongside the boat like a brightly decorated whale. The two of them worked hard retrieving the soggy sailcloth and finding it with all its stitches intact. They next discovered that, during all this excitement, their fishing line had wrapped around the propeller under the boat. So it was a diving trip for the skipper...

It is time again for me to take a look outside for any hazardous traffic. The glorious red, white, and blue colors of Laelia's spinnaker are visible under the bright light of the full moon. It is ethereal like the scenes in Maxwell Parrish paintings. There is not a soul or ship in sight. The only sound is the susurration of water against the hull punctuated occasionally by the sound of stampeding horses as Laelia surfs down a big wave.
Laelia at sea
16 47 N, 031 34 W, 2350 UTC, Friday, 19 Nov. 2010

A little after midnight, I scanned the horizon for signs of shipping traffic. There was nothing. There was only water, a little wind, and the sky. I then looked up at the rigging. There was no sail because we were motoring.

What are those white stumps on top of the solar panels just under the boom?

They looked like the large bearskin caps worn by the Buckingham Palace Guards, but in white. *Could they be mushrooms? Why would mushrooms grow on solar panels? Not likely.*

Despite the glaring moonlight, it was too dim to see clearly. I got a flashlight and, in bright light, I noted that they were large birds. Three feather-covered stumps with their heads tucked under their wings asleep. I left the hitchhikers alone except for a few photos. They were still there in the morning.

"They have long legs for wading and no web," Judy observed and suggested that they could be egrets. They flew away when there was too much activity on deck. We wished them well, but the nearest land was 500 NM away.

The wind was around eight knots. Neither the spinnaker nor the jib did very well in such light air. I hauled out the screecher, a light-wind sail just for conditions like this. It took some time to set it all up properly since I hadn't used it for several years. The bright red, lightweight sailcloth filled easily and was not so affected by the boat's rolling motion.

Our lunch menu consisted of the Cajun bean soup again and the last Cape Verde avocado on board. Cooking bean soup is an art. A

500-gram bag of dry beans didn't look like much. But, after soaking and boiling, these beans swelled beyond reasonable bounds to produce a breathtakingly large pot of soup. A few bags of dry beans could probably nourish the entire ship for the rest of the passage. Too bad there was no way to harness the hot air or we could jet-propel our little watercraft.

In the afternoon, we cut open the little pumpkin and cooked it. The mashed pumpkin was to become the central ingredient for making *Judy's famous pumpkin-pecan pie*. Thanksgiving was only a few days away.

For that evening, the dinner menu featured potato salad, canned Norwegian salmon, and very ripe fresh pears.

Thanksgiving at Sea
The latest forecast showed that there would be more intense wave action in our path on Thanksgiving Day. Judy decided that she would make her special pumpkin pecan pie earlier rather than later. So she went about mixing the magical brew while I went off watch and slept. There were no newt's tails on board, so she settled for some dark corn syrup and pecans. The piecrust was rediscovered somewhere in the freezer.

All was well until she went to place the fully loaded pie shell into the hot oven. This was a precarious job even on land, as the filling in the pie shell was still very liquid at this stage of preparation. Not surprisingly, the boat lurched at the most inopportune moment, causing the filling to slosh the wrong way.

It was not a complete disaster; only a small portion of the filling went on the galley carpet. I was asleep at the time so there was no eyewitness report as to what language was spoken by Judy during the incident. Upon baking, the pie showed no ill effects. Photos were taken to commemorate the heroic accomplishments.

Lunch today was potato salad and Gouda cheese with the remaining loaf of the German bread. We sliced it thin to make the loaf last. Before long we would have to bake our own bread.

By early afternoon the NE wind had come up to nine knots true. I decided to turn off the engine and unfurl the light-wind sail to continue our WSW course. We were gradually moving more southward in order to put a buffer between Laelia and the Polar "frontolysis" mentioned in the forecast. The forecast had also recommended staying above the 16th parallel N because of the convection activity in the south. Convection activity meant lots of squalls with possible thunder and lightning as well as rain. It could be a thrilling experience, but not something we'd like to risk again.

Judy spotted a pod of dolphins near the boat. Some appeared gray with light spots. The dolphins acted like they wanted Laelia to go play, but at 3.5 knots Laelia was like a big, lumbering slug as far as they were concerned. Soon the dolphins all went away.

Dinner was mashed pumpkin, meatloaf, and cooked beets with malt vinegar dressing. Yes, it was a lot of work preparing such an extensive menu. The pumpkin was left over from making the pie. Judy had baked the meatloaf some time earlier in Santa Cruz de la Palma. All it needed was a little heat. The cooked beets were bought in La Palma already vacuum packed.

We knew there would be days like this when nothing much happened. There was nothing to look at outside except water, water, and more water. The E to ESE wind had not gone over eight knots all day. With seven knots of wind our lightweight screecher could power Laelia at three knots. But when the wind dropped to four knots, Laelia was only drifting along at one or two. The autopilot had to work much harder at such a slow speed. There was not enough water moving past the rudder to maintain steerage. It was time to turn on the engine. We are certainly not sailing purists and were unabashed about using the engine.

Both lunch and dinner menus had that familiar look. Lunch was potato salad and tuna fish sandwiches. Dinner was meatloaf, mashed pumpkin, and sliced cucumbers. We finished the potato salad.

The moon had risen. It was still quite full, casting shimmering reflections over the water behind us. The tropical breeze was comforting, but without the scent of tropical flowers. Well...there were no plumerias anywhere near.

The only excitement all night was when a cargo ship was spotted on the AIS screen 18 NM from us. Its name was Hyundai No. 202 and it was heading for a destination in Benin. This was the first ship we encountered in many days.

The next day started ominously on the radio net with a medical emergency on an American boat back a few hundred nautical miles from us. The boat had a satellite phone on board, but needed a phone number for the hospital in Cape Verde. The radio propagation was not the best, but the information was eventually relayed to the boat. It appeared that they would be diverting to Cape Verde.

The wind picked up so we set the spinnaker and had a rollicking ride all day. At fifteen knots of wind, Laelia with the big spinnaker could sail at six or seven knots, depending on the course and wind direction. The boat would jump and rush up a wave and then surf down the other side. The swells were a pain in managing the sails, but all that side-to-side motion added to the sense of being on a roller coaster ride all day. There were whitecaps everywhere. Dark squall columns were all around. There was rain nearby, but Laelia remained dry.

This was also the day we had planned to do a lot of cooking. With prior warning by the forecaster, Judy had made her famous pumpkin pecan pie two days previously. So the pie was already set and chilling in the refrigerator next to the very special "Judy's traditional lime-jello," made with apples, pecans, cherries, and green jello. There was still the turkey to be baked, the dressing with chestnuts to be cooked, and mashed potatoes and turkey gravy to be prepared.

Believe it or not, by 1400 UTC (around midday at Laelia's longitude), the Thanksgiving dinner was on the table in the cockpit. I took photos of the festive table that included a handheld GPS leaning on a tub of gravy. That way we were reminded where we were with every bite.

We stayed on Cabo Verde time as our boat time. Consequently, sunrises and sunsets were taking place a little later (by our boat clock) on Laelia each day as we progressed west. From past experience, we had learned that it was easier (for us) to make changes only as needed. At some point we would change the boat clock to match that at the landfall. There were boats that changed their boat clock one hour at every 15 degrees longitude. We found that too confusing and we were never able to do it consistently. We kept a separate UTC clock (Greenwich time), because communication with other boats was always by UTC time.

The wind had stayed below 17 knots all day, so we decided to leave the spinnaker up for the night. All was well until all of a sudden, the chute folded and started to flap and twist and made very un-sailboat-like noises. Judy was on watch. She tried to turn the boat this way and that, trying to open up the chute. Nothing worked and it was too dark to see anything.

Finally, we realized that the spinnaker sheet (control line) had come apart from the clew. We had no choice but to pull the sock down and drop the spinnaker on the deck. By then the wind had dropped to below 12 knots. In light wind with the boat rolling in the swells, it would have been difficult to keep the spinnaker from self-destruction. It was a Happy Thanksgiving day at sea on Friday, 26 November 2010.

Thanksgiving dinner in the Atlantic (15 59.914 N, 041 17.881 W)

Thanksgiving altered our routine somewhat. For days, we were still working on finishing the leftovers. The turkey sandwiches were very good with cranberry sauce on our own homemade bread. For dinner we had, for a break from turkey, sweet-and-sour chicken on brown rice.

We saw fish jump in front of the bow. Not flying fish, but some sort of silvery looking small fish. The skipper of the Australian boat, about 500 NM behind us on the same track, wished he had his lures out to catch those fish. We were not fishing because we were over-provisioned already. I thought we should plan a few parties on board and disburse some of those healthy beans and oatmeal on hungry mariners.

Friday evening, just a little after sunset, we spotted the silhouette of a tanker backlit by the glowing horizon. We were rather disturbed that we couldn't find it on the radar or the AIS screen. Our active radar reflector didn't detect any signal from the ship either. For all practical purposes, it was a stealth ship.

Later in the night, Judy saw a glow reflected from clouds at the horizon. She thought the glow must have originated from that ship. It was unsettling not to find the radar signal associated with it. Much later we detected a faint radar target about one mile away. We thought it might have been a fishing trawler. These were things that could go "bump in the night." They made us feel less secure.

It was the end of the third week after our departure from Santa Cruz de la Palma and the second week from Cabo Verde. We still had plenty of food, but the supply of fresh fruit was dwindling. The papayas went first. Green bananas we had bought in Cape Verde were also long ripened. The last three forlorn-looking bananas were eaten almost a week ago. There were still a few mushy apples left. Apples didn't do well without refrigeration...not even golden delicious apples. There was one last orange still in the cockpit fruit hammock, looking quite inviting. There were also a few dried and yellowish looking limes left. The orange would be shared tomorrow at teatime. Later the limes would find a way to provide us with some vitamin C.

A couple of days later, as the wind was picking up, I was about to trade the red screecher for the jib and mainsail when Judy heard hailing on the VHF radio, which meant someone nearby.

"Sailboat heading west near latitude 15 degrees 39 minutes north...please come in. This is Panic Attack at 15 degrees 39 minutes..." A woman's voice came over the radio.

"Panic Attack, this is Laelia. We are heading west at 15 degrees 44 minutes north. Over."

"We are the sailboat about five miles to your south. We can see your bright red sail. It's beautiful. Over."

"Thank you. Are you with the ARC Rally? Over."

"No, we know about the Rally, but we are on our own. We left Lanzarote anchorage in the Canary Islands two weeks ago. Over."

"We left Santa Cruz de la Palma three weeks ago, but wasted a lot of time diverting to Cape Verde," Judy responded.

"We didn't have to stop. I would have liked to see the Cape Verde Islands, but several people on our boat were anxious to get to the Caribbean. Over."

"Well, it's actually very friendly at Mindelo, but the check-in was slow," Judy said.

They continued to compare the latest weather report.

"Thanks for the chat. Have a good journey. Over," Judy said.

"It's great talking to you. Good night. Panic Attack out."

"Laelia out."

We confirmed that the catamaran, Panic Attack, was visible on the water and detectable on the radar screen. I thought perhaps the boat would now be a hazard at night, but they quickly sailed on, leaving Laelia behind in their sea-spray dust. Anyway that was another reason I decided to put our mainsail back up. No sailor, however laid back, likes to be passed by another.

The rough seas and big swells from the night before continued into the morning. It was difficult to move around on the boat without holding onto something. For that matter, standing still was not too easy. On the bright side, the steady fifteen- to twenty-knot NNE wind driving the big mainsail and full jib had kept Laelia dashing forward at a good speed. From time to time we saw over eight knots.

The SSB whip antenna for the radio had been repaired in Santa Cruz de la Palma. We made a splint with two broom handles lashed to the antenna and liberally applied with layers of duct tape. It was ugly, but strong and functional...at least in calm weather.

The interminable back and forth and side to side as well as up and down motions did the impossible. The antenna was about to fall into the ocean yet again. The splint needed to be reinforced with more duct tape, but that required someone to climb up and stand on the stanchion to apply first aid to the radio antenna. It would have been a precarious job even in daylight over calm water. At that moment, with the rollicking sea state, I had trouble just holding on and standing still on deck. I wisely decided to give the midnight high-wire aerial act a pass.

By midmorning, it was like entering a dream world; all of a sudden mild sunshine, blue sky, and a soft breeze took over. The swells abated and the sea was flat. The gentle wind shifted to ENE then mostly east and the boat slowed to a crawl at three knots. With wind coming from the stern, the jib, in the mainsail's wind shadow, was listless. The sail plan didn't work at all with wind from dead astern. It was time to furl the jib, drop the main, and to raise the light wind screecher again.

While trying to get the screecher ready, I spotted some torn threads. Perhaps the sail would hold up for a few more hours if the wind didn't get too strong. Then, I remembered a saying about "a stitch in time..." Next thing I knew, I was sitting on the foredeck with needle and thread, sewing. On my hand was a sail maker's palm to push the needle through the sailcloth. I was baking in the hot sun and occasionally basted with a splash of cool seawater as the bow smashed into on-coming waves.

My... how I love this luxury yachting experience!

After the repairs, the light-wind screecher stayed up for more than forty hours. The big red sail turned out to be very versatile and not affected by big swells. The sail could manage winds from four knots all the way to 17 or 18.

With only another 600 NM to the Caribbean, the boat traffic seemed to be picking up. This morning, Judy hailed a sailboat about five nautical miles on our port. It was an Italian boat heading for Antigua. We saw two ships on AIS far enough away not to pose any threat.

Later that night the ship UCB Savannah, heading towards Africa, was 12 NM away, but on a collision course with Laelia. The CPA (closest point of approach) varied as Laelia's velocity varied with the swells and at one point was only 24 feet. The ship at 16 knots of speed plus that of Laelia at 4.5 knots meant the two vessels were closing in on each other at about 20 knots. We had less than half an hour to make things right.

"UCB Savannah, UCB Savannah, this is sailing vessel Laelia, Laelia." Judy hailed the ship over the VHF radio.

"Laelia, this is Savannah, I'm the watch officer on the bridge," the ship replied.

"This is Laelia, do you see us on your radar? We are 12 nautical miles on your bow. Over."

"Laelia, I saw you on my radar already and will make course adjustment to port. Savannah out."

"Thank you, Laelia out."

Just to make doubly sure I turned on both engines, getting ready to run for our lives, if necessary. We did not have enough time to drop the sails, but with 10 to 12 knots of wind from the stern, we could put on some speed with the sails up. Until we saw the ship's green navigation light clearly by binoculars, we were prepared to change course and speed to increase the CPA. Eventually the ship passed "starboard to starboard" at 1.1 NM CPA.

The night watch was becoming more demanding as we approached land. We had enjoyed the security of being hundreds of miles from nowhere, with no land and no ship for many days. All that security was slipping away as Laelia bravely plowed ahead one mile at a time and one day at a time.

Carib Isles, Here We Come.

The moon was low on Laelia's stern. It was a bright yellow crescent like the grin of the Cheshire cat lurking behind us. The shimmering light reflected off the water made a trail of gold. Two hours before sunrise, I confirmed Judy's observation from several days earlier that we could now see the Southern Cross (Crux). It was low on the southern horizon appearing faintly through the haze.

While Judy was preparing for her radio net in the morning, she announced, "We are 485 nautical miles from Antigua." It took some time to gather the necessary information before the net when she would report Laelia's position, true wind strength and direction, sea state, and percent cloud cover. If there were any unusual sightings, further explanations would be required. The Rum Runner's Net is a friendly and informal net with no strict reporting format.

We needed to decide on a landfall. Antigua was one of the three possible landfalls. Antigua and St. Martin both had the best services and available boat parts. Laelia would need a few repairs. Those were also interesting islands to explore. Antigua was the most up wind of St. Martin and Martinique and would keep our options open. Unless the weather made Antigua unsuitable, we were likely to make landfall there.

We were almost out of bread. Since we had plenty of flour in our provisions, the ship's baker decided to make another two loaves. This time it was to be whole-meal seed and grain bread with wheat and barley flakes, kibbled rye, sunflower seeds, linseed, and millet.

The whole mixture came in one package with directions. Apparently this British company founded by Thomas Allinson had been selling flour since 1892. He made it very easy. The bread was outstanding. Judy and I each had a slice with butter and orange marmalade while the bread was still hot at teatime.

It was rock-and-roll time again with white water churning all around. Laelia was heading west by northwest braving fifteen knots of north wind.

Fifteen knots? That's just a gentle breeze at the afternoon garden party in California.

With the big main and jib, Laelia could whip up six or seven knots of speed on a reach in fifteen knots of wind. At that speed, even a small one-meter wavelet rushing at the bow feels like a tall mountain. As Laelia crashed into a swell instead of leaping over it in a single bound, we felt the savage impact. The pounding of the waves kept up...the next wave and the next...the never ceasing swell.

The newly splinted radio antenna was going through a rigorous test of material strength. As the boat leaped, rolled, and dove, the antenna bent 90 degrees and more. Material fatigue developed in due course. With one leap too many, both splinted dowels snapped into splinters into the sea. Now the antenna was supported precariously by two thin guidelines and a few layers of tattered duct tape.

Will the antenna last through the long tortuous night?

Disasters, even minor ones, come in threes. Up high on the main sail, one of the Harken cars linking the mainsail to the mast track came undone. A sprinkle of ball bearings, the size of peas, rained down on our heads and skittered across the deck. We needed the cars to slide the mainsail up and down the track and to hold the sail to the mast. Fortunately there were nine other cars to keep the sail on the mast, but a dangling, hapless car was unsightly. It was one more part needing to be replaced.

14. The Caribbean Sea

Departing English Harbor, Antigua (17 00.215 N, 61 45.645 W), 20 January 2011. Arriving Prickly Bay, Grenada (11 59.815 N, 061 45.806 W), 03 March 2011. Departing Spice Island Boatyard, Prickly Bay on 08 Decemeber 2011. At sea, near the Colombian Coast, 320 NM from Guna Yala, Panama on 15 December 2011. Time included visits to Machu Picchu, Peru and to California.

Collision in Freeman Bay

Laelia was anchored in English Harbor, Antigua. It was the Caribbean headquarters for the British fleet during the 18th Century. At one time, Horatio Nelson was exiled to the island as punishment for letting Napoleon escape from a naval blockade. Now Antigua is a national park.

There were bunkers and ammunition sheds preserved from the past. Foundations for the cannons were still visible as we walked the trails. Goats roamed wild on the island...at least until time for the feast. One night a week there was the Caribbean steel band playing into the wee hours on the hilltop above the anchorage. We indulged in the BBQ under the stars while mesmerized by the tropical melodies.

Christmas on the island had bikini-clad Santa's helpers with bunny ears, sipping Champagne in high heels. The rest of the revelers were in fine costumes or swimsuits and floppies.

There was a gathering of fine mega yachts in Antigua. Our

daughter served as a volunteer boatswain's mate on the tall ship Tenacious, Jubilee Sailing Trust, out of Southampton. We waited for her and her husband's arrival and had a chance to see famous yachts such as the 88-meter Maltese Falcon at the dock. Antigua is like an enchanted nautical fairyland, full of magic and riches.

Laelia was securely anchored in a patch of water labeled as Freeman's Bay on the chart inside English Harbor. We were away from the vessel to explore the island. When the anchor was firmly set, it was generally safe to leave Laelia unattended for many hours. What we didn't count on were inexperienced sailors on chartered boats not understanding that anchored boats swing when the wind shifted.

Upon our return to Laelia, Ty and Judith, on another vessel in the anchorage named Fairwinds, greeted us: "Your boat was hit while you were gone!"

"Oh, no. What happened?" we both asked.

"There was this boat, Mystery, anchored near your boat that swung around... it hit your bow. We tried to save your boat and Judith almost got crushed. But, she raised the back platform on Mystery and prevented major damage to Laelia."

"Gee, thanks. I am glad you didn't get hurt. I wonder how much rode they dropped into the water," I said.

"The guy showed up at his boat right away. He said he had 200 feet of chain in the water," Ty replied.

"My god, that's way too much rode in a crowded anchorage like this," Judy said. "Do these people know anything about anchoring?"

Ty and Judith were still quite excited from their morning adventure. Laelia was floating quietly. A moderate chunk of fiberglass had been taken out above the waterline on the port bow and there were scratches over two square meters of the gel coat. There was no water leakage inside Laelia.

"I think I'll have to file a report with the Harbor Master." I was making mental list on what needed to be done. On land an accident like this would call for a police report followed by insurance claims.

Later, Ty gave me a "Collision Report" to be filed with my report to the Harbor Master.

Collision Report
Location: English Harbor, near entrance to harbor.
Wind direction: out of the east, light to moderate
Boat struck: Laelia owned by Howard and Judy
Boat, which caused accident: Mystery out of Wilmington, DE
Witness to accident: Ty Ebright and Judith Fabian
Name of witness Boat: Fairwinds, a Belize 43
Time of accident: around 11 am on 12/16/2010
Narrative: Ty and Judith were working on Fairwinds, in the galley and in the outside cockpit. We commented that the two other boats looked very close. We stopped working and observed through the binoculars. The Boats were no more than 50 feet from the bow of Fairwinds. Laelia was gently facing into the wind but Mystery was violently swinging in front of Laelia. We then observed the starboard stern of Mystery striking the port bow of Laelia.

Ty then described the actions he and Judith had taken to save Laelia from further damage. His report went on:

The boat continued to crash together. Judith then swam back to Mystery and climbed the swim ladder. She hoisted the back platform to an upright position. She did this just before an impact that would have destroyed the back platform and done severe damage to Laelia.

No more than 5 min later, the owners of Mystery returned to their boat and assumed control. Ty tried to point out the damage and they seemed not to want to look...

The owners boarded their boat and then tried to bring in their anchor and move forward. They were only able to go forward around 10 feet and the anchor could not be raised. It looked as if it had snagged on an underwater obstacle.

I stopped by the boat, Mystery, to meet the owner, Rick M. He apologized for the mishap and promised that he and his girl friend, K., would keep their boat in the harbor until the matter was settled. He and I agreed that we should ask the boatyard to do an estimate of the damages first thing the next morning.

Early in the morning, Rick and the Manager of the Yard accompanied me to examine the damages. Not surprisingly, the damage was clearly in the thousands, although the official estimate would not arrive until a few days later. Rick was visibly shaken, but made no protest. Little did I know what plan he was hatching.

"Hey look, Mystery is gone. It's not there anymore." Judy was first to notice when we returned from a short trip ashore later in the day.

"That's strange. He seemed so sincere yesterday when I talked to him," I said.

We searched the anchorage visually from Laelia's deck to make sure Mystery hadn't just moved to another spot in the harbor. We later discovered a wad of cash that amounted to $250 inside Laelia under a partially opened hatch. The accompanying note indicated that they had to leave and the cash was to cover the damages.

That was outrageous. Rick already knew that the repair cost would be much more. Mystery had flown the coop. All I could do was to file my Incident Report with the Harbor Master.

Incident Report
English Harbor
Attachment: Collision Report by Witness
Incident: Collision of two vessels at anchor
I named the vessels, skippers and witnesses involved, and continued:
   Damages: Survey of damage was by Deon Hector, Manager of Antigua Slipway around 07:30 AM local time on 17 December 2010. Survey of damage was carried out in the company of Rick M. and Howard Wang
   The incident is not settled. We are expecting the estimate from Mr. Hector at the Antigua Slipway.
End Incident Report by Howard Wang, Skipper of Laelia

As we were telling our sad story to an old-time Antigua boater, he asked, "What did you say was the boat's name?"

"It's Mystery, a sail boat...about a 36-footer," I said.

"I've seen that boat before. It's a charter boat company. Look them up," he said.

"Well, that seems to fit...that couple didn't seem to know much about their boat. They are probably first-time charterers."

It didn't take long for me to find Mystery on the charter

company's website with pictures and descriptions. When I called, the manager claimed not to be aware of the whereabouts of the errant vessel, but later he seemed to know a lot about the incident. I wondered if he had anything to do with the sudden disappearance of the vessel from the anchorage.

I thought this guy behaved like a weasel. He wanted me to take Laelia to his harbor for him to see the damage. He also wanted his people to survey the damage and do the repairs. After several days of wrangling, he agreed to pay only a fraction of the estimated cost. I couldn't continue the squabble. Time was on his side. We were on the move...as soon as Laelia was patched up.

Antigua is a beautiful island, but there were other islands vying in the wind. We made short stops at several other islands including Guadeloupe, Martinique, and Saint Martin/ Sint Maarten.

The Wonders of Dominica
Except for hurricanes, Caribbean Islands generally have consistent winds and calm seas to serve as havens for sailboats. We should have stayed the entire season, but we were anxious to move on. As we sailed south along the chain of islands, I kept Laelia mostly on the protected lee of the islands. The stronger winds were felt between islands in the gaps.

As we approached each island, I asked, "Do you want to stop at the next island?"

"Well...only if there is something special," Judy answered.

"Then, we'll skip it...what's another island anyway." We missed quite a few islands that way. We were anxious to head home.

We dropped anchor in Prince Rupert Bay, Dominica not far from the shack on the beach, the Purple Turtle Beach Club. The Cabrits National Park was perched on a high point of land sheltering Laelia from the prevailing winds.

Within the Park was Fort Shirley, the site of a rebellion by the British 8th West Indies Regiment on 9 April 1802 due to poor treatment by the then governor. Many of the five hundred black soldiers were killed during the gun battle or were hanged afterward. The governor was also indicted, charged, and tried, but not convicted. Due in part to the injustice of the incident, it resulted in the emancipation, in 1807, of all black soldiers in the Caribbean regiments. By 1834, slavery was abolished within the

British Empire except in India.

Dominica is special because there is more pristine wilderness on the island and it is the only place in the world to see the Sisserou Parrot (*Amazona inperialis*). We saw several on our tour of the jungle, but they were in flight at considerable distance.

Although the Caribs were not the first inhabitants of Dominica, they were the dominant population in these islands when Columbus arrived on his second voyage in 1493. From that time on, the Caribs fiercely battled the British and the French for more than one hundred years. Now there were about two thousand Caribs remaining in special territories. During our tours, we met only one woman who was reportedly of Carib descent. At the time, she was busy selling Carib handcraft.

Departing Dominica, our destination was Prickly Bay, Grenada, where there was a boatyard so we could leave Laelia on the hard for the Caribbean hurricane season between June and November. It was located far enough south that I thought it was less likely to receive a direct hit, although Grenada had been ravaged by hurricanes before.

A Death in the Harbor

Grenada was a friendly harbor. It had a large dinghy dock where we could tie up the dinghy to go ashore. The dock led to a bar and grill restaurant serving as the local watering hole for cruisers.

At the morning radio net, there was an announcement that a young man had died after his dinghy collided with a piling not far from the dock. The man lived on his boat and had been in the harbor several years. We didn't know him, but others seemed to feel the loss deeply.

"That piling is a real menace. Damn...it's right there as you round the corner," said a rotund man at the afternoon happy hour.

"Yeah, I know...it doesn't even have any lights on at night," someone replied.

"That piling used to have a light, but it burned out and it was never replaced," said a grizzled old salt. "It's the Caribbean you know...island time...nothing new."

"It's a real shame...Rick was always a lot of fun. I don't understand how he could have forgotten about the piling," said a young woman.

"Well, he was probably going a little fast as usual..." said someone who didn't finish the sentence that everyone was thinking: He probably had a few too many beers before the collision.

It was not an unusual downfall for cruisers that have been on the water for many years. Having a few beers at happy hour becomes a habit. Alcohol didn't hook everyone, but it was not an uncommon problem.

By the next morning, there were yellow ribbons wrapped around the piling. Bunches of flowers appeared and more ribbons. The warning light on the piling was never replaced.

A Tour of the Island

Grenada is a colorful island with exuberant hues that only tropical islands seemed to possess in abundance, without even trying. We learned about nutmeg and mace, the main commercial crop on the island. Our tour guide was a big woman with a hearty laugh.

She said loudly, "I love Americans...they saved us from Communism."

She seemed genuine and not saying that just because there were mostly Americans on the tour. She asked about the different nationalities among the mixed group and went on to tell us about the battles and how US medical students were rescued.

There was a monument at Leapers Hill to commemorate the last of the native Caribs in Grenada. In 1651, the Caribs were battling the French, but were vastly outnumbered and outgunned. When they were finally cornered with their backs to the cliff, instead of surrendering and being butchered, they jumped down the cliff. All we have left now is a plaque in the park.

Laelia at the Boatyard

Grenada is on the southern fringe of the Caribbean hurricane zone. There had been hurricanes every five or six years on the average. At the time of our arrival, it had been six years since Emily in 2005 and seven since a direct hit by Ivan in 2004, which devastated 85% of the structures on the island and killed 39 people. Many boats were destroyed.

After the haul out, Laelia was strapped down in the boatyard with heavy nylon webbings affixed with steel spikes in the ground.

I was relieved that we didn't have to store the mast separately, although all sails and canvas had to be stowed. It was a lot of our labor stripping the sails, but we used it as an opportunity to take the sails and canvas to the sail-maker for repairs. The canvas work was left with the sail-loft for the months we were away.

While we were in the boatyard, we saw a boat we recognized being hauled for storage. It belonged to an Australian couple we had met in Gibraltar. We knew both of them well and had meals with them on the dock. The skipper had died from a heart attack during a recent passage. His wife made a valiant effort to resuscitate him to no avail. She welcomed the autopsy required by the West Indies governments, because she desperately wanted to know if there was any chance she could have saved him. We heard second hand that it was such a massive heart attack that it was doubtful that even an emergency room could have saved him.

Sudden illness at sea can happen to any of us. There would be no emergency help at sea. It was a sobering thought. I was fortunate that my bypass operation was already two years old.

High Altitude Interlude

We made plans to return to California for our regular medical visit.

"What else can we do while the boat is on the hard?" I asked.

"Well, maybe we can go somewhere different," Judy replied.

"Like where? What's on your bucket list?"

"I've wanted to see Machu Picchu since I was in elementary school, but it's out of the way...maybe we can go later."

"Mmmm...why not sooner, what are we waiting for? We aren't getting any younger. Machu Picchu is high up in the mountains, right?" I was plotting ahead. I had suffered from altitude sickness many years earlier when climbing Mount Whitney. Altitude sickness is a very debilitating condition. Considering the altitude of Machu Picchu, I would rather go sooner than later.

So we went to Peru. We rented an apartment for several months in Lima, then visited Arequipa, Cusco, and Ollantaytambo in the sacred valley, and Machu Picchu. We also saw the Nasca Lines, sampled the jungle on the tributary of the Amazon, and visited Lake Titicaca, where villagers lived on artificial islands made from floating reeds. It was these villagers who inspired Thor Heyerdahl to sail from Peru to French Polynesia in 1947 on the raft Kon-Tiki.

During the night, a Tasman Mermaid was approaching Laelia with unknown intentions. Well, Tasman Mermaid was a 468-foot cargo ship by that name. It was steaming straight at us, according to the AIS screen. Visually the Mermaid was still too far away to be seen at 12 NM through all that rain and mist. I couldn't be sure that the Mermaid's skipper could even see us on radar because the rain creates a lot of noise to obscure radar images.

The Mermaid at 19 knots could run us down in 38 minutes without even being aware of the dastardly deed. I noted that the AIS calculated a CPA (closest point of approach) of a fraction of a mile. A little close, since Laelia tends to bounce around at various speeds and courses; the accuracy of the CPA is only as good as the input data. I made use of the engine to increase Laelia's speed over ground and noted an increased CPA.

It gave me assurance that Laelia could escape the grasp of the big Mermaid by running faster. By adjusting Laelia's course and speed, we slowly increased the CPA to more than two NM. It was not until I could see the Mermaid's navigation light that I could relax.

Judy was on the morning radio net that started with a weather report. It confirmed that we are having some unseasonable rain and wind. *I could have told them that.*

Then the net controller added the advice: "Cruisers should plan on hunkering down for the next few days. Not only will there be squall after squall and high winds, but the swells will be three meters and up."

Been there and done that, but we will hunker down as soon as we find a place to anchor.

15. Guna Yala

Arriving at Porvenier Island, Guna Yala (San Blas Archipelago), Panama (009 33.383 N, 078 56.922 W), 18 December 2011. Arriving at East Holandes Cays (09 35.266 N, 078 40.699 W), 21 December 2011. Checking out and departing Porvenier Island, 29 December 2011.

Approach to Porvenier
I had put the waypoints in the GPS chart plotter to guide Laelia to a safe starting point for entering the anchorage at Porvenier. Still, in waters where reefs could be just under the surface, it was a good idea to travel in good light, calm water, and a pair of watchful polarized sunglasses. What we had learned, especially in Fiji, where the conditions were similar, was that with the sun behind us we had less reflection from the water surface and could see the submerged obstacles.

A careful lookout for hazards was important. Just this season, we heard that a boat tried to enter an anchorage at night, despite the waypoints, hit a reef and had to abandone the vessel. With all that in mind, we timed our arrival around 1000 hours local time.

Just as we were closing on the first waypoint, there was a sliver of blue sky and a dash of sun. *Wow, how exciting*! Farther back, a giant dark squall with blackened skies was chasing us. It was very sobering. *We better hurry*. On the fringes of the squall were a few smaller clouds with rain and small rainbows, which looked miniature compared to the giant inky squall. If I had a tripod and an umbrella to protect the camera from the rain, I could get a fabulous picture of the dark, black, angry sky with fringes of lighter gray clouds and rainbows. Those were fleeting thoughts as I diverted my attention.

Already the sun was gone and we were under a total cloud cover. The water looked dark blue and opaque. The rain and heavy mist ensured that the visibility was no more than half a mile. Undaunted (there was no alternative), Laelia aimed for the first waypoint, about one nautical mile from the anchorage. By design that first GPS waypoint could be approached safely from most directions.

As we approached the anchorage, we took note of Sail Rock, a dark and gloomy rock guarding the entrance. Most of the water in the anchorage was sixty feet or deeper.

"Watch out! There is a reef right in front!" Judy said. Indeed, there was a long spit of a reef projecting out from another little island. The water was lighter colored than the surrounding water, and probably had sea anemone all over it. I pushed the throttle to reverse.

Clunk, clunk, clunk!

Mmmm, that does not sound like the happy purring of a reverse gear. I quickly put the engines in neutral. Laelia was still heading towards the reef.

"Damn! I don't need this to happen now!" I cursed as I figured out that the port engine was still good. With only the port side in reverse, we managed to stop the boat and turn away from the reef

Oops! I hope that's not a sign of more pending need of repairs with the starboard transmission. I was not feeling too cheerful at the thought. To mess with the transmission meant hauling the boat out of the water again. It was a gnawing unpleasant feeling.

Eventually, we anchored not far from a small French boat. I went into the starboard engine room and looked over the transmission. All looked normal. *What could be wrong?* I turned off the engines, changed into swim trunks, and went under the boat to take a look. I was glad to see a big wad of polypropylene hanging from the prop. It meant that the folding prop with all that junk on it was not able to open properly and was off balance. This problem could be fixed! I went back up to the surface and asked Judy for a knife to free the propeller. I surfaced with the knife in my teeth and held my catch high...a polypropylene sack and some rope.

Indigenous People of Guna Yala

Isla Porvenier was the Port of Entry to the San Blas (Guna Yala) Islands on the Atlantic side of Panama. These islands are home to the Guna indigenous people. At the time of our visit in 2011, the spelling of "Kuna Yala" was commonly used, but the correct spelling, preferred by the indigenous people, is "Guna."

After anchoring and removing the polypropylene from the propeller, we felt pretty good. For the first time in ten days we had a good night's sleep without standing night watch. I still woke up to check Laelia's GPS position several times during the night. The anchorage was not big, but the holding in sand was excellent. The anchor never budged from where we dropped it in the water.

I kept a record of the GPS positions as Laelia swung about the anchorage with the wind. It was always a good feeling to see the exact same positions repeating themselves. It meant the boat was swinging about with the anchor firmly embedded in the sandy substrate at the bottom.

The sky was still cloudy with occasional rainsqualls. The wind continued to blow relentlessly, but with the barrier reef blocking the swell from the open ocean, it was much more comfortable on board. In front of us was the little island (Isla Porvenir) where we could check in with Panamanian Immigration and Port Office. Around the government building there were a few Panamanian soldiers looking very bored. Their presence was probably intended more as a show of force than for protection.

The Guna population and the Panamanian government were in a prolonged uneasy truce. The native people wanted to maintain their own way of life and were distrustful of the government. It was common to see indigenous people demonstrating in Panama City against constructing a mine or cutting trees on Guna land. Guna natives and the Afro-Caribbeans were usually the lowest paid laborers in the modern Panama City.

Not quite a century ago, brute-force efforts by the government to suppress the Guna natives' traditional ways resulted in a short rebellion with some Panamanian police being killed. As a result, more Panamanian soldiers were dispatched to teach the natives a lesson. If it had not been for the interference of an American adventurer and the US Navy, there would be far fewer Guna natives alive today. Since 1925, there has been an agreement to allow some degree of autonomy to the natives.

We tourists were transients in their country. Although we knew little of the indigenous people's way of life, we couldn't help but admire their spirit of independence and their tenacious effort to preserve their heritage. When in doubt, I tended to side with the underdog.

The offices on the little island were very basic. The windows were wide open to let the trade winds blow straight through the squat little building. The Panamanian Immigration Officer asked a few questions, but showed little interest, and checked our departure papers from Grenada. He stamped the passports and charged US $15 per person before giving me a receipt.

In the next office, the Port Captain typed in every detail of a cruising permit application form on an electric typewriter, painstakingly, one stroke at a time. It cost US $193 for the one-year cruising permit. After separating the triplicate copies and a flurry of stamping, I got the permit.

What is he going to do with all the papers? Where will he find enough space to file all those precious documents?

I refrained from asking aloud. It is best to limit conversation with officials to a minimum...and not volunteer any information.

We weren't done yet. There was yet a third office where a young Guna woman showed me the schedule of charges for visiting Guna Yala. (That was what the Guna natives call this part of the world instead of the Spanish name of Archipelago de San Blas.) She had long black hair, a round face, and a coppery complexion. I could have mistaken her for a Chinese or a Vietnamese.

The cost was US $2 per visitor and US $20 for an ordinary sailboat. Luxury yachts would have to pay US $50 and a cruise ship US $300. There was absolutely no question that Laelia was just as ordinary as a sailboat could be. More triplicate copies of receipts and more stamping, then we were all done.

Porvenier is a small island not much bigger than a football field, but with a barrier reef several times the area of the island. There was a rather short runway across the middle of the island originally built by the Americans during WWII. It would have been a strategic location for defending the Panama Canal. There was a lot of loose sand and other construction material piled here and there. Apparently the runway was being extended onto the reef to make it longer for larger, modern airplanes.

They are expecting a lot of people wanting to fly here?

There were a dozen structures for short-term lodging and some palm trees, but there was not much to do. Porvenier could serve as a jumping off point for boat charters or a place for taking water taxis to the many hard-to-reach little islands. I suppose flying to Porvenier would save tourists many hours of bouncing around in a four-wheel drive through the jungle and a wet boat ride.

The largest building on Isla Porvenier was one with a roof of palm leaves and bamboo inner supports. It was intended to appear "native." It had a sign declaring itself a restaurant. I took a peek inside. There were tables and chairs enough for twenty or thirty people, but it was dark. There were bare electric light bulbs dangling on wires, but they wouldn't be turned on until the cruise ship visitors arrived. There was a kitchen, but no one to do the cooking at that moment. Why would cruise ship passengers pay money to come here to eat substandard food when they could have it all on the ship? Perhaps there could be some entertainment in native costumes?

Not far from Isla Porvenir, there was an island with a Guna village. From our position in the anchorage, even with binoculars, it appeared to consist of poorly built and densely packed shacks. On the other side of the anchorage, there were a few wind-swept islets barely above water with a few palm trees, but otherwise uninhabited.

Occasionally, the natives would paddle in their dugouts called "ulus," which were genuine dugouts made from hollowed tree trunks. On closer inspection, many of the ulus leaked and had rotted parts. Traditionally men paddled ulus to fish at sea. Some called them the cowboys of the sea

The Guna indigenous people originally lived in the mountains of the mainland. After the Spanish conquest in the 1500's, they gradually retreated to the coastal regions of present day Colombia and NE Panama. Many of them further migrated to the islands of the archipelago for protection as well as to avoid mosquitoes.

According to the guidebook, the indigenous population of Guna Yala was around 53,000 at the time. Living on these isolated small islands provided some degree of cohesion, allowing them to better maintain their native culture. Traditionally, they were matrilineal, but many of them converted to Christianity. Today they still live with their traditional religion as an integral aspect of their daily lives and social organization, but many of them are also Christians of various denominations.

Molas

We often saw Guna women paddling their ulus (dugouts), wanting to sell us molas. Mola making is a very intricate handcraft, a stitchery specific to the Guna natives of the San Blas Archipelago. They first sew two pieces of material (usually cotton) of different colors together with basting stitches, with the planned design drawn on the top layer. Then they cut away the top material along the design to reveal the color underneath. The raw cut edge of the top layer was notched at intervals and turned under and sewed to the layer underneath. For a 2-layered mola, this would be the finished product. Additional layers were added as desired. Some of these molas can have up to 7 layers of different colors with intricate designs.

Before contact with Europeans, Guna women painted their bodies with designs. In more recent centuries, Guna women wore tops with panels of mola front and back and also as designs for skirts. (Mola actually means "blouse" or "clothes" in the Guna language). The molas were to ward off evil spirits. The women also wore many rows of beads on their legs and arms as well as gold nose rings and headscarves. Most of them avoided being photographed.

These Guna natives were quite good bargainers. They would give and take on transactions. Well... one of them certainly knew how to take. I was outdone early on by a Guna woman. We bargained and I selected a number of pieces and paid her the agreed amount. It wasn't until she was long gone in her dugout that we realized that she had taken several pieces of our selections back with her. The result was that we paid much more and got less than what we thought we were buying. Well, it came under the category of "live and learn."

East Holandes Cays

We did a 16-NM hop to another reef system four days before Christmas. It was a long strip of barrier reef stretching six or seven miles. Wherever it was above sea level, it was an island with a lot of palm trees. What we saw was a string of little islands linked together by invisible submerged reefs. We understood that there were 21 of these little islands in this area called the Holandes Cays. The swells crash onto the windward of the reefs generating an incessant loud roar day and night and sending up white spumes five or six feet into the air. We watched all that fury from the protected anchorage on the leeward side of the reef.

We got word that cruisers were planning a Christmas potluck on the little BBQ Island at this anchorage. That sounded inviting, so we hopped over.

We remained at an anchorage nicknamed Swimming Pool. It didn't look like a swimming pool, but it was shallow where most of the boats were anchored in ten or fifteen feet of water. We preferred deeper water at around 30 feet, where there were fewer no-see-ums and mosquitoes. Also, the roar of the surf was not as loud. Judy got to meet and talk to many folks whom we had only contacted over the radio.

On the morning radio net two days before Christmas, it was reported that during the night there was a boarding in the Nagana anchorage about 5 NM east of our location. Two Guna natives had attacked a French single-handed sailor with machetes. The sailor was tied up and robbed. That was not good news.

At our anchorage there would be a Guna boat coming with supplies to set up a little "tienda" on BBQ Island. We needed supplies and it would be an outing ashore. It had been two weeks since we left Grenada. With the launching and all the activities related to departure, we hadn't done a very good provisioning run in Grenada. Consequently, our supply of perishable foods was down to a carrot or two, a few onions, and a couple of not too reputable apples.

We rode the dinghy to the BBQ Island. There was a little thatch hut surrounded by coconut palms that the Guna villagers used as a shelter when they visited. Other than the hut, it was just white coarse coral sand and NE trade wind. It smelled of salt air and the roar of the waves crashing on the windward reef was never ending.

The supplies were not impressive. The giant carrots, with various rotten parts already cut away, looked grotesque. The only stalk of celery was already wilted beyond resuscitation. The potatoes carried so much mud that it was hard to tell where the potato began. We bought onions, several cucumbers, and two small heads of cabbage, three oranges, and a cantaloupe.

Our primary adventure was in dealing with the dinghy at the beach. One would think the beach should have calm water, being on the leeward side of the trade wind and surrounded by reefs. It was definitely calm compared to the outer reef, but it was not calm enough.

We landed without incident. Both of us got out of the dinghy quickly and helped pull it to higher ground on the beach. While we were shopping, a few big waves came in and "pooped" the dinghy. It was filled with water and sand, and was too heavy to move. I opened the drain plug to let the water out, but just as it emptied, another big wave would come and start the process all over again. I bailed as fast as my arm could move until the water was down enough to launch the boat. I put the drain plug back, turned the boat bow towards the water.

When we got the boat part way into the water, Judy went partially on the boat and we all shoved off, with a few other people pushing. There we were, a few feet from the sandy beach trying to make a getaway. I dropped the outboard down so the prop was in the water, pulled out the choke, and tried to start the engine before another wave hit us.

For once, it started on the first pull. The soft purr of the outboard was pure music to my ears. I turned the dinghy to face into the waves. Needless to say, we were drenched in salt water and our "Crocs" shoes were filled with coral sand. We survived yet another adventure. In the scheme of things, it was nothing major, but enough to keep us on our toes. Overall it was not too bad for a peaceful Christmas Eve.

Christmas Day 2011
The Christmas Party with gift exchange would allow us some social activity. It was potluck finger food because there were no tables and chairs at the BBQ Island. The cruisers also put together a gift basket for the Guna village that was nearby. We contributed

a can of spam, a bag of beans, and a number of toys for the basket.

The party was quite a treat. Judy baked a big pan of brownies for the potluck. There were more than sixty plus people from more than sixteen boats in attendance. They all brought food so there were more than we could eat. There was a game of gift exchange and music from a keyboard powered by a portable generator. It was a full day and we were content.

West Lemmon Cays
After the Christmas party, we departed the Swimming Pool anchorage on a half-day sail to West Lemmon Cays. It was a blustery bright sunny day. There were two entrances to the West Lemmon anchorage, one on the north and another south. We entered from the south to avoid dealing with the swells and currents on the windward, north side.

Upon arrival, we encountered a German-flagged, three-masted, 50-meter sailing schooner named Thor Heyerdahl. It was too deep drafted to enter the channel so it dropped anchor near the entrance, exactly on our waypoint. With reefs on either side of the narrow channel, we had little maneuvering room in the current. Even more annoyingly, two of its young passengers were frolicking in the channel. We couldn't run over the couple and we didn't want to run aground on the reef. All we could do was wave them aside from our path as we sped by. We had to move rapidly to maintain steerage. They had no idea of the risks in which they had put themselves.

Our first sight upon entering the anchorage was a sailboat aground and abandoned on the reef at the north entrance. It had probably been there for at least a week. All its sails were already stripped and lines were whipping about in the wind. We later heard that the boat had tried to enter the anchorage at night in the dark. The skipper had missed the entrance by about twenty feet.

In all the years we had been sailing on Laelia, we had entered a harbor in the dark only four times. Once was on our return to the Channel Islands Harbor, our homeport, marked by lights well known to us. The second and third times were both on our arrival at Bundaberg, Australia. That channel was also well marked. Only the fourth time, our night entrance to Kupang, Indonesia was a mistake that could have resulted in a collision.

At West Lemmon Cays, there was a small bar under a thatch roof on one of the small islands. After we dropped anchor, we launched our dinghy to get a cool drink. The bar's owner was a German named Yogi who was a former cruiser and a charter boat captain. He married a local woman who wanted to settle on firm ground. He was tired of the chartering business anyway and agreed with the one condition that he must have a dog. He now had a Rottweiler that was friendly on land, but would defend the master's boat fiercely. We couldn't even go past by dinghy near his boat without creating a frenzy of barking and growling.

We discovered with pleasure that the bar also served a big plate of chicken, rice, and salad for five dollars. We ate our dinner by the water with sand between our toes. It was a quiet little island. Life could be peaceful here, but perhaps a little too tranquil. There was nothing to do.

Occasionally a Guna ulu would show up to sell molas. We met two of the quite famous mola makers. Lisa was a transvestite and was willing to pose for a photograph. We also bought some very intricate molas from Venancio. There were water taxis departing for other islands. Laelia was at a secure anchorage here, so we decided to explore the Carti Islands where the anchoring was known to be difficult with deep water and poor holding. A water taxi allowed us a relaxed visit without having to worry about Laelia.

Carti Island

We went to Carti Sugdub Island by water taxi. It was the only island we visited that was densely inhabited by Guna natives. There were a few small stores, a school, and a museum of Guna culture. The museum was small with an earthen floor, but the curator did a good job of teaching us some aspects of Guna history and culture.

A short distance away was a backpacker's hotel with a small restaurant downstairs. Cruise ships stopped in the nearby waters on their way to or from the Panama Canal. Visitors would arrive on the island by tender. No doubt on the days with the cruise ship hovering, the museum would be full and all the molas would be on display for sale.

Although there was a school on the island, the young people we met seemed very lacking in arithmetic skills. The teenagers had a difficult time in totaling up purchases. They added one item at a time, but seemed unable to multiply when there were several items at the same cost. With each transaction, they had to call in older family members to help with the calculations.

We learned at the museum that the Guna natives believed that their spirits departed their bodies when they slept. Consequently, their sleeping bodies would become defenseless. A carved doll was placed in the room as their vigilant counterpart. While they slept, their spirit would enter the dolls and keep watch over them as their guardian.

We were given a chance to buy several dolls to be placed on our boat to confer spiritual protection on us. Judy, ever practical, very diplomatically declined: "Oh, thank you, the dolls are beautiful, but we don't have any space on our boat."

It wasn't simply about buying a doll, but incurring an obligation. Whoever became the owner of the doll would be duty-bound to keep it forever. The doll must never be damaged or destroyed. Of course we couldn't simply toss such personal alter egos over board. Judy was right that our boat was already cluttered with too many things.

"Where can we park a couple of dolls to watch us sleep?" Judy whispered to me just in case I was tempted to buy a doll or two.

We were the only visitors on the island at the time except for a young man from Boston who was on a round-the-world motorcycle journey. Unfortunately he was unable to find transport off the island to go to Colombia and had been stuck on the island for four days already.

Cargo ships were not allowed to pick up passengers in Panama City, but could accept passengers from the San Blas Islands. That was why he went there. What he didn't realize was that no sane captain would bring a precious cargo ship into such reef-infested waters to pick up a single passenger and his motorcycle. We listened to his plight sympathetically, but couldn't offer him any help.

Later we discovered a local captain on a small ship that would ferry backpackers between Colon, Panama, San Blas, and Cartagena, Colombia. We sent the captain the following email message on behalf of the young traveler:

To: Mark at Fresh Air Charters:
We met a young man on Carti Sugdub Island on Tuesday, 27 December 2011. His name is Daniel staying at the hostel above the restaurant by the concrete dock at Isla Carti Sugdub. He would like a passage from there to Colombia together with his motorcycle. He has been there for four days now and is very desperate. We have no way to reach him, but he has been in touch with Yogi at West Lemmon Island. That is all we know and hope you can help him.
Howard and Judy
Catamaran Laelia

Our water taxi trip was down wind on the way to Carti, but the return trip was just the opposite. The wind was not a serious problem, although it blew salt spray on board the open boat making us wet. It was the speeding boat crashing against the oncoming swells that gave us the physical beating. Every time we were lifted by a swell, the boat would crash back down with a great, big, bone-jarring splash. To be sitting in such a boat was cruel physical punishment indeed. With every bounce, I could feel the hard bench we were sitting on not giving a millimeter.

With each crash of the boat, I imagined that my spinal column was being compressed. I could feel myself becoming shorter as we went along. We were not wearing kidney belts. I tried to use my arms as shock absorbers to ease a little of the punishment. But, on one of these downward crashes, I landed wrong and ended heavily on my right nether "cheek." No doubt it was bruised seriously. I didn't cry out or show my distress, but for days afterwards, I had to sit sidesaddle on my left.

We enjoyed the tranquility at the anchorage, but it was time to move on. We departed West Lemmon on a short sail back to Porvenier to check out of San Blas. Upon entering the anchorage, the first sight was a sailboat aground on the reef. We had been there less than two weeks earlier when the reef was unadorned by any wreckage. It was on a well-known reef called the Sail Rock with its GPS coordinates given in the guidebook. Again we were told that the boat had tried to enter the anchorage at night. Although we had been there before and even had the tracks from our previous visit on the chart-plotter screen, we still would be very reluctant to enter the anchorage in the dark.

Aside from checking out with Customs and Immigration, there was nothing else to do on Isla Porvenier except to hoist anchor and head towards Portobello, our next destination.

16. The Panama Canal

Arriving at Portobelo, Panama (09 33.323 N, 079 39.688 W), 29 December 2011. Arriving at Shelter Bay Marina, Colon, Panama (09 22.082 N, 079 57.029 W), 03 January 2012.

Portobelo Harbour
We departed Isla Porvenier early and arrived at Portobelo Harbour in midafternoon. It was a magnificent big harbor with depths ranging from seventy to thirty feet of water over a considerable distance. The muddy bottom also provided firm holding for the anchor. On land we were now only a bus ride away from the Panama Canal. Laelia could sail to Shelter Bay Marina in a few hours. It was a good place to spend New Year's 2012.

Columbus originally named the harbor "Puerto Bello" on his fourth voyage. It was the most convenient harbor on the Atlantic side to transship all the treasures gathered in Peru and elsewhere in the Americas. Galleons in the Pacific brought treasures to "Panama Viejo" (or Old Panama), near the present-day Panama City on the Pacific coast. Then, pack mules carried the loot overland across the Isthmus to Portobelo, where the treasures were delivered across the Atlantic to Spain.

We visited forts on the Caribbean side designed to protect the port against attacks by pirates like Henry Morgan. We explored Fort San Geronimo (Fuerte San Jeronimo) in Portobelo. The heavily defended port had additional bastions, Fort Santiago, located farther west from Portobelo on the south shore of the harbor. Overrun by vegetation, there also appeared to be remnants of gun batteries on the hillside overlooking the harbor. There were structures at the waterfront left from what must have been a wharf. They were mostly rock stumps at the water surface, a navigation hazard at night for speeding dinghies. Fort San Geronimo was in need of restoration. Many cannons were rusting on the ground. Similarly, the large two-story Customs House, used for counting and weighing thousands of tons of gold before it was shipped to Spain, was in need of repairs and maintenance. So much vegetation was growing on the roof and in the gutter that I feared the structure would not last many more years.

The Panamanian government certainly had put little money in this town. The roads were in poor repair and dwellings appeared dilapidated. The only bridges we saw that still served the community were built in the late 1500's. Portobelo appeared to have had a strong Chinese influence. The Chinese owned both supermarkets and the Ferreteria (hardware store), but strangely there were no Chinese restaurants in town. The best food was at Captain Jack's Hostel, a restaurant and bar catering to cruisers and backpackers with decent prices and free wifi. We had dinner there with fellow cruisers from s/v Stardust on New Year's Eve and watched fireworks from the balcony.

We met a sad-faced gentleman and his wife. He appeared to be in his late fifties and well tanned; his wife was much younger. He drank his beer listlessly.

"I lost my boat eleven days ago," he said to no one in particular.

"Oh, I'm sorry to hear that. What happened?" I replied. I could tell that he needed to voice his sadness to put it behind him.

"It happened close to Colombia...there was this rough current. I just wasn't able to maneuver my boat away from the reef. I lost everything I had. I was on that boat for twelve years you know...and it's now all gone."

"I'm so sorry, what will you do now?" I said awkwardly, not knowing how to lighten his sorrow. Perhaps just having someone to listen was of some help.

"I don't know...we are both still alive." His wife put her arm around him as he continued, "We'll manage...one day at a time...somehow."

"Yeah, that's right, that's all we can do...one day at a time. The sun will shine again." We all drank to that.

After they left, there was a discussion among cruisers of boats lost in the area. We counted as many as twelve boats that had run aground on a reef during just November and December of 2011.

This was certainly not a boat-friendly patch of water. Part of the problem was that boaters were not acutely aware that this was reef country. Having navigated atolls and coral reefs in the Pacific, Judy and I had developed an unconscious respect for the risks. Of primary importance was to navigate in good visibility above and below the water surface. Many of the boats were lost at night entering harbors where the hazards were obvious in daylight.

Panama Canal Transit
On New Year's Day, 2012, Laelia was still anchored in the Portobelo Harbor, where no treasures remained, just quiet poverty and a few ruins. We invited friends from s/v La Luna and s/v Stardust to a chili and bean dinner on Laelia before they set sail for the Canal Zone the next day. We departed a few days later.

Our destination was the Shelter Bay Marina as the starting point of our canal transit from the Atlantic to the Pacific Ocean. The Isthmus of Panama is oriented east and west. As a result, our canal passage was generally from north to south. The nearest city to Shelter Bay, our starting point, was Colon on the Atlantic (or Caribbean) side, and Panama City was on the Pacific side.

To reach Shelter Bay Marina, we had to enter the breakwater that served to protect the Atlantic terminus of the canal from swells and surges. There were more ships than we had ever seen gathered in one place, just outside of the breakwater, some moving and others anchored. We sensed danger in a jungle of big ships and monstrous anchor chains.

As we approached the breakwater entrance, Judy hailed the Cristobal Light Station, "Cristobal Light Station, Cristobal Light Station, this is sailing vessel Laelia. Over."

"Cristobal Light Station. Go ahead."

"We are planning to enter the breakwater and will be heading for the Shelter Bay Marina. Over," Judy informed them. The Light

Station replied, "Proceed with care to shipping traffic. Over."

Despite the fact that it was daylight, it was difficult to distinguish the many anchored ships from those in motion. They were not moving very fast, but with over a hundred ships in the vicinity, we could get in the way of these lumbering behemoths. We had already furled the sails with both engines at the ready so we could weave through the anchored ships without the distraction of sail tending.

"You see that ship ahead...the white hull? It's moving...he's heading in the direction of the breakwater entrance," I said.

"I see him," Judy replied while on the helm.

"I think we can cut across the channel and follow it," I said.

As we speeded Laelia towards the channel, the ship in motion at about eight knots seemed to have slowed, then came to a stop.

"What's going on? Why is it stopping?" I was puzzled and a little frustrated by the confusion. Had the ship continued, we would have dropped in behind and followed it.

Perhaps Laelia can cut in front of the ship instead and head for the entrance. The entrance appeared to be clear. Just to be cautious, I checked the AIS screen before we headed for the entrance.

Whoa! There was an AIS warning in red blinking alarm mode on the screen. There was a tanker exiting the canal some distance away still, but heading straight for the breakwater opening. It became clear that the other ship was stopping for the tanker to come through. If we insisted on cutting across the channel now, we would be crossing the bow of the tanker in motion.

If we are fast, we can probably make it across instead of the interminable wait. At least that thought crossed my mind.

Had we zipped across, the tanker would have no maneuvering room and would most likely blow its horn five times to let us know that we were in imminent danger...and to broadcast the skipper's displeasure. Since we had no desire for that kind of attention or for adventures involving close encounters with big tankers, Laelia stopped outside the buoyed channel and waited for the mighty tanker to pass before following the other ship into the breakwater entrance. In crowded harbors, prudence is a survival trait.

Shelter Bay was formerly a US Naval base, but had been converted into a modern marina with excellent facilities. Our friends Bob and Becky on s/v Stardust, whom we had been in touch with by radio, greeted us and helped us tie up in the marina.

We had already contacted by email an agent named Erick whom we had read about in a Noonsite report on the Internet. He informed us that the canal fee would be $500 for vessels less than 50 feet in length and his fee would be $350. Plus there would be an inspection fee of $55 and a security fee of $44. The total came to $949. He would supply us with twelve tire fenders and four approved lines, each 125 feet long, at no additional cost. We wouldn't have to pay the bond normally required to cover any damages caused by our vessel to the canal.

As soon as we engaged him and provided a list of answers about the boat, he acquired from the Canal Authority a Ship Identification Number (SIN) for us. Laelia was now officially in the queue to transit the Panama Canal. During the busy season of February and March, there could be a wait list of as long as three or more weeks for small craft. He also obtained for us an official advisor to assist us with the transit.

The inspection on the second day after our arrival, arranged by the agent, took a couple of hours, not only to measure the boat, but to check Laelia's seaworthiness, ability to anchor, and whether she had adequate engine power to transit the canal without delay. On the official form, the only correct answer to minimum boat speed was eight knots, but in practice they would accommodate boats motoring at five knots.

Thursday evening our friends Bill and Joan, who had made the Pacific crossing (the Puddle Jump) at the same time as us on their own boat a few years ago, arrived at Shelter Bay Marina after a long flight from California and an extended taxi ride from the airport. They would join us on the canal transit. Having had a bad experience previously with friends aboard Laelia for the first five days of the Atlantic crossing, we were a little "stirred, but not shaken." We knew their interest in transiting the Canal and had invited them on board. Bill and Joan are seasoned blue-water sailors and we had stayed in their home in California a number of times. We knew for certain that both of them had good dispositions.

By Friday, our agent informed us that we would transit the

canal on Tuesday, 10 January. That gave us three days to get ready. The transit from Atlantic to Pacific for small sailboats was now required to take two days, beginning at mid-morning. (In the reverse direction, from the Pacific to the Atlantic, the transit required only one day). That meant we would have to feed everyone on board two lunches, one dinner, and one breakfast. We counted a maximum of as many as nine persons on board, including the four of us, two people from s/v Stardust who would help with line handling, two paid line handlers, and our advisor.

The canal transit could be hot on a small boat, so there had to be plenty of cool drinks. So we provisioned and pre-cooked as many items as practicable.

The menu turned out to be teriyaki roast chicken breast for make-your-own sandwiches with mayonnaise and sauces for lunches. Peanut butter was also available as a backup. For dinner we had spaghetti with meat sauce, vegetables and dessert. Breakfast was scrambled eggs with sausages and fried onions. Hot water was available for coffee and tea. We put a big cooler with ice in the cockpit to keep the soda and water cold. That way everyone could get their drinks as they needed them. Beer was only available at dinner after we anchored.

With spare time before the transit, we visited historic Fort San Lorenzo guarding the mouth of the Chagres River on the Atlantic (Caribbean) side. The Spanish built the fort to defend against marauding pirates from invading inland along the Chagres River.

We scouted out Gatun Locks, the nearest locks to us on the Atlantic side. We could watch the ships from either direction entering the locks and leaving. The locks were double lanes side by side. We saw two ships going in the opposite direction through the locks at the same time. On the banks of the locks were small electric locomotives on rails, called mules, at least four to each ship, with retractable steel cables to keep the ships centered.

The entire Panama Canal is a series of artificial lakes, channels, and locks. Gatun Lake has the highest water level on the isthmus and provides water pressure for all the locks. The Gatun Locks, a series of three locks, raise or lower ships between the Atlantic Ocean and Gatun Lake, a height difference of 85 feet (25.9 m) from the Atlantic sea level.

On the Pacific side, the Pedro Miguel, Miraflores Lake, and

Miraflores Locks acting as three locks raise or lower ships, between the Pacific Ocean and Gatun Lake, 85 feet to the Pacific mean sea level. In practice, the net elevation changes vary around 15 feet, depending on the Pacific tides.

Gatun Lake, the 32-mile of dredged channel, and eight miles of Culebra Cut are all situated between the locks on the Atlantic side and those on the Pacific side. The water in the lake serves not only to provide water pressure for the locks, but also for generating electricity and storing fresh water for the community.

Although not obvious, another important role of Gatun Lake is in controlling the erratic and dangerous Chagres River. During the rainy season, the Chagres in the past would increase to mighty heights, flooding the banks, and washing away anything in its path. Gatun Lake contains that water and puts it to productive use.

On the day prior to our transit, our agent brought tires all wrapped in black plastic. We checked the tires to make sure there were no wires sticking out of the rubber to cause damage to the hull. We were told to tie the tires on with ropes that were strong enough to keep the tires alongside, but would be able to break and release if the tires got tangled up with rafted boats. That was to protect the lifelines on the boat from getting torn off if the fenders became tangled. Our lines were quite strong, so we assigned one person with a pair of scissors to cut the fenders loose if they tangled.

Laelia at the Gatun Locks
Our instructions were to depart Shelter Bay at 1100 hours with all crew and line handlers and to arrive at the Flats anchorage to wait for our advisor to come aboard at 1300 hours to give us further instructions. This first part went by with no problem, but even with the best preparation, the unexpected can happen...and did happen.

Our understanding was that every small craft was required to have four lines with handlers and adequate fenders. Our agent provided 12 tire fenders and we had our usual complement of ten large fenders. The idea was that we needed to be ready for any configuration of lockage.

Although we had requested center lockage, it was possible for the Canal Authority to require us to raft to another boat or tug.

Frequently, several sailboats were rafted together during a lockage. In that event, the fenders become very important. It was possible, but unlikely, for the Canal Authority to ask small boats to tie to the sidewall, which was very rough and full of slime.

When we arrived at the Gatun Locks, there was a ship about 700 plus feet in length entering the lock ahead of us. Of the small craft, there was only Laelia and a moderately sized powerboat of about 50 feet. We were told to raft up to the powerboat for the lockage. For reasons no one could fathom, the powerboat skipper requested to be on side-tie to the lock.

After the powerboat was tied to the sidewall, we approached next to the powerboat to raft up. That was when things became questionable. The powerboat did not have adequate fenders. He had only two or three small fenders that looked inadequate for that size vessel.

Things got really exciting when the water became turbulent as we were being lifted by incoming water. The boats were sitting low in the channel along the lock wall. The dock lines dangling straight down from the bollards were not very effective in keeping the powerboat in place. I could hear the powerboat crunching against the wall. He tried to use his engine to power away from the wall. Of course that created a whipsaw effect that involved two rafted boats. There was a flurry of activity to move fenders to keep the two boats from smashing to pieces.

In the midst of all this, the skipper of the powerboat asked our advisor to borrow the tires from Laelia for use on the wall to protect his boat. There simply wasn't time for that. I thought it was pure pandemonium created by an incompetent miser.

The skipper of the powerboat might have saved himself about $30 by not renting fenders at $3 each, but would probably need to spend a few thousand to repair his hull. He might also have picked the side lockage because he had only two line handlers instead of four, saving him about $120. He could have rafted to us in center lockage, requiring only two line handlers on each boat. The Gatun Lock had three locks in series. Each time, we had to tie and untie. We did the remaining two locks better, but it was still unpleasant with the powerboat on a side tie to the wall.

Upon exiting Gatun Locks, we were now in Gatun Lake. Our

advisor showed us where we should anchor for the night, a place not far from the locks in about fifty feet of water. The holding in mud was good. He told us that another advisor would arrive at 0630 hours in the morning. Our crew sighted a few crocodiles on the mud bank in the waning light of the evening. We had dinner on board, followed by a board game. The two young line handlers played their music on the deck.

It was still dark at 0600 hours the next morning. I was starting to get breakfast ready. Judy was brushing her teeth and saw through the porthole flashing signals from an approaching vessel. It was the advisor arriving a half hour early, when we actually expected him to arrive late. Luckily, everyone was stirring already. It took no time at all for everyone to be at breakfast, including the advisor. We were under way before 0630 hours.

Judy served as helmsperson for part of the passage, then Joan, followed by Bill and Bob. As skipper, I was required to drive in the locks. The advisor guided each of us as we passed ships and dredges. It was impressive to realize the size of Gatun Lake; it covered an immense area between the two sets of locks.

We followed the dredged channel in Gatun Lake from buoy to buoy. We could see, outside of the dredged area, dead trees and stumps. Had we been a slower boat, the advisor might have decided to take a short cut away from the channel through the jungle to save time

We spotted a few crocodiles at a distance. The first wild life close by was the rare "Blue Morpho" butterfly. Joan was the first to realize what it was. The large wings were a deep blue with black fringes, and they were iridescent. The butterfly was flitting back and forth behind Laelia, shimmering and welcoming our arrival. It was my first sighting of a butterfly in the Morpho genus.

As we went along, our advisor pointed out locations of interest. He noted the new home of Manuel Noriega who had recently been repatriated to Panama to serve out his prison sentence. It was a small hillside with an extensive amount of barbed wire. We learned that Panamanians were generally happy to have had Noriega deposed, but very disturbed by the heavy-handed way in which the US had dealt with Panamanian sovereignty.

Among the many landmarks, the Culebra Cut was the most

infamous. This was where the Panama Canal sliced through the Continental Divide. The builders had to turn the mountain into a valley to make possible a waterway connecting Gatun Lake to the Pedro Miguel Lock.

Unfortunately, the geological formation of the Culebra was composed of unstable layers of lava rocks and blue shale. When the blue clay became wet, the rocks slid off the slopes in an avalanche, killing and destroying. The Culebra Cut caused more accidents, costs, delays, and unending engineering headaches than any other part of the canal. Diseases added to the heavy toll on human lives.

As we went through the cut, it did not look very imposing. We saw barren terraced slopes on either side of the waterway. From the scene at hand, it was hard to imagine the hardship, the pain, and the maimed bodies that made the excavation possible. In part this was because we were only looking at what little remained of the mountain. It required effort to imagine that we were passing through what had been a solid mountain more than 300 feet high and more than a third of a mile wide for a stretch of eight miles. The entire mountain had been blasted away by dynamite, picked up by steam shovels, and carried away by cars on tracks. Over 100 million cubic yards of rocks and debris had been hauled away, but the significance of such number was hard for the mind to encompass.

Perhaps a better way to appreciate the immense scale of the project is to look at what was created from all the rocks and clay from the cut. The entire district of Balboa (676 acres) was landfill from the Culebra Cut. Similarly, the Amador Causeway connecting Balboa and the offshore islands of Naos, Perico, and Flamenco was built from the rocks and debris from Culebra. Now, the causeway served as a breakwater to block the current silting the approach channel to the canal on the Pacific side.

Pedro Miguel and Miraflores Locks

In contrast to our drama at Gatun Locks, our lockage through Pedro Miguel and Miraflores Locks was almost an anticlimax. We were delighted that we were the only vessel in the locks. It was unusual for a small craft to go through lockage alone. Small boats simply didn't pay enough to justify the amount of fresh water used in the transit.

We requested center lockage and Laelia was indeed alone with two lines to each sides of the Canal. It seemed so simple. As the water was lowered, the lines were let out, keeping the boat centered. Then we motored into the next lock. I noticed that it was difficult to steer and had to use the throttle to adjust the direction of movement.

We could see the observation deck on shore at Miraflores crammed with hundreds of tourists. Judy could hear the announcer on the public address system telling the tourists about the vessel in the lock: "...a catamaran named Laelia... on her final leg of an eight-year circumnavigation...returning home to California."

At that point, we could hear cheers and saw hundreds of cameras flashing. *We are celebrities!*

What we didn't know at the time was that we were on the Miraflores webcam. Our Dutch friends, Denise and Etienne, on s/v La Luna had alerted their friend Filip in Belgium to look for Laelia. As a result, Laelia's lockage at Miraflores was recorded and forwarded to us. It was a priceless recording to be treasured.

The remainder of the passage was uneventful. We exited the Miraflores Locks and dropped off our advisor. Then, after we went under the Bridge of the Americas, we arrived at the Balboa Yacht Club. Right away, our agent came to Laelia to pick up the line handlers, tire fenders, and lines. From the mooring at the Yacht Club, we could watch all the canal traffic coming and going.

The Panama Canal was for its time the biggest and most expensive project ever attempted. Some thought it would enhance world peace by improving transportation. Others considered the canal to be vital for a naval power to control both the Atlantic and Pacific oceans. Its creation involved people from more than ninety countries. Many bigger-than-life personalities participated in intrigue or contributed to the technological knowhow, while many tens of thousands of people were engaged in the building of the Canal.

A majority of the laborers were unskilled and black, but not all. For example, Paul Gauguin, the artist, was hired as a common laborer during the French era (1887). He was among those considered to be a "tropical tramp." The unskilled laborers were mostly recruited from Jamaica during the French effort. During the American period (1904-1914), most of the unskilled laborers were from the island of Barbados in the Caribbean. There was a proposal to recruit Chinese laborers, but it was met with popular objections from both Americans and Panamanians. The apparent reason was that the Chinese tended to settle and become commercially successful.

**Laelia in the Miraflores Locks, Panama, 01/11/12 13:43:37
(Screen shot courtesy of Filip Lembregts)**

Quite aside from the unprecedented amount of money, first from French private enterprise and later from the US government, the construction of the canal cost a combined 20,000 to 30,000 lives due to accidents and sickness, with the majority of deaths caused by tropical diseases such as dysentery, pneumonia, yellow fever, and malaria.

It was the popular belief that the diseases ultimately stopped the French effort in building the canal. No doubt that was a major contributing factor, but the final coup de grace was a scandal involving corruption in the French government that brought the canal company (Compagnie Universelle du Canal Interoceanique de Panama) to its knees in bankruptcy.

Carlos Finlay, a Cuban, proposed that the mosquito was the disease vector. He was ridiculed for his conclusions derived from exhaustive research. At the time, the popular belief was that yellow fever was transmitted by toxic vapors or by direct contact. There was also the belief that the lack of personal hygiene and inadequate moral character enhanced the disease. Walter Reed, after whom the Walter Reed National Military Medical Center in Washington, D.C. was named, confirmed Finlay's conclusions that yellow fever (in urban areas) was transmitted primarily by a particular species of the mosquito (*Aedes aegypti* formerly *Stegomyia fasciata*).

Later, with the pestilence vanquished (at least among the white workers), with better management and improved living conditions of the workers (again there was a color divide), the Canal Project was eventually a success. It is a magnificent story of human endeavor involving bigger-than-life personalities dealing with projects of immense scale and complexity never before attempted. It was a time of brave optimism and the willingness to do what no one had done before. (David McCullough's book, *The Path between the Seas*, is an excellent read about the creation of the Panama Canal.)

Laelia Needs A New Rudder
Having been on a boat for many years, we both knew there would be unexpected events. There wasn't much anyone could do to anticipate these problems. It was just a matter of keeping alert and dealing with events as they transpired.

We never planned to hang around Panama as long as we did. Laelia berthed one week in the Shelter Bay Marina preparing for the canal passage. On 10 through 11 January 2012, it took us a total of only 27 hours to complete the actual canal transit, including an overnight stop in Gatun Lake. Then Laelia stayed on a mooring buoy at the Balboa Yacht Club, off and on, until 18 February, with time away and at the boatyard. We were in the Panama Canal Zone for a total of 46 days, unplanned.

After the canal transit, we felt good and wanted to celebrate. It was unanimous that we should do a little sailing in Panamanian waters with Bill and Joan, who had flown all the way from California. Our destination was a cluster of islands called Isla de Las Perlas, not far west of the Canal Zone. These two hundred plus islands at one time produced large quantities of pearls.

Pearls did not bring the islanders good fortune. Balboa discovered pearls at these islands in 1513. Later Gaspar Morales killed many of the natives and treated others cruelly in an effort to obtain more pearls. The Spaniards forced the native divers to continue to bring up pearls. The blood and tears of an enslaved population were mostly forgotten in the passage of time.

Within two years of the arrival of the Spanish conquistadors, native islanders were no more. After that, slaves were brought from Africa to dive for pearl oysters. A profitable market existed for pearls as well as for the mother of pearl from oyster shells. The pearl oysters began dying off from a peak in 1925 and almost completely disappeared by 1948.

We sailed to Isla Contadora, one of the bigger islands in the archipelago. It was on this island, five hundred years ago, that the conquistadors inventoried pearls and gold from elsewhere. Now there was still a customs house standing, although in poor maintenance. There was a small town with several restaurants and many expensive vacation homes. We, of course, appreciated the large anchorage with plenty of swinging room for Laelia.

On a hot afternoon, I thought it was a good opportunity to check the zinc under Laelia and replace it, if needed. I dove in the crystal clear water and went below the boat. Immediately, I noticed that the port rudder was missing.

"Guess what...we have only one rudder," I said as I surfaced.

"Oh no, not again," Judy responded.

The last time Laelia had lost the port rudder was in 2008. A new rudder was constructed as a replacement in Bali. Unable to find any one-and-one-half inch stainless stock, a smaller stainless rod was welded inside a stainless pipe. Then, the pipe/rod was machined to exact diameter for building the rudder. It all looked good when the rudder was done, but in retrospect there were predictable problems.

Now fast forward to the moment in the anchorage at Isla Contadora. That same replacement port rudder broke. The cause was probably corrosion in the rudderstock, known technically as galvanic corrosion. Boaters know, at least in the back of their minds, that not all stainless steel is the same. Normally stainless steel is resistant to corrosion, but if two different kinds of stainless steel are in electrical contact, the amount of corrosion is much greater than either in isolation. Also, welders generally know to use the appropriate welding rods to weld stainless steel. The wrong kind of welding rod could also result in greater galvanic corrosion.

Experts on marine corrosion might say: Howard, you are lucky that the replacement rudder lasted as long as it did. We were also fortunate we didn't know about the broken rudder before the canal transit or we would not have been allowed to make that attempt.

We were also thankful to have discovered the broken rudder in Panama. Here at least there was technical assistance and specialized material was available, even though nothing was very cheap. We were also lucky that we found Adrian, the one person who knew how to build a new rudder and was willing to take on the project. At the time, he was working to build up his sailing kitty to prepare his own vessel for an Antarctic expedition.

While we were at it, we decided to replace both rudders. The remaining starboard rudder had previously been bent...just a little. It was bent when we ran aground departing Port Suakin, Sudan. Since that time, the starboard rudder had been held in place with duct tape and hose clamps. It was still working, but I couldn't be sure for how much longer. It seemed prudent to make two identical rudders while we had the mold. To make things more trying, Laelia had to be hauled out of the water. So we had to go to the yard and pay for the haul-out.

After days of labor, production problems, and scheduling delays at the yard, Laelia was sporting two identical rudders and carried a spare...although a slightly bent spare.

Sights in Panama
We did some sightseeing even before we discovered the missing rudder and while we were waiting for the repairs. Panama City is a large modern city with an old town (*Casco Antigua*) that is under

extensive restoration. Here we saw run-down homes and shops as well as tastefully renovated high-end shops housed in old colonial architecture.

Not far from the modern downtown is the *Panama Viejo* (Old Panama). This part of the city was burned down in 1671 when the buccaneer Henry Morgan sacked the city of 10,000 residents. It was the Pacific port where the Spanish unloaded from ships the gold and treasures that they had collected in the New World. Now, *Panama Viejo* was in ruins, but there was plenty remaining to show that it had been a substantial city.

We met a taxi driver who offered us an all-day fare for taking us to tourist sights. Although he didn't speak much English and our Spanish was pretty weak, we managed to communicate well enough. The group of us went all the way out of the Panama City to a wildlife reserve. The highlight was a two-toed sloth. We had to wait some period before it moved around on the tree slowly...it was slothful.

It was the Asian New Year and there was a Lion Dance performance at the Convention Hall. Our driver knew the location, but had never seen a lion dance before. We had to listen to the Chinese delegates, representing the Chinese government, giving a very long speech in Cantonese and again in Mandarin. Then it was translated into Spanish. The three long, tedious speeches were the antithesis to the exciting lion dance. It appeared to me that the Chinese government was trying to woo the Chinese residents in Panama City. The lion dance was well done, but the speech was a clumsy effort and counterproductive.

In Panama as well as across the Caribbean and the Pacific Islands, we have noticed the Chinese influence seemingly sponsored by the government in a patient, long-range effort to expand its sway.

17. North to Costa Rica

Departing Balboa Yacht Club, Panama (08 56.240 N, 079 33.351 W), 18 February 2012. Departing Costa Rica Yacht Club, Puntarenas, Costa Rica (09 58.948 N, 084 47.782 W), Tuesday, 13 March 2012.

Departing Panama
We finished installing the rudders on Laelia, paid our bills, and checked out with the Port Captain in Panama. The wind was with us on our second trip to Isla Contadora. Having been on land for so long, we needed to acclimatize ourselves to the idea of going to sea again. It seemed everything was at the wrong place and we kept forgetting to do necessary boat chores. We hoped that a short hop to a familiar anchorage would reacquaint us with the seafaring life. When we headed out again, we had ENE wind and sailed SW towards Punta Mala on the SW point of the Gulf of Panama.

In Spanish, Punta Mala means "bad point." By now, we were automatically suspicious of any point of land that protruded into the sea. We expected confused currents and shifty winds. Punta Mala was no exception; it had a bad reputation of nasty swells and sudden storms. At the time, the wind was fair and we had a one-knot current in our favor. We rounded Punta Mala after dark with no drama, although I was on my guard the entire time. Many of our friends and family told us that they were praying for us. We certainly thank them.

From here forward, our course would be generally in the NW direction, as it is the outline of the Central American Pacific Coast. The winds had been erratic. It had blown in just about every direction. We had no wind at times and the sea was mostly calm.

With very flat seas, it was easy to notice irregularities at the water surface. One time, we saw a lump ahead of us on the horizon. Judy got out the binoculars to have a better look, but it remained a lump at the water surface with no distinguishing features.

"It's just a rubber tire...a fender that fell off," I said.

"Look...the lump has a head sticking out of the water," Judy exclaimed.

Before we could take a second look to be certain, everything disappeared. "It must have been a turtle." We both came to the same conclusion.

A little later, we saw another lump, but this time it had a seagull standing on its back. It was just like in the cartoon BC where a bird was hitchhiking on the back of a turtle.

As we got closer, the seagull flew and the turtle dove under the surface. We scrutinized the surface for more of those lumps for the next few hours while the sea was still flat. We counted at least two more turtles that afternoon, all of them southbound. It was difficult taking photos of shy animals that disappeared when we got closer. The telephoto lens was wonderful, but couldn't take sharp photos from a moving sailboat.

We estimated the distance from our destination and calculated arrival time to make sure we would reach port in daylight. At one point, when I had just finished trimming the sails smartly for Laelia to glide along in light wind, I noticed a stronger breeze starting to pick up. I watched the meter as the boat's speed over ground (SOG) went up to just below eight knots. At that speed, we would end up arriving too early in the dark. So I reefed the sails. No sooner had I finished reefing than the wind dropped to the point that we had to turn on the engine.

Our intended destination on that leg was Golfito, Costa Rica. It is a protected harbor tucked away inside a larger body of water, the Golfo Dulce, surrounded by pristine tropical jungles. Laelia entered Golfo Dulce in the wee hours of the morning while it was still pitch dark. Judy was on watch when she detected a vessel following behind Laelia at ten knots. She determined from the AIS screen that it was a 148-foot National Geographic vessel, the Sea Lion.

"Sea Lion, Sea Lion, this is sailing vessel Laelia, Laelia. Over."

"Laelia, this is Navigation Officer on Sea Lion. Over."

"We are a sailing catamaran...do you see us on your radar? We are motoring at about four knots. Over."

"Yes, you are loud and clear on the radar. I also see your AIS data. Over."

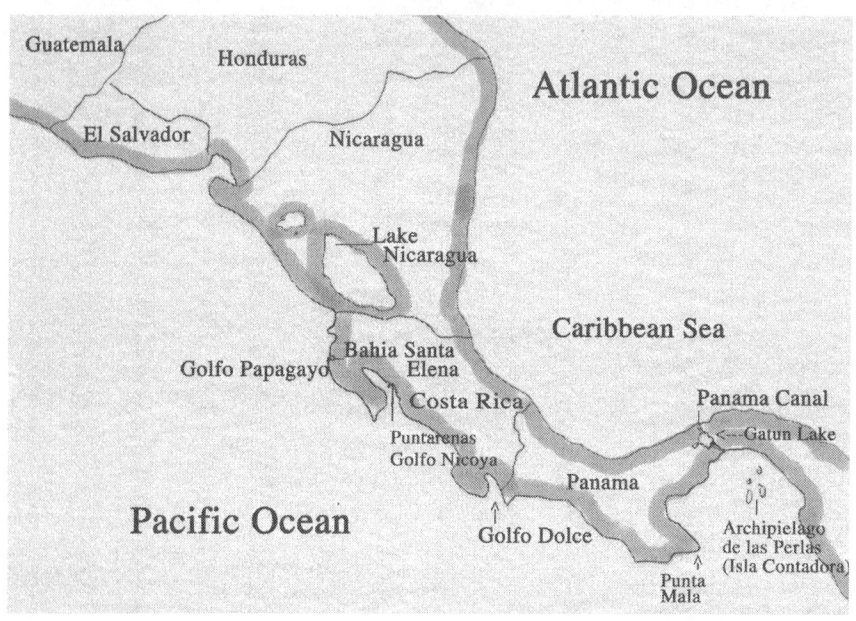

"Oh good. We don't always know if our AIS signal is strong enough. Thanks for the info. Over."

Judy asked if this was a National Geographic survey ship.

"No, we are actually a passenger ship...a cruise ship. We are smaller and can go to places that big cruise ships can't get to go."

"Where are some of the more interesting sights around here?"

"Well, tomorrow we'll anchor off the Orchid Garden and the passengers will get a chance to tour the garden." The conversation continued for a short while.

In the early morning light, as we entered the channel for Golfito

Harbor, we met a welcoming committee of dolphins. At any one time, there were as many as four or five dolphins swimming alongside each bow of the catamaran. One would swim on its side with its ventral surface almost touching Laelia. Then it would move ahead as if leading Laelia along. It would accelerate and leap forward out of the water with exuberance. Then another group of dolphins would come and continue the game. The whole sequence would repeat with more dolphins. It was almost as if the dolphins were trying to teach Laelia how to play like they do. We delighted in the energetic display.

We wanted to stop at Golfito to visit Casa Orquidea, which is well known to orchid fanciers worldwide. After Laelia was tied to a mooring, we made arrangement to see the Orchid Garden by water taxi. The owners of the garden had bought the place some thirty years ago as a small banana and pineapple plantation on the shore of Golfo Dulce. Over the years they became experts on orchids and were helping to preserve indigenous species.

They also grew vegetables, spices, and fruits for their own consumption and sold the excess. We had a chance to try their tree-ripened star fruit. Unlike the store-bought star fruits that are often sour, these tree-ripened fruits were very sweet. We were treated to a glass of star fruit juice.

One plant we had not expected to see was the so-called "miracle fruit." Our son had told us to keep an eye out for this fruit in the tropics. Here we were, face to bush with one. The bush was about three meters tall with sparse red fruits of 2 cm by 1.5 cm in diameter. The fruit looked a little like an ornamental miniature pepper. We were told first to taste a pickle plant, which tasted sour, like a pickled cucumber. Then we were to taste the miracle fruit, which was mildly sweet. After that, the pickle plant tasted much less sour and somewhat sweet.

The miracle was that somehow the fruit had changed our taste perception to make sour things taste sweet. It was interesting, but more biological than miraculous. The miracle fruit (*Synsepalum dulcificum*) contains only a small amount of sugar to give a mild sweetness of its own. But, it also contains a substance called *miraculin*, which when in an acidic solution, activates the sweet receptors on the tongue to provide the unexpected sweet taste.

We enjoyed the taxi system in Golfito. The taxi, a sedan, would keep picking up passengers as long as it had space. Each passenger would pay 700 colones (about $1.50) for any destination on the main road. To go off the main road it would cost an additional 100 colones per street. It was convenient and not too expensive.

Golfito had only one main street and two other streets in parallel. At one time, it was the banana capital of the world. It was a company town. The United Fruit Company controlled and provided everything. With the worldwide drop in the price of bananas, the company had departed. Golfito was left with nothing.

The town has good potential, with a deep-water gulf and a well-protected harbor. It also has several national parks nearby, pristine forests, and a lot of wild life.

Unfortunately, there was not much infrastructure at the time to support visits by amateur explorers like us. A transition to a tourism-oriented economy was growing, but slowly. We did notice foreigners coming to Golfito to buy property. It was indeed a world away from all the hustle and bustle of modern civilization.

Parque Nacional de Manuel Antonio

We knew little about the Manuel Antonio National Park until we studied the guidebook. Despite the fact that it was among one of the smaller parks in Costa Rica, it attracted more visitors than many of the others. The main reason for its popularity was its rich wild life.

There was a small anchorage at a beach inside the park boundary. We dropped anchor between a giant rock outcrop and the beach, as recommended by the guidebook. The holding was good and the rock blocked swells from the Pacific Ocean. We felt pretty secure as we tested the holding by pulling hard on the anchor with the throttle in reverse.

Early in the morning, we went ashore. We were dragging the dinghy up the beach so it wouldn't get washed away at high tide. Several young men asked if they could help...of course! They were full of energy and dragged the dinghy all the way up to the trees. It was high and dry, but just to be extra secure I tied the dinghy's anchor rode around a small tree. We weren't sure how high up the tide would come later in the day.

Even before we found our way to the ticket booth for the park, we came across the first of many reptiles that scamper around the beach and the walking trails. We thought they were iguanas, but never quite got the identification clarified.

There were many local naturalists available to serve as guides on a tour through the park. They carried monocular telescopes on tripods to help people see the animals that stayed high up in trees. There were two–toed and three-toed sloths. Apparently, the two-toed variety was more aggressive, but we didn't put that claim to the test. We had seen three-toed species in the jungle of Panama, but this was our first encounter with the two-toed sloths in the wild.

We had heard Howler monkeys before, but never laid eyes on one in the wild. They sounded like fearsome creatures with their deep pitched growling reverberating loudly through the jungle. The sound effect was intimidating. We met up with a whole tribe of them hanging out, literally, on a large tree almost a hundred feet above our heads. Taking photos of them was difficult with the tree casting a heavy shadow. I got a few photos, but nothing impressive.

We saw many more animals, especially reptiles and monkeys. Before long the tourists were leaving the beaches. The park would close at sundown. We headed to the beach to our dinghy. The dinghy was still high up on the beach, but there were no helpers, young or old. We huffed and puffed a long time moving the dinghy to the water's edge.

By this time, there was an incoming tide together with the surf rolling in. It was not the kind of giant surf to delight surfers, but challenging enough for launching a dinghy. Judy got in first and we loaded all our things while the dinghy floated in shallow water. I kept it pointing into the waves and gave it a mighty push to gain some momentum. At the last moment, I would jump in, lower the outboard, and start the outboard before the next wave rolled in...at least that was the plan.

What actually happened was a little different. When I pulled on the cord to start the outboard, it didn't start...I pulled it again and still no go. By this time the surf was starting to roll in and the dinghy turned sideways. The surf picked up the dinghy and began tipping it precariously.

My...it could capsize...with us still in it.

It didn't tip over, but it got swamped and filled to the brim with seawater. I must have pulled the starter cord one more time because the outboard started to purr. That was a very calming sound.

"It's like sitting in a bathtub," Judy observed and started to bail with a quart-size plastic container. It would have taken her hours to empty the dinghy.

Another wave was beginning to roll in. The dinghy was now more stable with the extra weight...could it still flip over? I didn't want to find out.

"Forget about bailing...let's just head on back," I said as I turned the dinghy into the wave. The dinghy moved sluggishly because it was so heavy with all that water plus the two of us.

"Well, we are not in any danger of sinking," Judy said, as water was still dripping from her hair. She is beautiful that way, but it wasn't quite the wet romantic beach scene.

The dinghy sat low in the water with a full load. The five-horse outboard engine was barely above water, working at maximum throttle as it moved laboriously, carrying all that wet weight.

It was a comical sight, but there was no one to appreciate the hilarity.

The Cloud Forests

Our next destination was Puntarenas in the Golfo Nicoya for several reasons. North of Puntarenas was a high-risk passage with a dangerous "Papagayo" wind in our path. It is a "gap wind" blowing from the Caribbean Sea, across the Central American Isthmus, over Lake Nicaragua, towards the Pacific Coast. I thought we should wait for optimal weather at Puntarenas, the nearest port to the Papagayo wind. It was also the nearest port to Monteverde, the cloud forest, where we could do some sightseeing while we waited.

The Monteverde Cloud Forest Biological Reserve is world famous. Its brochure announces: "The tropical cloud forests are enormously rich ecosystems, supporting 20% of the world's plant diversity and 16% of vertebrate diversity in only 0.4% of the earth's surface...with over 100 species of mammals, over 400 of birds, 120 of amphibians and reptiles, tens of thousands of insects, and over 3,000 species of plants, including the largest orchid diversity in the world with 500 different species."

How can we resist visiting such a unique niche in the world?
Monteverde has an interesting history. In 1951 forty Quakers escaped from the US to avoid penalties for refusing to be drafted into the military during the Korean War. They chose Costa Rica because it was the one country that had abolished its army in 1948. While the Quaker families were waiting in San Jose, trying to decide what to do, they were offered considerable land in the mountains. The land was undeveloped with no electricity and no running water. At the time, there were only a few Costa Rican families living in Monteverde. The Quakers arrived by horse and oxcart. They did well as pioneers and prospered.

Today, Monteverde is not only a thriving tourist destination, but also a prime area of biological interest with its animal and plant diversity and a unique tropical cloud forest environment. More than 10,000 bird watchers come here each year just to see the single species of endangered quetzal among other avian species.

We rented a four-wheel-drive car in Puntarenas and drove up the mountain. It was only forty miles, but it took two hours with half the journey on steep and windy dirt roads. Due to a reservation mix-up, we ended up staying at a better, but more expensive hotel.

What we didn't know at the time was that the half owner of the beautiful hotel was one of the youngest of the original Quaker settlers in Monteverde. Little Ruth Campbell had her first birthday in San Jose just before her father, John Campbell, and two others rode horses to look over the land they had been offered.

The hotel described itself as "the half Costa Rican-half Quaker, family-owned hotel." Although we were disappointed that the Quaker History Museum in town was no longer operating, the Hotel El Establo had some old black-and-white photographs taken by John Campbell. There was a picture of Ruth in front of her birthday cake and a group photo of the entire original community.

Climate of Monteverde

As I mentioned, we were waiting for the Papagayo winds to settle on the Pacific side of northern Costa Rica and Nicaragua, but we had not considered the path of that wind. We knew that the Papagayo wind is created by clockwise, high pressure, cold air on the Caribbean side of Central America against the low pressure on the Pacific side. The pressure difference propels the air to move across the Continental Divide of the Central American isthmus. The heavy cold air gains speed as it rushes over the mountains and accelerates down the slopes, races across Lake Nicaragua, towards the Pacific.

Here in Monteverde, we were only a few hundred feet from the Continental Divide. The winds we were trying to avoid at sea were moving at a furious rate over our heads and around us. We could see clouds racing across the sky. The moisture penetrated the forest and looked like mist. The heavier clouds became rain. With the wind gusts, the wind-driven rain became horizontal from time to time.

It didn't rain continuously, but sporadically all day long. Of the four days we were there, only on our last day did we have more sunshine than clouds, but Judy was sick that afternoon and slept all that sunshine away.

While Laelia was waiting at Puntarenas to avoid the Papagayo, we came up the mountain, into the very path of the maelstrom. Well, it was not quite like discovering the source of the Nile. The locals told us that the wind and the rain only happened from time to time. Some days were even nice and warm.

We were not complaining. After all, we had come here to experience this special environment. We went on a night walk hoping to see nocturnal animals. Our guide showed us all sorts of interesting plants and insects such as the walking stick. It was so well camouflaged that it became invisible after our guide released it back onto the bush.

We also saw tree frogs in a shallow pond. They came there at night to mate. We estimated at least fifty or more frogs in a little puddle of water. It must have been quite a party, but by next morning, we couldn't find any of them hiding in the surrounding plants. These frogs were already decreasing in numbers and are expected to die out in Monteverde as the climate becomes warmer.

For a number of hours, the smart animals were comfortably warm in their hideaways, nice and dry, while we, the big mammals, were looking for them in the wind driven rain.

We went on a guided tour of the Cloud Forest Reserve. Immediately, we saw one of the most prized sights of the bird watchers...the quetzal. It was a juvenile male without its iridescent tail feathers yet. We then saw a mature male with its long tail feathers and bright plumage. It was all through the telescope set up by the guide. The quetzals eat primarily avocados and there were plenty of wild species of avocados in this forest. We saw some avocado trees of incredible size and discovered the wild turkey...a rather large bird and very easy to see.

More frogs were sighted at the Frog Pond, where they were housed in large glass enclosures. After dark is the best time to see these frogs when they become active. On the other hand, the best time to see butterflies is when it is warm and sunny. At the Butterfly House, we got to see the Blue Morpho butterflies close up. While I was trying to photograph them, one landed on my head. The problem was that there was not too much light and these butterflies moved fast.

We were fortunate that there was a reserve. Much of the development was so successful that the cloud forest was quickly disappearing. The land had been cleared for raising dairy herds and farming. Preservation of the reserve was due to the efforts of biologist George Powell and his wife, who recognized the imminent loss of a natural treasure. They and one of the early settlers, Wilford Guindon, joined forces to establish the reserve in 1972. Most of it was under strict protection and only 3% was open to visitation. Efforts were made to return the cleared land to its original state.

A Bureaucratic Nightmare
Departing Puntarenas had not been easy, due to the cumbersome bureaucracy. It was just another example that sailing away from home and work was not the ultimate freedom, as some might imagine.

On Friday, we decided to do some of the departure paperwork while we still had the rental car. Transportation was important because the Port Captain in Puntarenas could only do the paperwork for vessels traveling within Costa Rica. Now that we were leaving the country, we had to check out with the Port Captain in Caldera to obtain a "Zarpe Internacional." Zarpe is a port clearance document and Caldera was a $20 taxi ride away. We didn't know where Caldera was, except that it was not within walking distance.

We finally arrived at the Port Office in Caldera on a miserably hot, scorching morning, and waited. When it was finally my turn, the Port Captain explained to me that, although I had all my papers, I still needed to go to any BCR bank to pay the required fee of $20. I asked for the bank account details so I could make the payment to the correct department.

"You don't have to worry about that...the banco will know what to do. They have all the forms," said the captain.

"I'm sure you are right, but I would feel better if I could have the account number for depositing the money. The form will be in Spanish and the bank will not be able to help." I knew from past experience that these bank clerks would absolutely not volunteer any information unless I asked direct questions or could produce some documents.

The captain was very patient with me and photocopied the request form from another boater for me to use as a template. He then gave me the list: Banco BCR, Immigration Office, Customs, and Puntarenas Municipal Office. I would have to pay another $20 to the Puntarenas Municipality, but they had their own cashier. I already knew where there was a bank and the Immigration Office when we checked in. I decided to push my luck and asked for the address of the Customs.

"Oh...Customs is no longer in Caldera, they moved to their new building about halfway between Puntarenas and Caldera on the highway." The captain very obligingly drew a map for me. Also, he just remembered that Immigration had also moved.

"My office will close at 4 PM...a las cuatro punto! And I do not plan to be here tomorrow, Saturday." He said this very formally.

He was probably the most patient, nicest official I had ever met. I thanked him profusely in English and in Spanish. It was a long list of offices we had to get to in order to get our papers stamped and signed...a test of endurance.

Why can't these offices be in the same town? Or even in the same building?

Knowing that there was a time limit, we quickly went searching for the customs office. Judy did the driving and I navigated. We found it easily after stopping to ask for directions only once. There were four staff persons there doing nothing. They acted like they didn't know what to do with my papers; they huddled and then made some phone calls. Finally one person reluctantly took the papers and entered a lot of data on a computer terminal. It seemed like forever, but I was in and out of the Customs in a little more than one hour. *We are on a roll.*

We decided to skip lunch so we could get the list completed and drive back to Caldera before the Port Office closed, a las cuatro punto. The BCR Bank was extra busy on a Friday. I had to take a number and wait. Again, the clerk acted like she had never done the transaction before, even with the template in front of her. I had to show my passport so she could exchange the $20 to exact local currency before I could pay her. She did everything at half speed. Eventually, she managed to receive the payment and gave me a receipt, all in slow motion. Two tasks completed and two more to go!

At the "Municipalidad" (City Hall) someone directed me to the office. I waited like everyone else, and there were many of them. Finally, I was told to pay at the cashier's desk. They didn't seem to care why I was paying, so long as money was flowing their way.

Actually, I still didn't know why I had to pay. I had already paid the Yacht Club for all the services I had received. But I was exhausted, and at that point I didn't care. I just wanted to get the nightmare over with and sail away. Costa Rica is a beautiful country, but running an efficient bureaucracy was not their forte.

The Immigration Office was further away and it took us several tries to locate it. Again there were four or five people all doing nothing. They acted like they had never done the job before until the Jefe (boss) arrived back. All of a sudden they were all busy.

The boss, an Indian lady in her sari, looked at my papers and declared they were fine, but she wanted to see Judy also. This was very unusual. In every port I, as captain, had gone to check in and out with both our passports. The crew was not directly involved. I thought this Jefe was one of those bureaucrats who wanted to feel her power by making others miserable. I kept my cool and maintained an unemotional appearance, figuring that a psychotic meltdown would be counterproductive at that moment.

Luckily, Judy was patiently waiting in the rental car and could be verified in person. In retrospect, the Jefe was actually pretty sharp in doing her job; she was making sure this big Chinese guy wasn't running some kind of a sex trafficking ring through her immigration office. By that time it was already past 3:30 PM, and getting back to the Port Office in Caldera by 4:00 was doubtful.

In any event, our immigration clearance was only good until the next day, Saturday. If we couldn't depart by Saturday, she would not clear us on Friday. The Port Captain had already informed me that he would not be there Saturday. At that point, I knew I was beaten. I needed to let it go. We would come back to Immigration on Monday morning, clear with the Port Captain on Monday afternoon and depart on Tuesday morning at high tide. It was not meant for us to depart that Saturday.

We returned the rental car, did some shopping for more provisions, and ate at a Chinese restaurant. We came across a taxi driver who spoke English and asked him to come on Monday morning to take us to the Immigration Office.

On Monday afternoon the Port Captain was on a freight ship doing a check-in, so his clerk was getting the papers ready. She told us that the customs clearance had already expired and that the immigration stamp didn't have a time of clearance indicated. Furthermore, I only had a copy of the National Zarpe from Quepos, Costa Rica. Apparently, the Port Captain in Puntarenas should not have taken my original Zarpe.

It was only because of my obsessiveness that I had made a photocopy of the Zarpe. Luckily, my Spanish-speaking taxi driver was able to ask the clerk to call and clarify that there was an original. The taxi driver explained to me that the clerk had to be careful to get everything just right. Well, I suppose that's what bureaucracy is all about.

We waited for the Port Captain for about forty-five minutes. Miraculously, he was willing to overlook all the irregularities and signed the Zarpe to let Laelia depart Costa Rica legally. That was the end of that particular bureaucratic nightmare.

If one's dream is to sail the seven seas, the Bard of Avon has some relevant thoughts, *"...perchance to dream...ay, there's the rub"* for who knows what kinds of dreams might come...perchance it's a dream of bureaucratic torment.

18. The Precarious Bash North

Departing Puntarenas, Costa Rica (09 58.948 N, 084 47.782 W), 13 March 2012. Arriving Marina Chiapas, Mexico (14 41.946 N, 092 23.527 W), 20 March 2012.

The Deadly Papagayo
We were not looking forward to sailing from Puntarenas north because of the fierce Papagayo "gap winds" (or Papagayo Jet) blowing from the Caribbean Sea across the Central American Isthmus. The dangerous condition was notorious, but we had no choice.

I had selected Bahia Santa Elena as our destination anchorage for the first leg of our Pacific passage from Costa Rica. It is a small bay, described in the guidebook as a safe haven near the border between Costa Rica and Nicaragua. The region is not more than twenty miles from Lago Nicaragua, where the Papagayo wind blows across unobstructed. It was very probable that we would desperately need a sanctuary in that patch of water.

Bahia Santa Elena was only 140 miles away from Puntarenas. Sailing at five knots, we should arrive in around 28 hours. By departing Puntarenas in early morning we hoped to insure arrival in daylight with a margin of about six hours.

We checked out at the Port Office Monday afternoon and were ready to depart early Tuesday at 0615 hours. By casting off the mooring line at high tide, we wouldn't have to navigate against the current departing the Puntarenas estuary. We were required to have a local pilot to lead us out of the shoals. When the pilot's panga didn't show at the appointed time, we had to contact the office by radio.

More delay ensued when the starboard propeller caught one of the two mooring lines and Laelia had to be cut free. With the panga leading the way, Laelia finally reached deep water at 0835 hours. We had lost an hour already.

Along the way north, there were strong currents, contrary winds, and fishing nets slowing Laelia's progress.

"Look, there is a whole fleet of fishing boats," Judy reported.

"Yeah, I counted at least 25 of them," I replied.

As we got closer, it was apparent that some of the boats were towing fishing nets. We had to zigzag around these obstacles. We desperately wanted to avoid entering an unknown harbor in the dark and under possibly seriously dire conditions.

As we sailed north, even fishing boats were becoming a rare sight. Laelia was in desolate waters. We were on our own with no possibility of help. Overhead both the Southern Cross and the Big Dipper were visible in a clear inky sky. All was well.

Through the night, the shifting wind picked up and the waves grew bigger. The strongest winds were from the NE with sudden gusts that would slam Laelia, which was on a NW course, from the side with a loud bang. One powerful gust hit Laelia especially hard. It sounded like a freight train.

Wow...sixty knots...sixty-seven? I was reading the anemometer.

We had experienced fifty-knot winds in Cook's Bay in Moorea, but that was with Laelia anchored securely in the harbor. We had never been in this kind of wind while underway. Catamarans have more initial stability than mono-hull sailboats, but once capsized, catamarans would stay upside down with complete stability...indefinitely. Fortunately, I had reefed all the sails by that time and we were motoring with both engines. Laelia did heel, but not to the point of flipping over.

At daybreak, the wind eased as the sun peeked over the low mountains to the east, but was still blowing at 15 to 17 knots. The sea was calm enough that Judy was able to stay up. I kept checking the time and speed, calculating our arrival time at Bahia Santa Elena. It would be close.

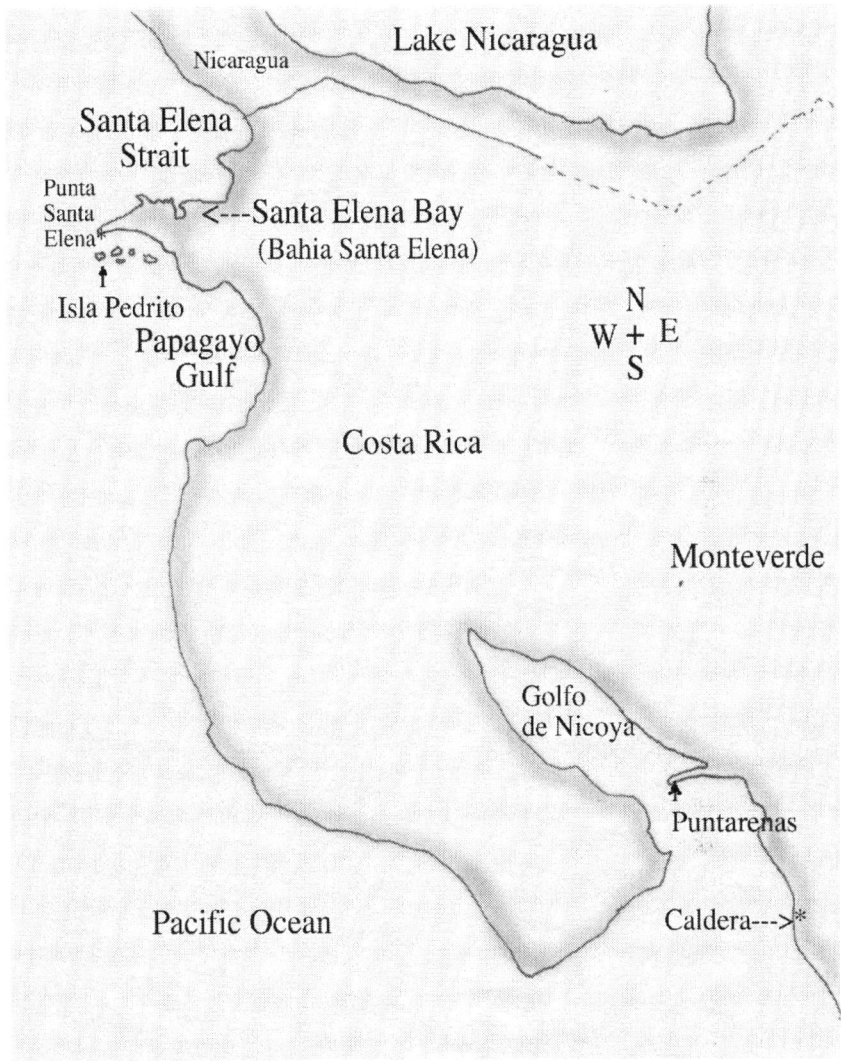

From Puntarenas to Santa Elena Bay

We saw turtles on the west side of Papagayo Gulf, swimming south. I asked them where they were going, but received no answer. It was spring. They were no doubt heading for some deserted beach to lay eggs.

We passed Isla Pedrito, a rocky islet at the western-most point of a chain of small islands, then Murcielago Bay. As Laelia rounded Punta Santa Elena at 1425 hours, we immediately had wind on the nose at 36 knots NE and big waves crashing against us. There was no longer any landmass to shield us from the fury of the Papagayo blowing from Lake Nicaragua. The entrance to our refuge at Bahia Santa Elena was about ten miles away, but Laelia was only making good two to three knots.

Sunset came at 1754 hours. I turned on the tricolor, our nighttime navigation light, with a sinking feeling. From our approach, the entrance of the bay was not obvious. We saw only sloping ridges of land dipping into the sea. The entrance to our refuge was tucked between a pair of those land ridges.

We were now navigating in twilight; darkness was imminent. If we didn't find the entrance soon, we would be lost. We knew we were close according to the electronic chart, but we couldn't be certain that the chart was accurate. We had never been there before. There was no substitute for confirming the entrance, a navigable opening to Bahia Santa Elena, by eye. We kept going and looking. As we passed each land ridge, it was one disappointment after another.

"Look, there is the entrance," Judy exclaimed suddenly.

We turned and entered the bay in the last remnants of twilight. The wind decreased and the waves calmed. We headed for the east side of the bay and anchored as soon as we reached fifty feet of depth. Even as we were still paying out the anchor chain, the sky was becoming pitch black. The moon was nowhere. I couldn't see my hand in front of my face. Judy, at the helm, normally communicated with me by hand signals. As I released the anchor chain in darkness, we had to shout.

Suddenly, there was a ray of light from closer to the shore. We gathered that there were a few fishing vessels warning us that they were about. They were safe from us. We were firmly anchored in the nick of time at Bahia Santa Elena.

There was still wind in the protected anchorage, but much lighter, and the wave action was mild. We were able to rest and sleep in safety. With the rough conditions during most of the passage, Judy had to sleep a lot to avoid seasickness. As a result I was sleep-deprived and needed the respite.

There was no service at the bay. It is inside the Parque Nacional Santa Rosa. We didn't go ashore. We arrived on a Wednesday evening, waiting for a calm day to depart. Thursday, we were still shell shocked. Friday, the weather was no better.

Arriving in Mexico

We were anxious to continue our journey. The Ides of March had passed a few days earlier. There weren't too many more days before the beginning of the Mexican hurricane season in June. We had hoped for a stay in Mexico to recuperate before heading back to San Diego by early May, if possible.

We knew it was dangerous to keep a firm schedule while sailing at sea. It was important to be patient and wait out unfavorable weather. We had seen in the news that several boats had met unfortunate ends by sailors risking bad storms to meet a schedule. Often, the victims of the disaster were never found; only debris from their boat was discovered.

I studied the weather on Friday...several times. I inspected the engine and prepared Laelia for rough seas. The wind was blasting unabated. At this point we were still within the Costa Rican border. Much of the infamous gap wind blowing across Lake Nicaragua was still ahead of us. From Bahia Santa Elena, we still needed to reach the Nicaraguan coast through a stretch of open water.

It would be dangerous if we chanced upon seriously bad weather. I knew Laelia could handle a strong wind, but it was the big waves that could doom us. Waves grow with consistent wind. Sailors call the distance the wind blows without obstruction the "fetch." I wanted Laelia to cross the Strait of St. Elena so we could hug the Nicaraguan coast to avoid the worst of the rough seas. The wind strength would be about the same near the coast, but the wave height, with limited fetch, would be less.

By Saturday the weather report seemed to improve. We could wait for more subdued conditions, but it was unclear that the wind would ever be much better. At 0500 hours in the morning, the wind was still howling in the dark. We hoisted anchor at 0640 hours by dawn light. As soon as we cleared the landmass at the entrance to the bay, the wind picked up to 20 to 30 knots from the northeast.

For the initial part of the passage we sailed NNW taking advantage of the NE wind with a double-reefed jib and engine at low RPM. The waves were sharp, around three to four feet, from the north. The going was slow and not comfortable as Laelia bashed into the waves. The conditions gradually calmed as we approached the Nicaraguan shore. Laelia also sailed more to the NW, following the coastline. We were able to shake out the reefs in the jib and gained speed.

We looked longingly at the harbors we passed. There was Bahia San Juan del Sur and another bay called "Lot's Wife." We passed Honduras, El Salvador, and Guatemala. We were anxious to head northward, not knowing what delays might haunt us along the way.

We knew for certain that another feared gap wind was waiting at the Isthmus Tehuantepec in southern Mexico. It was a fierce wind that was known to have blown a 100-ton ship off course. During the peak season when the Tehuantepec wind is more active, a long wait for calm condition is not uncommon.

For crossing the Bay at Tehuantepec, it was convenient for northbound sailing vessels to stop at Puerto Chiapas, the southernmost port on the Pacific coast of Mexico and an entry port where we could check in with Mexican immigration and customs.

Judy hailed the marina as Laelia entered the commercial harbor of Puerto Chiapas. The marina manager gave us a list of directions to a newly dredged corner of the harbor. The marina was completely new with some facilities not yet installed. For that reason, there was a generous discount on the dock fees.

We arrived at low tide with exposed mudflats in parts of the channel. With Laelia's shallow draft, we navigated the channel with only one more call to the manager for further guidance. We discovered later that he could see Laelia's mast from the marina and was able to give detailed instructions.

After we docked, the Mexican Navy arrived to inspect Laelia with a police dog. The officers and their security detail were polite and very professional, although the paperwork was tedious. The rifle-toting soldier even asked for my permission, then requested that I accompany him while he searched the staterooms. I was very impressed by their thoughtful behavior. The police dog obeyed the command and sat by the bow the whole time.

Chiapas is famous for its coffee beans. We toured a plantation founded by a German immigrant family. It was a long drive on mountain roads by bus, but we learned much about growing coffee and enjoyed a scrumptious lunch.

19. Completing the Circumnavigation

Departing Chiapas Marina, Mexico (14 41.946 N, 092 23.527 W), 27 March 2012. Laelia at sea, crossing her outbound track in the vicinity of Cabo Corientes, Mexico (20 32.58 N, 105 43.74 W), at 0839 UTC, Sunday, 08 April 2012.

Braving the Tehauntepec
The infamous "Tehuantepec" was nothing to mess with at sea. Its mere mention in hushed tones was with respect, tinged with fear. With little warning, it can blow ocean-going ships off course and capsize sailing vessels. It's a gap wind that roars across the isthmus of Southern Mexico. The high-pressure cool air from the Gulf of Mexico, funneled by the mountain passes, rushes across the narrow landmass, blasting down to the Gulf of Tehuantepec on the Pacific side. The strong, gusty wind has been known to roar at hurricane-strength of over 100 knots and reach 100 miles off shore with swells that could be felt 1,000 miles away.

"How long are you staying at Chiapas?" our dock mate at the marina asked us.

"I'm waiting for calm conditions at the Tehuantepec before sailing north," I said, "We've been waiting for almost a week already."

"How does it look?"

"Well, the pressure is coming down in the Gulf of Mexico...maybe a weather window is coming up," I responded.

"That's good news. Tehuantepec's not too active by this time of the year, but between November and early March people have waited as much as a month. I know... I've been through here before."

By studying the weather conditions before departing, the probability of confronting the infamous gap wind was lowered, but the guidebook warned that "sucker gusts" are possible any time of the year. The recommendation was to stay within the 30-foot depth line. That meant staying close to the shore to avoid big waves generated by the wind. The trouble with that recommendation was the much longer distance we would have to sail to get past the gulf.

It was a trade-off between staying a longer time in the hazardous zone versus sailing a shorter distance farther away from shore. I took an intermediate strategy by sailing only part way into the gulf, but not so close to shore.

The Gulf of Tehuantepec was not too far north of the Chiapas Marina. The distance put Laelia on a night passage across the Tehuantepec after the first day out from the Chiapas Marina. We made the run on both engines with all the sails furled and hatches secured. I was on night watch with my tether on. There was a steady wind, but nothing threatening. Just as I was thinking that the scare was only hype, a gust hit us. Laelia was knocked off course.

Wow! This is like a bomb.

The wind gust lasted for only about five or six minutes, but felt longer and gave me an adrenalin rush.

Although the prevailing wind on that part of the Pacific coast is from the NW, locally there is often an offshore wind in the morning and a stronger onshore wind in the afternoon. I thought we could take advantage of these winds and sail instead of running the engine against the NW headwind.

In the morning I would sail off shore. By afternoon I would take advantage of the contrary wind and sail back closer to shore. The only problem was that there was no wind at all for a couple of hours during the wind shift with Laelia stuck off shore. It was a lot of effort sailing in a strong wind, but not gaining much distance going north. It was more or less a failed experiment.

While I was doing all that, there was another boat in the vicinity, a *Westsail 32*...a solidly built vessel constructed in the days before engineers realized the incredible strength of fiberglass.

It had hulls made from inches of solid fiberglass and was reputed to be indestructible, but heavy. Unkind sailors called them Westsnails; others referred to them as crab-crushers.

While Laelia was tacking back and forth mightily, morning and afternoon, and floundering in between the wind shifts, the Westsail 32 was chugging along. We noticed it from time to time, but paid no attention.

At some point the Westsail hailed us on the VHF radio: "Hey, we are famous, we beat a catamaran! We didn't think that was possible."

They seemed very excited about sailing faster on that leg. I wasn't so amused.

Rats! I didn't know we were racing.

Judy was on the radio with them for some time. We later had lunch with the couple in Zihuatanejo. They were on an emotional high upon almost completing a circumnavigation of the world after more than twenty years. Their homeport was Manzanillo, not many miles north.

The husband and wife team was originally from Sausalito, California, but had lived on their boat in Manzanillo before starting out on their circumnavigation. They had stopped in various countries to replenish their sailing kitty. Having credentials as an English teacher who specialized in drama, the wife was able to obtain employment as a drama teacher in schools.

Laelia continued north; our next destination was Puerto Vallarta, a short hop away.

At 0839 UTC, in the wee hours of the morning locally, on Sunday, 8 April 2012, Laelia crossed her outbound track, not far from Cabo Corrientes, Mexico (20 32.58 N, 105 43.74 W). It had been a little more than seven years since we had sailed past this point on our way to the Pacific Islands.

We had completed our circumnavigation of the world. We had seen for ourselves that the world is round and people everywhere around the world are not all that different.

The Announcement

Friends and Family:

On Sunday morning, 08 April 2012 at 0839 UTC, we crossed Laelia's outbound path as we rounded Cabo Corientes, Mexico. Thus, we've completed a circumnavigation of the globe aboard Laelia. The journey of more than thirty thousand miles took seven years and brought us to 41 different countries. We are delighted and would like to share this moment with you.

    Although the loop is closed, the homeward journey is not yet finished. We will continue heading north to Ventura, California. For now we will rest for a few days, dry out a few items, and do the laundry. It will give us a chance to do some needed boat maintenance and replace the broken radio antenna on Laelia. With the next favorable weather cycle, we hope to round Cabo San Lucas at the tip of Baja California. After that, we will bash north along the Pacific Coast and head for home.

    Thank you for your encouragements and being there for us.

We wish you all the best,
Howard and Judy
Nuevo Vallarta, Mexico

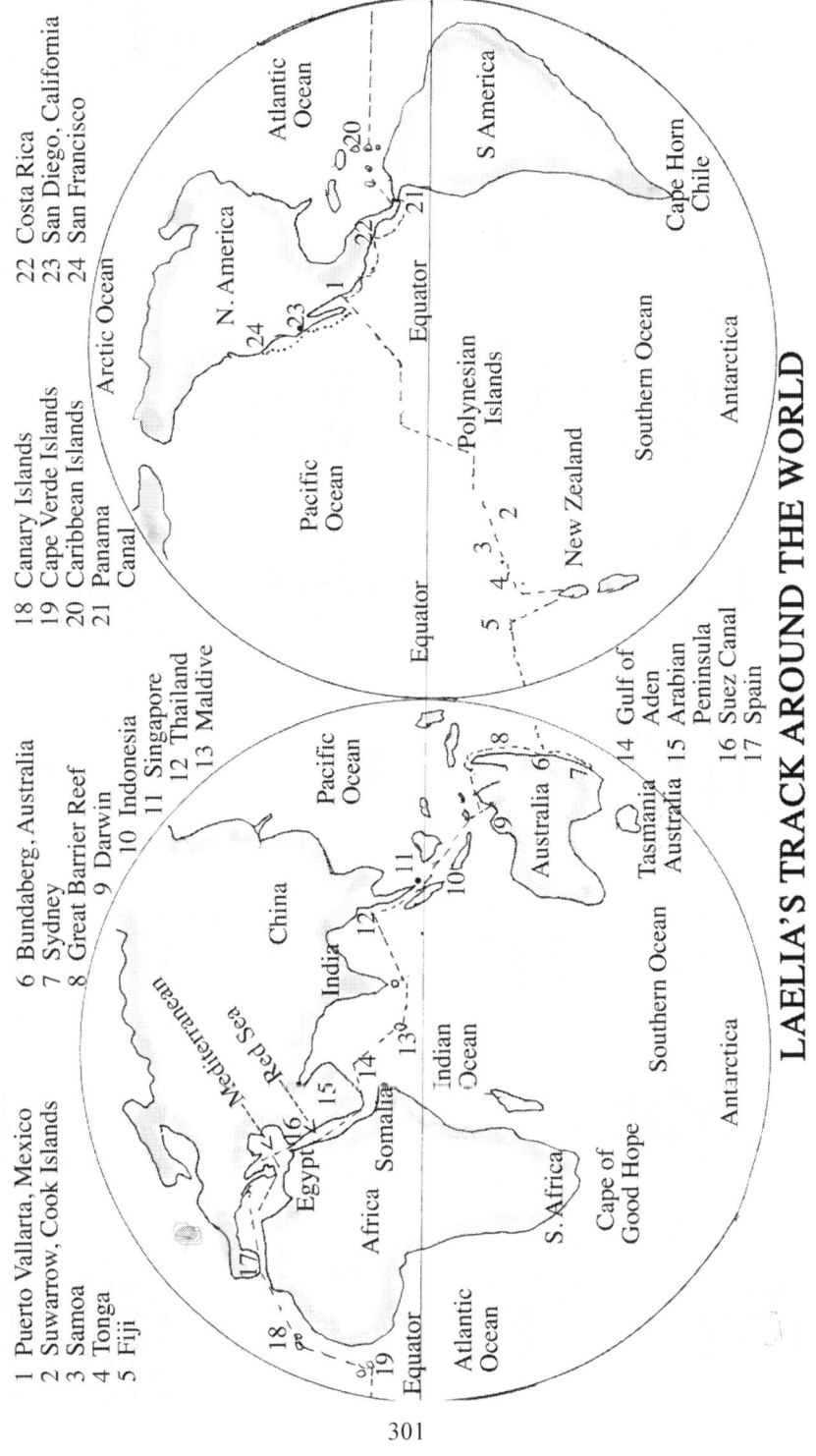

Epilogue

Laelia tied up at the Customs and Police Dock in the San Diego Harbor. Two Customs Officers came and looked at our USCG Documentation, passports, and asked a few questions about our previous port. They didn't feel compelled to come on board. Before they left, they told us where the quarantine bin was for throwing away any vegetables and fruits. That was it. It's official...we are back in the United States of America.

Our nephew, Mark, who lives in San Diego welcomed us home at the dock. He helped us raise the string of forty-two courtesy flags from all the countries we have been to in the past eight years. The sun was bright and the wind made the flags flutter and crackle. It was a fitting celebration.

Our friends, Lane and Gail, embarked a cruise ship in Florida, and finally caught up with us in San Diego Harbor on Mother's Day. "Wow, you two are so brave to sail around the world," Gail said.

"Thank you, but you know we aren't that courageous. You have known us a long time; we are pretty cautious people," I said.

"We follow all the safety precautions...I always insisted that Howard put on the tether before going on the foredeck. I don't ever leave the cockpit when we are at sea," Judy said.

"Well, sailing around the world...it's so daunting," said Gail.

"Yeah, I suppose you are right...looking back, it seems like a lot, but it didn't happen all at once. It was living one day at a time...and dealing with one problem at a time," I replied.

"What does it take to sail around the world?" asked Lane.

"It was probably important that we tried to learn as much as possible. That made us less afraid...fear has a way of eating into our ability to reason. Even when we slipped up, we tried to learn from our mistakes. It's living life one day at a time, just like millions of other people all around the world."

Judy wanted a home again. That was the implicit promise before we sold our house in Ventura. Our beloved Laelia went to a new owner in Long Beach Harbor and we became landlubbers.

About the Authors

Howard and Judy were born in 1942. Howard emigrated from Hong Kong, in 1957 to Seattle, Washington where he went to Cleveland High School. Judy grew up in Long Beach, California and went to Long Beach Poly High School. They met on the Caltech campus in Pasadena where Howard was an undergraduate. At the time Judy was a student nurse at the Los Angeles County Hospital School of Nursing. After their marriage, Judy worked as a Registered Nurse while Howard studied neurobiology as a graduate student at UCLA. Howard was also a Postdoctoral

Research Fellow at UCB and MIT. For thirty-three years they lived in Santa Cruz, California, where Howard taught and did research at UCSC and Judy continued working as a nurse. Howard learned to sail on small boats at the University of Washington Sailing Club in Seattle when he had a summer job on campus, and continued sailing as a member of the UCSC Sailing Club. Judy is not fond of small sailboats; she didn't learn how to sail until after her fiftieth birthday. Howard and Judy are both members of the Ventura Sail and Power Squadron. They now live in Santa Barbara, California...boatless.

Made in the USA
San Bernardino, CA
21 March 2018